First World War
and Army of Occupation
War Diary
France, Belgium and Germany

48 DIVISION
Divisional Troops
Royal Army Medical Corps
1/3 South Midland Field Ambulance
1 March 1915 - 31 October 1917

WO95/2752/3

The Naval & Military Press Ltd
www.nmarchive.com
Published in association with The National Archives

Published by

The Naval & Military Press Ltd

Unit 10 Ridgewood Industrial Park,

Uckfield, East Sussex,

TN22 5QE England

Tel: +44 (0) 1825 749494

www.naval-military-press.com

www.nmarchive.com

This diary has been reprinted in facsimile from the original. Any imperfections are inevitably reproduced and the quality may fall short of modern type and cartographic standards.

© **Crown Copyright**
Images reproduced by permission of The National Archives, London, England, 2015.

Contents

Document type	Place/Title	Date From	Date To
Heading	WO95/2752/3 1/3 South Midland Field Ambulance		
Heading	48th Division 1-3rd Sth Mid'd Fld Amb Mar 1915 To Oct 1917		
Heading	War Diary And Summary 1/3rd South Midland Field Ambulance R.A.M.C.T. March 1915		
War Diary	Chelmsford	01/03/1915	31/03/1915
Miscellaneous	War Diary Summary to March 31st. 1915	31/03/1915	31/03/1915
Heading	War Diary 1/3rd Sth Mid Fd Ambulance April 1915 Vol II		
Miscellaneous	1/3rd South Midland Fd April 1915		
War Diary	Hardifort	01/04/1915	04/04/1915
War Diary	Caestre	04/04/1915	04/04/1915
War Diary	Fletre	04/04/1915	07/04/1915
War Diary	Armentieres	08/04/1915	12/04/1915
War Diary	Romarin	12/04/1915	30/04/1915
Miscellaneous	C Form (Duplicate) Messages And Signals		
Miscellaneous	A Form Messages And Signals		
Heading	War Diary For Month Of May 1915 Vol III		
War Diary	Romarin	01/05/1915	31/05/1915
Miscellaneous	1/3rd South Midland F.A-May 1915		
Heading	48th Division 1/3 S.M. Field Ambulance Vol IV June 1915		
War Diary	Romarin	01/06/1915	25/06/1915
War Diary	Leferme	25/06/1915	25/06/1915
War Diary	Delporte	25/06/1915	25/06/1915
War Diary	Bailleul	25/06/1915	25/06/1915
War Diary	Le Ferme	26/06/1915	26/06/1915
War Diary	Delporte	26/06/1915	26/06/1915
War Diary	Vieux Berquin	27/06/1915	27/06/1915
War Diary	Ham En Artois	28/06/1915	28/06/1915
War Diary	Auchell	28/06/1915	30/06/1915
Diagram etc	Diagram		
Miscellaneous	C Form (Duplicate) Messages And Signals	04/06/1915	04/06/1915
Heading	48th Division 1/3 S.M. Field Ambulance July 15 Vol V		
War Diary	Auchell	01/07/1915	20/07/1915
War Diary	Lillers	21/07/1915	21/07/1915
War Diary	Doullens	21/07/1915	21/07/1915
War Diary	Mondicourt	21/07/1915	21/07/1915
War Diary	Coigneux	21/07/1915	27/07/1915
War Diary	St. Leger	27/07/1915	28/07/1915
War Diary	Vauchelles	28/07/1915	31/07/1915
Diagram etc	Diagram		
Heading	War Diary For 1st To 31st August 1915 1/3rd South Midland Field Ambulance Vol VI		
War Diary	Vauchelles	01/08/1915	31/08/1915
Heading	War Diary For September 1915 1/3rd South Midland Field Ambulance		
War Diary	Vauchelles	01/09/1915	30/09/1915
Heading	War Diary October 1915 1/3rd South Midland Field Ambulance R.A.M.C. (T) Oct 1915		

War Diary	Vauchelles	01/10/1915	31/10/1915
Heading	War Diary November 1915 1/3rd South Midland Field Ambulance 48th Division Vol VIII		
War Diary	Vauchelles	01/11/1915	30/11/1915
Heading	War Diary Of 1/3rd S.M. Field Ambulance-48th Division For The Month Of December 1915 Vol IX		
War Diary	Vauchelles	01/12/1915	31/12/1915
Heading	48th Division 1/3rd S.M F Amb Jan Vol X Jan 1916		
War Diary	Vauchelles Les Authie	01/01/1916	31/01/1916
Heading	War Diary Of 1/3rd South Midland Field Ambulance For February 1916 Vol XII		
War Diary	Vauchelles Les Authie	01/02/1916	21/02/1916
War Diary	Souastre	22/02/1916	29/02/1916
War Diary	Vauchelles Les Authie	29/02/1916	29/02/1916
Heading	War Diary For Month Of March 1916 1/3rd South Midland Field Ambulance R.A.M.C. (T.F.) Vol XIII		
War Diary	Souastre	01/03/1916	11/03/1916
War Diary	Couin	12/03/1916	31/03/1916
Heading	War Diary Of 1/3rd South Midland Field Ambulance For April 1916 Vol XIV		
War Diary	Couin	01/04/1916	30/04/1916
Miscellaneous	Summary Of Daily State Of Sick And Wounded April 1916		
Heading	A.F.C. 2118 War Diary 1/3rd S.M. Fd Amb May 1916 Vol 15		
War Diary	Couin	01/05/1916	31/05/1916
Miscellaneous	Summary Of Daily State Of Sick And Wounded May 1916		
War Diary	Couin	01/06/1916	30/06/1916
Miscellaneous	Summary Of Daily State Of Sick And Wounded	01/07/1916	01/07/1916
Heading	War Diary For The Month Of July 1916		
War Diary	Couin	01/07/1916	15/07/1916
War Diary	Warloy-Baillon	16/07/1916	17/07/1916
War Diary	Millencourt	18/07/1916	26/07/1916
War Diary	Vadencourt	27/07/1916	29/07/1916
War Diary	Beauval	30/07/1916	30/07/1916
War Diary	Franqueville	31/07/1916	31/07/1916
Heading	War Diary Of 1/3rd South Midland Field Ambulance For The Month Of August 1916		
War Diary	Franquville	01/08/1916	01/08/1916
War Diary	Longvillers	02/08/1916	09/08/1916
War Diary	Beauval	10/08/1916	10/08/1916
War Diary	Raincheval	11/08/1916	13/08/1916
War Diary	Louvencourt	14/08/1916	26/08/1916
War Diary	Bertrancourt	27/08/1916	31/08/1916
Heading	War Diary Of 1/3rd South Midland Field Ambulance For The Month Of September 1916		
War Diary	Bertrancourt	01/09/1916	07/09/1916
War Diary	Bus Les Artois	08/09/1916	13/09/1916
War Diary	Orville	14/09/1916	18/09/1916
War Diary	Monplaisir	19/09/1916	30/09/1916
Heading	48th Division 1/3rd Field Ambulance Oct 1916		
Miscellaneous	From O.C. To A.D.M.S-48th Division	01/11/1916	01/11/1916
War Diary	Ivergny	01/10/1916	01/10/1916
War Diary	Grenas	02/10/1916	03/10/1916
War Diary	Mondicourt	04/10/1916	15/10/1916

War Diary	Henu	16/10/1916	19/10/1916
War Diary	D.26 Central	20/10/1916	21/10/1916
War Diary	Couterelle	22/10/1916	22/10/1916
War Diary	Halloy	23/10/1916	25/10/1916
War Diary	Bresle	26/10/1916	26/10/1916
War Diary	Becourt	27/10/1916	31/10/1916
Heading	War Diary Of 1/3rd South Midland Field Ambulance For The Month Of November 1916		
War Diary	Becourt Hill III Corp Real Station	01/11/1916	30/11/1916
Heading	War Diary Of 1/3rd South Midland Field Ambulance For The Month Of December 1916		
War Diary	Becourt Hill (III Corps Real Stn)	01/12/1916	14/12/1916
War Diary	Becourt Hill	15/12/1916	31/12/1916
Heading	War Diary Of 1/3rd South Midland Field Ambulance For The Month Of January 1917		
War Diary	Becourt Hill	01/01/1917	07/01/1917
War Diary	Albert	08/01/1917	08/01/1917
War Diary	Airaines	09/01/1917	28/01/1917
War Diary	Mericourt	29/01/1917	29/01/1917
War Diary	Somme	29/01/1917	31/01/1917
Heading	War Diary Of 1/3rd South Midland Field Ambulance R.A.M.C. T.F. For The Month Of February 1917		
War Diary	Eclusier (Near) G 15 C.5.0	01/02/1917	06/02/1917
War Diary	G 15.c.5.0	07/02/1917	28/02/1917
Heading	War Diary Of 1/3rd South Midland Field Ambulance For The Month Of March 1917		
War Diary	Eclusier G.21.c.5.0 Divisional Main Dressing Station	01/03/1917	25/03/1917
War Diary	Eclusier	26/03/1917	31/03/1917
Heading	48th Div War Diary Of 1/3rd South Midland Field Ambulance For The Month Of April 1917		
War Diary	Doingt	01/04/1917	22/04/1917
War Diary	Templeux La Fosse	23/04/1917	30/04/1917
Miscellaneous	3rd South Midland Fd Ambulance R.A.M.C.T	01/06/1917	01/06/1917
Miscellaneous	Collection Of Wounded From An Advancing Army In Open Fighting	01/05/1917	01/05/1917
Miscellaneous		30/04/1917	30/04/1917
Heading	War Diary Of 1/3rd South Midland Field Ambulance For The Month Of May 1917		
War Diary	Templeux La Fosse Map 62c 1-40000 D.28d	01/05/1917	11/05/1917
War Diary	Halle	12/05/1917	12/05/1917
War Diary	Combles	13/05/1917	13/05/1917
War Diary	N.11.C	14/05/1917	31/05/1917
Miscellaneous	Appendix I List of Casualties Occurring during the Months	31/05/1917	31/05/1917
Miscellaneous	Appendix II	31/05/1917	31/05/1917
Heading	War Diary Of 1/3rd South Midland Field Ambulance For The Month Of June 1917		
War Diary	N 11. C	01/06/1917	30/06/1917
Miscellaneous	Appendix No.I		
Miscellaneous	Appendix No.II Copy of letter received from A.D.M.S., 48th Division d/20.6.17	20/06/1917	20/06/1917
Diagram etc	Diagram		
Miscellaneous	Appendix IV		
Miscellaneous	1/3rd South Midland Field Ambulance War Diary For The Month Of July 1917		
War Diary	N.11.C	01/07/1917	01/07/1917

War Diary	Gomiecourt	03/07/1917	03/07/1917
War Diary	Bienvillers	03/07/1917	20/07/1917
War Diary	Grenas	21/07/1917	22/07/1917
War Diary	Proven	23/07/1917	23/07/1917
War Diary	A.23.C.2.9	24/07/1917	31/07/1917
Heading	War Diary Of 1/3rd South Midland Field Ambulance For The Month Of August 1917		
War Diary	A.23.c.2.9 XVIII Corps Main Dressing Station	01/08/1917	31/08/1917
Miscellaneous	Battle Casualties To Personnel Of 1/3rd South Midland Field Ambulance		
Miscellaneous	Military Medal		
Heading	War Diary Of 1/3rd South Midland Fd Amb For The Month Of September 1917		
War Diary	School Camp	01/09/1917	01/09/1917
War Diary	St Janter Biezen	02/09/1917	20/09/1917
War Diary	Audruicq	21/09/1917	27/09/1917
War Diary	Duhallow ADS	28/09/1917	28/09/1917
War Diary	ADS Buhallow	29/09/1917	30/09/1917
Diagram etc	Diagramatic Plan Of Route Of Evacuations To A D S		
Heading	War Diary Of 1/3rd South Midland Field Ambulance For The Month Of October 1917		
War Diary	A D Stn Duhallow C.25.d.3.0	01/10/1917	10/10/1917
War Diary	Gwent Fm	11/10/1917	17/10/1917
War Diary	Chateau de la Haie	18/10/1917	26/10/1917
War Diary	Amb. Station	27/10/1917	31/10/1917
Miscellaneous	Appendix No.3 To War Diary Of 1/3rd South Midland Field Amb		
Miscellaneous	Appendix No.2 To War Diary Of 1/3rd South Midland Field Amb		

WO/95/2752/3

1/3 South Midland Field Ambulance.

48TH DIVISION

BEF

1-3RD STH MID'D FLD AMB.

MAR ~~APR~~ 1915-~~DEC 1918~~ to OCT 1917

TO ITALY

WAR DIARY AND SUMMARY.

1/3RD' SOUTH MIDLAND FIELD AMBULANCE ! R! A. M. C. T.

MARCH 1915.

Hour	Date	Place	Summary of Events	Remarks Reference etc.
9.30 am	Mar. 1st 1915	Chelmsford	Concentration Exercise	
9.30 am	2nd	Do	Field Day. CHIGNALL-ST-JAMES. Received orders that non-medical transport officers would not proceed abroad with Field Ambulance. Appointed Lieut Dacre acting transport officer vice Lieut Hanley.	
	3rd	Do	Lecture on "Discipline" by the C.O.	
	4th	Do	Experimental packing of equipment in new G.S. and Limbered Medical Store Wagons with view to ascertaining weights and best methods of packing.	
10.0 am	5th	Do	Unit took part in Field operations with 1st M. Inf. Brigade at BOYTON'S CROSS. C.O. completed twenty years service in Volunteer and Territorial Forces.	
	6th	Do	Route March	
9.30 am	7th	Do	Church Parades being cancelled a short route march was taken	
10. am	8th	Do	Lieut. Dacre proceeded to Aldershot for course of instruction on "Transport both and Horse" Management	
	9	Do	Kit inspection by Section Officers Attended lecture on the War by Capt. Chatterton	
5 p.m.		Do	Proceeded Field Ambulance Movements in Hylands Park	
9.30 a.m	10	Do	Attended lecture on Signal Communication by Capt. Wichnott RE.	

Hour	Date 1915	Place	Summary of Events	Remarks, References etc
	March 11th	Chelmsford	All sections engaged in preparing and laying out Equipment for inspection by A.D. of M.S.	
	12th	Do.	Inspection by A.D. of M.S. of all Ordnance and Medical Equipment	
	13th	Do.	Attended Open air Service, Chelmsford Recreation Ground	
	14th	Do.	Concentration March. Dundas cooked in the Field	
	15th	Do.	Examination of 5 men qualifying as 1st Engineers Mr. J. Wood Kell gazetted as Quarter Master and Hon. Lieutenant.	
	16th	Do.	Marched Short to Hylands Park for Practice in Field Ambulance movements and erection of Operating and Bell Tents.	
	17th	Do.	Whole Unit engaged in "General Guard Drill" Escort Duty. Took over temporary duty with Divisional Ammunition Column at Rothwell. Tested our Water Cart with Captain Dale Sanitary Officer and the D.A.D. of M.S.	
7.45 am	18th	Do.	Sectional Parades Hard fell in with view to practising field operations by 4 but owing to heavy rainstorm parade was dismissed without moving off.	
7.30 am	19th	Do.	Head Work Field Jobs and dutie. on Squires Market along with S.R. O. M.S. Gave demonstration in use of property to Wolseley Motor of Motor Wagons Staff - supplied five heavy Draught Horses	
8.30 pm	20th	Do.	Duty. Motors Lowland 23 - J.M.T. Expected to take over Equipment. Lowland	

Hour	Date 1915	Place	Summary of Events.	Remarks, References, etc.
	March 21	Chelmsford	Open air Service - Chelmsford Recreation Ground	
	22	Do	Route March. C.O. presided over Medical Board for examination of Captain Briggs. 16th Battn. Glos. Regiment for fitness for service.	
	23	D°	Leave of men boots, Army pattern, to all N.C.O's & men of Transport Section engaged in fifty seven Horses to Draught Horses. Eleven H.D. and two riding horses required to complete establishment arrived today.	
	24	D°	Whole Unit busily engaged in preparations for going abroad - Chevalet "Kenilworth" today, landing over to Civil authorities.	
	25	D°	Parade of every Officer, N.C.O. and man with complete personal Equipment, for inspection.	
	26	D°	Inspection of Unit by the A.D.of M.S.	
	27	D°	Orders received to proceed abroad tomorrow.	
	28	D°	Unit proceeded by train to SOUTHAMPTON for embarkation.	
	29		Unit embarked at SOUTHAMPTON for L'HAVRE	
	30		Arrived L'HAVRE. Disembarked and marched to N° 2 Rest Camp.	
	31		Entrained at Gare Maritime. L'HARVE	L'HAVRE

WAR DIARY.- SUMMARY-

To March 31st. 1915.

DIVISIONS: 1/1st. SOUTH MIDLAND.
UNIT,- 1/3rd. SOUTH MIDLAND FIELD AMBULANCE.
WARSTATION,- SWINDON.
STATIONS SINCE OCCUPIED, - DUNSTABLES HITCHIN - WARE -
WALTHAM ABBEY - NORTH WEALD BASSET - MARGARETTING-
CHELMSFORD - SOUTHAMPTON - Le HAVRE .-

TRAINING- ETC.-

Up till the time of leaving Chelmsford the training of the Unit was of an ordinary routine character. During the latter part of the month much of the time was devoted to preparations in anticipation of proceeding overseas and to the receiving and taking over of Horses, Vehicles, Stores, and equipment generally. It was somewhat unfortunate that in the case of the Horses and Vehicles and Harness, these were served out to us so near the time of our departure, - the Harness required much fitting, - the horses were unaccustomed to the type of harness as well as to the type of vehicles, and the consequence was that great difficulty was experienced, and unnecessary risks were run. Nevertheless, when the day came for our departure from Chelmsford, March 28th., the entraining (in two parties and in two separate trains) was carried out so expeditiously that both trains were able to depart before the scheduled time. We proceeded by train on that day to SOUTHAMPTON, where on the following day we embarked for Le HAVRE. The journey by rail and voyage across channel were accomplished without incident. On our arrival at LE HAVRE all details of disembarkation were speedily done, and in the afternoon we proceeded by march route to No. 2 Rest Camp at LE HAVRE. Here we spent the night of the 30th. to 31st. March, and in the early morning of the latter date we marched from the Rest Camp to the Gare Maritime, LE HAVRE, and entrained for a destination unknown. Here, again, out Time Table was excellently maintained. We were ordered to be at the Gare Maritime, Point 6, at 7 a.m. and on the stroke of that hour the head of the Column marched on to the platform. Again the entraining was so expeditiously carried out that the train was able to move off considerably before the scheduled time.

LT. COLONEL.
OOMG. 1/3rd. STH. MID. FD. AMBULANCE.

War Diary

1/3rd Sth Mid Fd Ambulance

April, 1915.

Vol. II

1/3rd. ends mothered 7. ● April, 1915.

The blank has been detached + filed under "totters" blank. 17 (d)

Army Form C. 2118.

WAR DIARY
or
INTELLIGENCE SUMMARY.
(Erase heading not required.)

1/3rd S.M. Field Ambulance.

Instructions regarding War Diaries and Intelligence Summaries are contained in F.S. Regs., Part II. and the Staff Manual respectively. Title pages will be prepared in manuscript.

Hour, Date, Place	Summary of Events and Information	Remarks and references to Appendices
April 1st 12 midnight - 9.30 A.M. En route by train.	Left LE HAVRE at 9.40 a.m. on the 31st ult. by train. Arriving ABBEYVILLE midnight. At 9 a.m. arrived CASSEL where we detrained and proceeded by march route to HARDIFORT which we reached at mid-day. Took over Girls School as Hospital and there installed Tent Sub-Division of "B" Section.	Reference Map ST. OMER 4. scale 1/80,000
HARDIFORT	Mr. CHAILLOU attached to Unit as Interpreter. Weather: bright sunshine. 1 Heavy Draught Horse taken on strength.	"
April 2nd HARDIFORT	Routine work: unpacked and repacked wagons and overhauled water carts. A glorious Spring day. 1 H.D. Horse (703) shot at CASSEL by order A.D.V.S.	"
" 3rd DO. 9.30 A.M.	Paraded at 9.30 a.m. and proceeded by march route to CHATEAU-DES-ILES for inspection by General Sir Horace Smith-Dorrien.	App. No 1.
7 P.M.	Received orders to move into S.M. Infy. Bgde on the following day.	
" 4th HARDIFORT 1 P.M.	Paraded at 1 p.m. and proceeded by march route via CASSEL and CAESTRE to FLETRE. Head of Unit marched into CAESTRE on the	Reference Map ST. OMER 4.
CAESTRE 4.45 P.M.	stroke of 4.45 p.m. as per orders.	App. No. 2.
FLETRE 5.40 P.M.	Arrived FLETRE 5.40 p.m. Two motor Ambulances joined Unit today.	" No. 3.

WAR DIARY
or
INTELLIGENCE SUMMARY.
(Erase heading not required.)

Army Form C. 2118.

Hour, Date, Place	Summary of Events and Information	Remarks and references to Appendices
April 5th FLETRE	Weather very wet. Instructions to move on first rail. Inspection of hmber and routine duties.	Reference Map. HAZEBROUCK Scale 1/100,000. S².
April 6th FLETRE	Routine work: Weather fine in morning; wet and cold afternoon & evening.	Do.
FLETRE April 7th 10. AM	Received instructions to report myself to A.D.M.S 4th Division at NIEPPE for instructions. Did so and was ordered to attach "A" Section and Transport to No. 11. Field Amb. at ARMENTIERES., "B" Section to No 10 Fd Amb at ROMARIN and "C" Section to No 12 Fd Amb at STEEN-WERCK. Hd. qurs. en route and detailed (Returns to append.) We distributions under Command of O.C.s Sections.	Do Apx. No. 4. Reference Map. HAZEBROUCK S².
April 8th ARMENTIERES 9 a.m.	Visited Dressing Station of No 11. 3d. Amb. with Lieut. Col. Kelly, and received useful instruction.	Do
10 a.m.	The D.D.M.S. 2nd Army visited this 3d. Amb. for Inspection.	
3 p.m.	Visited advanced Dressing Station and Regimental Aid Post at LE BIZET.	
April 9th ARMENTIERES 10 a.m.	Accompanied the D.A.D.M.S. IVth Div. on visit to Advanced Dressing Station of No 11. 3d. Amb. and Regimental Aid Post by Lane Invalier at LE BIZET. A rough and looking morning and later a storm of thunder and lightning.	Do

Army Form C. 2118.

WAR DIARY
or
INTELLIGENCE SUMMARY.
(Erase heading not required.)

Instructions regarding War Diaries and Intelligence Summaries are contained in F.S. Regs., Part II. and the Staff Manual respectively. Title pages will be prepared in manuscript.

Hour, Date, Place	Summary of Events and Information	Remarks and references to Appendices
April 10th ARMENTIERES.	As a result of agressive activity on part of enemy a considerable number of wounded had to be evacuated from Dressing station this morning.	Reference Map "HAZEBROUCK 5a" Scale 1/100,000
10 a.m.	Accompanied D.A.D.M.S. IVth Divn on tour of inspection of advanced Dressing Station of No. 10. 3d Amb. at PLOEGSTEERT and the Sick Station of Same kind at ROMARIN.	
April 11th ARMENTIERES. 9-12 a.m.	Stand morning in and around Dressing Station and Office. Weather bright and fine: everything clean and still.	
8 p.m.	Received instructions that had would not move with S.M. Infy Bgde I.H.Q. Hrs (mounted) died. On the following day but would remain to represent IVth Divn area and on the 15th instt take over all the duties of No. 10 3d Amb.	App no. 5.
April 12th ARMENTIERES. 10 a.m.	Received verbal instructions from D.A.D.M.S. 4th Div. to proceed to ROMARIN and report myself to Major Temple. O.C. No.10. 3d Amb. to which I was to be attached for a few days for instruction pending my head taking over.	
ROMARIN 3 p.m.	Reported at Hd Qrs No. 10 Fd. Amb. ROMARIN. Major Green proceeding to No 11 Fd. Amb. in my stead. 1 H.D. Horse died. (unwounded)	Reference Map HAZEBROUCK.
April 13th ROMARIN 9 a.m.	Proceeded with Capt Lothian on a round of inspection of Advanced Dressing Stations at PLOEGSTEERT, Sick Stations at ROMARIN Village and at LE BLEU farm and various Regimental aid Posts.	

(73989) W4141—463. 400,000. 9/14. H.&J.Ltd. Forms/C. 2118/10.

WAR DIARY or INTELLIGENCE SUMMARY.

(Erase heading not required.)

Army Form

Instructions regarding War Diaries and Intelligence Summaries are contained in F.S. Regs., Part II. and the Staff Manual respectively. Title pages will be prepared in manuscript.

Hour, Date, Place	Summary of Events and Information	Remarks and references to Appendices
April 14th ROMARIN. 9 a.m.	In office with Major Tonsdale to admistr. one H.D. horn (7043) died.	Reference Map. HAZEBROUCK 5E
10 "	Rode round with Major tonsdale on tour of inspection of Sec's and Advanced Dressing Stations. One heavy draught horse collected today from Remount Depot Withless county.	App. no. 6.
April 15th ROMARIN. 7 a.m.	Despatched orders as to march route etc. to O.C.'s Sections and Transport. "B" Section both over Advanced Dressing Station at PLOEGSTEERT. The 2nd Sub Division of "C" Section both over Sec's Station at ROMARIN. Bearer Sub Division of "C" Section Dame at LE BLEU FERME (a Signal of Five men of Same Section at Sec's Bay - LE BLEU COTTAGE. "A" Section remained at FORTRIE FARM ROMARIN establishes as Head Quarters of Unit. We also Ambulance wagons and transport were parked Two Wagons regimed at LE BLEU FERME: ROMARIN. PLOEGSTEERT and PETIT PONT.	Reference Map. do App. no 7.
2 p.m.	Completed taking over and No. 10 Fd. Amb. marched out. Two motor Ambulances to Complete- establishment joined Unit 60% Lieut HARTY Reed. to Base Sec's today	do
April 16 ROMARIN	Two motor Ambulances to Complete establishment attached today. Round of Units to Advanced Dressing & Deck Stations. Day fine. Divisional headquarters move from MERRIS to NIEPPE	

(73989) W4141—463. 400,000. 9/14. H.&J.Ltd. Forms/C. 2118/10.

Army Form C. 2118.

WAR DIARY
or
INTELLIGENCE SUMMARY.
(Erase heading not required.)

Instructions regarding War Diaries and Intelligence Summaries are contained in F. S. Regs., Part II. and the Staff Manual respectively. Title pages will be prepared in manuscript.

Hour, Date, Place	Summary of Events and Information	Remarks and references to Appendices
April 17. ROMARIN	Routine duties. Visited Sick and attended dressing Station. Weather Bright Sunshine. Motor Cycle (Reed to repair depot at BAILLEUL for repairs to rear.	Reference Map HAZEBROUCK 5A.
April 18th 10 a.m. ROMARIN	Accompanied A.D.M.S., S.M.D. on visit to Infantry to advanced dressing aid dock stations. Motor Ambulance (A 9749) Sent to BAILLEUL for repairs.	do
11 a.m.	Church Parade for A Section. Received verbal instructions from A.D.M.S., S.M.D. to send all Convoy from ? received by No. 12 D.R. STEENWERCKE to 12D.R.A. BAILLEUL. Weather warm bright Sunshine	
April 19. ROMARIN 10 a.m.	Sick Parade visited today the A.D.M.S. 2nd Army and A.D.M.S. 3 M.D. Motor Ambulance (A 9748) attained having undergone repairs. Motor Car (291) sent to Pont de Nieppe for repairs: returned with information that returns unable to be carried out until 22nd inst. Conducted kalks for men obtained at head quarters	do
5 p.m.	Accompanied A.P.M. on inspection of Case of Venereal disease. Weather warm bright Sunshine.	

Army Form C. 2118.

WAR DIARY
or
INTELLIGENCE SUMMARY.
(Erase heading not required.)

Instructions regarding War Diaries and Intelligence Summaries are contained in F.S. Regs., Part II. and the Staff Manual respectively. Title pages will be prepared in manuscript.

Hour, Date, Place	Summary of Events and Information	Remarks and references to Appendices
April 20th 10 a.m. ROMARIN to 1 p.m.	Accompanied D.A.D.M.S., 5.M.D. on tour of units to Sick and Advanced Dressing Stations, and regimental aid posts.	Reference Map HAZEBROUCK 5.B
5/5 p.m.	Lieut Heath A.V.D. visited aid inspected horses.	
	Weather - fine.	
April 21st 10 a.m.	Tour of inspection of sick and advanced dressing stations. H.D Horse (7043) died	
ROMARIN to 5 p.m.		
2.30 p.m.	Visited No.12 2A STEENWERCKE for motor amb. and information.	do
	Weather : chill in morning - fine later.	
April 22? 10 a.m. ROMARIN. 1 p.m.	Accompanied by D.A.D.M.S., S.M.D. visited sick and advanced dressing stations.	
	Our H.D. Horse (7041) Sent to m. V.S. LEVEAU.	
	Weather : bright warm sunshine.	do
April 23? 10 a.m. ROMARIN. 1 p.m.	Visited sick and advanced dressing stations.	
	with A.P.+Q.M.S. +D.A.+Q.M.G. visited Laundries & 185coy.	
	Weather : bright: high winds: roads very dusty.	do

WAR DIARY
or
INTELLIGENCE SUMMARY.
(Erase heading not required.)

Army Form C. 2118.

Hour, Date, Place	Summary of Events and Information	Remarks and references to Appendices
April 24th 10 am ROMARIN	Visited Cech Station with A.D.M.S. S.M.D. afterwards meeting	Reference Map
1 pm	Head Quarters of units at FORTIER FARM	HAZEBROUCK 1:5?
	Received orders to warn all such reported by own motor ambulances	app. A. B.
5 pm	Visited Headquarters S.M. Inf. Bgde. to inform Bde. Commdr. MO of a	
	list system of methods to be employed to combating asphyxiating gases	
	alleged to be now used by enemy.	
	Weather: Dull and cold. Dusty.	
April 25th 10 am	Visited BAILLEUL at request of G.O.C. S.M. Inf. Bgde. with view to obtain	Reference Map
ROMARIN	any information as to Cyprus how the poisoning by asphyxiating Gases on	
	our patients who might have passed through the Field Ambulances	do
	and Casualty Clearing Stations from recent fighting around YPRES	
3 pm	Visited and upheld small of engineers of G.O.C. S.M. Inf. Bgde.	
	Weather: bright ??? Rain showery night. ??? ???	
April 26 9:30 am	Visited Cech and advanced Dressing Stations	
ROMARIN 1 pm	Head Quarters Visited by A.D.M.S. S.M.D.	
	Saw riding and ??? A.D. ??? (when on ???) - to address Commdr.	
	at 8 ??? establishment	
	Weather: Bright warm sunshine.	
April 27 ROMARIN	Routine duties including Visit to Advanced Dressing ??? Stations	
	Weather ??? ??? ???	

WAR DIARY
or
INTELLIGENCE SUMMARY.
(Erase heading not required.)

Army Form C. 2118.

Hour, Date, Place	Summary of Events and Information	Remarks and references to Appendices
April 28th 10 a.m. ROMARIN	Visited Bath and advanced dressing stations.	Reference Map HAZEBROUCK 1:3
2.30 p.m.	Rode from LE PLETRE to arrange for payment of billets hastily occupied June. Weather: warm bright sunshine.	
April 29th. ROMARIN 9 a.m. – 1 p.m.	Routine duties.	
2 p.m.	Changed duties of Sections. "B" Section returning from A.D.S. to Headquarters & vice versa: "C" Section took over duties at A.D.S. "A" took over duties at Seek Station.	Do
2.30 p.m.	Service at A.D.S. held by the LORD BISHOP OF PRETORIA. Weather: very warm; bright sunshine: no wind.	
April 30th. ROMARIN 10 a.m.	Visited Seek and advanced dressing stations. Remainder of day routine work generally. Riding horse out lame for Wesleyan Chaplain returned to A.S.C. to-day. Weather: again very warm; bright sunshine; absence of wind.	Do
	Number of Sick and Wounded dealt with attached herewith. Vide Special Chart.	

Smith Lowe
Lieut-Colonel RAMC
The General Situation continued unchanged throughout the period.

"C" Form (Duplicate).   Army Form C. 2123
MESSAGES AND SIGNALS.   No. of Message

	Charges to Pay. £ s. d.	Office Stamp.

Service Instructions.

Handed in at .... Office 6.40 m. Received 6.55 m.

TO   Commanding 1/3rd Sm Field Ambulance

Sender's Number	Day of Month	In reply to Number	AAA
M.511	third		

Please note you are detailed to move with the South Midland Infantry Brigade aaa

FROM   ADMS

PLACE & TIME   1/1st Sm Division 6.10 pm

"C" Form (Duplicate) — MESSAGES AND SIGNALS.
Army Form C. 2123

No. 90 Redstone

Handed in at: 3pm **Office:** 3 pm **Received:** 12 ? m.

TO: H3rd M Field Ambulance

Sender's Number	Day of Month	In reply to Number	AAA
Bm 30	3/4/15	Bm 34	

Reference my Bm 34 the permission order that all the wheeled vehicles and two motor ambulances of number 3 field ambulance will march under our orders tomorrow Sunday aaa Your billeting party should meet Staff Captain at FLETRE church at 10 am tomorrow aaa You will march your ambulance independantly aaa route CASSELL aaa CAESTRE aaa FLETRE aaa You must time your march to pass CAESTRE at 4.45 pm and not before aaa You will be billeted at FLETRE aaa acknowledge

FROM / PLACE & TIME: SM1B 7 pm

"C" Form (Duplicate). Army Form C. 2123
MESSAGES AND SIGNALS

Handed in at 3 SM Office 8.05 Received 8.59

TO: 1/3rd S.M. Field Ambulance

Sender's Number	Day of Month	In reply to Number	AAA
BM 31	3/4/15		

Reference my BM30 division wire the whole of the third field ambulance less five motor field ambulances will proceed with you aaa there are seven motor ambulances in a field ambulance the two motor ambulances to proceed with you have been warned aaa message ends aaa I have received no acknowledgement from you for my BM30 acknowledge

(3)

FROM PLACE & TIME: SM1B 8.40 pm

"C" Form (Duplicate). Army Form C. 2123.
MESSAGES AND SIGNALS. No. of Message

Charges to Pay. Office Stamp.
£ s. d.

Service Instructions.

Handed in at................ Office........... m. Received........... m.

TO   O C 3rd S.M. Field Amb.

| Sender's Number | Day of Month | In reply to Number | AAA |
| 23 m S | 4th | | |

Report yourself today to a D M S
4th Division at NIEPPE for
instructions

(4)

FROM   A D M S 4/ S.M.D.
PLACE & TIME   9.30 am.

"C" Form (Duplicate).
MESSAGES AND SIGNALS.
Army Form C. 2123.
No. of Message

SM FAR   110

Service Instructions.

Handed in at...... 2 SM ...... Office ...... a.m. Received ...... p.m.

TO OC 3rd SM Field Amb
    4th Div.

Sender's Number	Day of Month	In reply to Number	AAA
MS 58	11th		

3rd Field Amb now attached
to the South Midland Infty
Brigade which is attached to
the 4th Division will not
return with the South Midland
Infantry Brigade tomorrow (12th April)
but will remain where
it is at present. On
the 4th Div. area. And
on the 15th April all
vehicles (motor and horsed) belonging
to the 3rd Field Ambulance
will move to ROMARIN and
the 2nd Field Ambulance will
then take over all the
duties from the 15th April
that the 10th Field Ambulance

FROM
PLACE & TIME   (5)

"C" Form (Original).
MESSAGES AND SIGNALS.

Army Form C. 2123.

No. of Message...........

Prefix	Code	Words	Received	Sent, or sent out	Office Stamp.
	£ s. d		From.........	At..........m.	
Charges to collect			By............	To	
Service Instructions.				By	

Handed in at.................... Office ....m. Received ....m.

TO (R) O6 5th S M Field Amb

*Sender's Number	Day of Month	In reply to Number	AAA

have been doing up to date

FROM — ADMS 1/1st S. Mid Div

PLACE & TIME — 6.10 pm

* This line should be erased if not required.

"C" Form (Duplicate). Army Form C. 2123.

MESSAGES AND SIGNALS.

No. of Message ....

Charges to Pay. 12.IV.15 Office Stamp.

Service Instructions.

Handed in at .... Office 12.20 m. Received .... m.

TO: Commdg 3rd South Midland Field Amb.

Sender's Number	Day of Month	In reply to Number	AAA
MS 63	12		

Please be prepared to collect remounts from railhead. Heavy draught also. Time of arrival will be notified later.

FROM: ADMS South Midland
PLACE & TIME: Div.

"A" Form. Army Form C. 2121.

MESSAGES AND SIGNALS. No. of Message

Prefix	Code	m.	Words	Charge	This message is on a/c of :	Recd. at	m.
Office of Origin and Service Instructions.			Sent			Date	
			At	m.	Service.	From	
			To			By	
			By		(Signature of "Franking Officer.")		

TO { Commanding ...

*	Sender's Number	Day of Month	In reply to Number	A A A
	SM1	15th		

Divisional Headquarters ...
MERRIS ...
... NIEPPE
Divisional Signal Office ...
closed at MERRIS ...
... and will reopen at
NIEPPE at ...

(4)

From: South Midland Division
Place:
Time:

The above may be forwarded as now corrected. (Z) J H Beckton
Censor. Signature of Addressor or person authorised to telegraph in his name

*This line should be erased if not required.
3662 M. & Co. Ltd. Wt. W929/549—100,000. 6/14. Forms C2121/10. Depty.-Asst. Director Medical Services
1/1st South Midland Division.

"A" Form.   Army Form C. 2121.

MESSAGES AND SIGNALS.   No. of Message _____

Prefix SM Co KC m. Words Charge   This message is on a/c of :   Recd. at 11 a.m.
Office of Origin and Service Instructions.   30   Date 24/4/15
YSM   Sent   From YSM
                    At   m.   Service.
                    To   By Cpl McMllen
                    By   (Signature of "Franking Officer.")

| TO | COMDG | 3RD | FIELD | AMBULANCE |

| Sender's Number | Day of Month | In reply to Number | AAA |
| MS 132 | 24 | ✓ | |

Motor ambulance convoy will not
call at PLOEGSTREET and
ROMARIN this morning AAA
Evacuate with your old (?) motor
ambulances

(8)

From MEDICAL   SOUTH   MID   DIV
Place
Time

2nd (S.M) Field Ambulance

"49th Div"

121/3506

ams.

6/5/15

WAR DIARY
FOR MONTH OF MAY 1915.

Vol III

May 1915

Army Form C. 2118.

WAR DIARY
or
INTELLIGENCE SUMMARY.
(Erase heading not required.)

3rd Field Amb. 48½ (S. M.) Division

Instructions regarding War Diaries and Intelligence Summaries are contained in F. S. Regs., Part II. and the Staff Manual respectively. Title pages will be prepared in manuscript.

Hour, Date, Place	Summary of Events and Information	Remarks and references to Appendices
MAY 1st ROMARIN — 10 P.M.	Situation on this front unchanged. Visited cash and advanced dressing stations at ROMARIN and PLOEGSTEERT respectively. 10 P.M. Received urgent message from O of C Advanced Dressing Station to send immediately one motor ambulance to LE BIZET FERME and two to Advanced Dressing Station. Weather: warm and bright.	Ref Maps Sheets 28 and 36. Scale 40,000.
MAY 2nd ROMARIN — 11 A.M.	Situation unchanged. Routine duties. B.A.D Horses to unless Casualties from the Aid Post South of unsaligna (R.30 A.M.O.S.) on the Waggons to FORTRIE FERME. Weather: cold, quiet and cloudy.	Do
MAY 3rd ROMARIN — 10 A.M. 5 P.M.	Situation unchanged. Visited cash and advanced dressing stations at ROMARIN and PLOEG-STEERT respectively. The supplies/lights of Green Crosses milles LE FORTRIE FERME & impart Graves outside the Motor Ambulance and on fire repair. Weather: Bright but colder and very dusty.	Do

WAR DIARY
or
INTELLIGENCE SUMMARY.
(Erase heading not required.)

Army Form C. 2118.

Hour, Date, Place		Summary of Events and Information	Remarks and references to Appendices
MAY 4th ROMARIN	8.30 AM	Established headquarters of Unit at DEREUMAUX FERME, ROMARIN.	Ref Map: Sheet 36 Scale 40,000.
	2 p.m.	Proceeded to BAILLEUL made inspection of A.D.M.S. to purpose of visiting Casualty Clearing Stations to obtain information as to reception of gas poisoning cases. Weather today dull followed by heavy rain in afternoon.	
MAY 5th ROMARIN	10 a.m.	Routine duties. Visited sick and advanced dressing stations. Weather dull, some rain.	Do
MAY 6th ROMARIN	10 a.m.	Proceeded to BAILLEUL to purpose of visiting No 8 Casualty Clearing Station and seeing gas poisoning cases.	
	5 p.m.	Visited sick station. Called there in emergency as (iv) men of the 5th C.I.D.S. Regt had been admitted seriously wounded through the accidental bursting of a trench bomb in the use of which the had been receiving instruction. One Officer instructing and one private were killed outright. All wounded treated and immediately evacuated. Weather today very warm; a perfect Summer day.	Do

WAR DIARY
or
INTELLIGENCE SUMMARY.
(Erase heading not required.)

Army Form C. 2118.

Hour, Date, Place	Summary of Events and Information	Remarks and references to Appendices
MAY 7th ROMARIN	9.30 a.m. Proceeded to HAZEBROUCK with A.D.M.S. 12.30 p.m. Routine duties in office. One M.D. Horse died today. Weather - warm and sultry.	Ref Map. Sheet 36. Scale 40,000.
MAY 8th ROMARIN	9.30 a.m. Proceeded to NIEPPE to report officially to newly appointed A.D.M.S. 10.30 a.m. Attended as member a Medical Board held at office of A.D.M.S. upon Capt F J CLAYTON 5th R Warwick Regt. 12 noon Routine Sick Station. Weather: warm and dry, bright sunshine.	Do
MAY 9th ROMARIN	10.30 Attended at office of A.D. of M.S. to purpose of conferring with him and Lt Col Wootten 1/1 S.M. Fd. Amb. upon question of re-arranging our area of collection of wounded from trenches. Decided that the 1/1st S.M. should collect from the area of trenches occupied by GLOS. and WORCESTER BGDE. and that the 1/3 S.M. Fd. Amb. should collect from area occupied by S.M. Infy and WARWICK BGDES. 12.30 Visited @ch station - ROMARIN	Do

WAR DIARY
or
INTELLIGENCE SUMMARY.
(Erase heading not required.)

Army Form C. 2118.

Hour, Date, Place	Summary of Events and Information	Remarks and references to Appendices
MAY 9th. ROMARIN. 2 p.m.	As it was considered at Conference with A.D.M.S. this morning that L would probably be advanced to SERACUDS the Advanced Dressing Station at PLOEGSTEERT. I proceeded to LE FORTRIE FERME with view to taking over certain buildings there for Sick Station. Un present Sick Station at ROMARIN to be used as Advanced dressing Station.	Ref. Maps. Sheets 28 and 36 Scale 20,000.
6 p.m.	Village of PLOEGSTEERT heavily shelled during the afternoon rather in direction of PETIT PONT to inspect possible roads of evacuation in the event of the PLOEGSTEERT — ROMARIN road being impossible during action. Weather — warm and dry.	
MAY 10th. ROMARIN 10 a.m.	Joint of inspection of Regimental Aid Posts and Regimental stretcher bearers with A.D.M.S. and D.A.D.M.S.	D ɔ
2.30 p.m.	Joint of inspection with Second in Command with view to finding suitable building for Dressing Station. Weather. Day warm, Night freezing.	

WAR DIARY or INTELLIGENCE SUMMARY

Army Form C. 2118.

Hour, Date, Place	Summary of Events and Information	Remarks and references to Appendices
MAY 11th ROMARIN 10 A.M.	Rode round to WHITE GATES, HYDE PARK CORNER and view "THE PIGGERIES" to LE GRANDE MUNQUE Fm with view to making the farm a wagon rendezvous under new Scheme, and with Sanction of A.D.M.S.	Ref Maps - Sheets 28 and 36 Scale 40,000
2.30 P.M.	Made tour of Inspection with 9 B.G.R.A. & O.C. Div R.E. & Reg-mental Aid Posts and to discuss new positions for the same in the trenches.	Do
	Ensured Advanced Dressing Station today (PLOEGSTEERT) taking over present Such station at ROMARIN for trenches of 108th Brigade and rounded.	
	Weather very warm, bright sunshine.	
MAY 12th ROMARIN 9 A.M.	Routine duties.	
12 Noon	36 A.D.M.S. II Army & A.D.M.S. S.M.D. visited Head Quarters today — also Advanced Dressing Station at ROMARIN	Do
2.30 P.M.	Attended Conference at Office of A.D.M.S. S.M.D. & O.C. Field Ambulances and Regimental Medical Officers, to discuss methods of combating effects of Poisonous Gases.	
	Received orders to erect Baths at Enstagements for reception of Pack Animals.	

Army Form C. 2118.

WAR DIARY
or
INTELLIGENCE SUMMARY.
(Erase heading not required.)

Instructions regarding War Diaries and Intelligence Summaries are contained in F.S. Regs., Part II. and the Staff Manual respectively. Title pages will be prepared in manuscript.

Hour, Date, Place	Summary of Events and Information	Remarks and references to Appendices
MAY 12th ROMARIN	Weather again warm and bright becoming dull + cloudy in evening.	Ref Map. Sheet 36 Scale - 1/40,000
MAY 13th ROMARIN 10 AM	This morning attended Conference in SOMERSET HOUSE, BOIS DE PLOEGSTEERT with the Acting Brigadier of the S.M. Inf. Bgde and O.C's Regiments of this Brigade together with O.C. R E and Regimental M.O.s to discuss and consider new positions of Regimental Aid Posts.	Ref. Map. Sheet 28. Scale - 1/40,000
1 P.M.	Today had opening and loft-lands erected in field with view to expanding and if necessary superseding Dress and Wounded Dressing Station at ROMARIN Village.	
	One H.D. horse (Church of Chrysth) today. Weather - Rain and roads again muddy.	
MAY 14th ROMARIN 11 AM	Major Chappell R.E. consulted with me today with reference to Bore Hole Wells for patients now being constructed in field adjoining head quarters.	Ref Map. Sheet 36 Scale - 1/40,000
	For several days we have employed number of Officers men in preparation of respirator pads and mouth plugs for protection of men in trenches against asphyxiating gases. So far have held mill in the undermined (column some 3600	Do

Army Form C. 2118.

WAR DIARY
or
INTELLIGENCE SUMMARY.
(Erase heading not required.)

Instructions regarding War Diaries and Intelligence Summaries are contained in F.S. Regs., Part II. and the Staff Manual respectively. Title pages will be prepared in manuscript.

Hour, Date, Place	Summary of Events and Information	Remarks and references to Appendices
MAY 14th ROMARIN	Issue boots and some 7000 small arms ammo cartridges. Today 1800 more of the town have been shelled with "whiz bangs" whilst the battery above 6 tanks bought. Weather again fine. Sharp frost during night.	Ref. Map. Sheet 26 Scale 40,000
MAY 15th ROMARIN 10 a.m.	Attended Conference at Headquarters S. Fr. Infy Bde. with acting Brigadier. O.C.'s Regiments of Brigade. Officers representing Supervision & Artillery. In addition to matters mainly concerning Officers of fighting units. The Outposts & respective posts and some posts in Saueulain were discussed.	Do
3 p.m.	Visited Office of A.D.J.M.S.	
6 p.m.	Received visit from A.D.J.M.S. with information discussed various matters chiefly relating to respiration pads. Total now issued 3 & 50. Mouthpieces 11.500.	
	Weather: again day and pleasant.	
MAY 16th ROMARIN 9 a.m.	Church Parade.	
9.30	Visited dressing station and inspected billets of 5th Glou. Regt.	
11 a.m.	Received visit from Major Christie R.E. and arranged to send him 2 NCOs & 28 men as working party for construction of regimental out posts in Bois de PLOEGSTEERT.	Do

WAR DIARY
or
INTELLIGENCE SUMMARY.

(Erase heading not required.)

Army Form C. 2118.

Hour, Date, Place	Summary of Events and Information	Remarks and references to Appendices
MAY 16th ROMARIN	2.30 p.m. Attended at office of A.D.M.S. for conference with Capt. Brown R.A.M.C. of the 19th Fd. Amb. in to methods adopted in his ambulance at advanced dressing station and regimental aid posts.	Ref. Map. Sheet 36 Scale - 1/40,000
	4.30 p.m. Visited Divisional Ammunition Column; impholed sanitary arrangements at that unit at MERRIS.	Do
	Weather again warm and bright.	
MAY 17th ROMARIN	10 a.m. Went to MERRIS - with view to effecting exchange between Lieut SULLIVAN M.O. Div. Amm. Col. and LIEUT. SPRAGUE R.M.O. 5th Glos.. the latter officer is suffering from Rheumatism and as the work of the Div. Amm. Col is at present lighter than that of a unit in the trenches it was considered by A.D.M.S. that if a suitable exchange could be effected it would tend to the efficiency of the Service.	Do
	The "attached" motor ambulance was safely returned today.	
	Sent motor Ambulance returns from having puis motor pans repairs today.	
	All more respirator pads healed and ready to issue.	
	Received instructions to collect the motor cycle at STEENWERCK today but when sent for was informed it had been collected by one of the other Fd. Ambs. of this Dvn. in Error.	Do
	Health: Very good: have been shewing steady all night and today: found a/c in Telegraph.	

WAR DIARY
or
INTELLIGENCE SUMMARY.

(Erase heading not required.)

Army Form C. 2118.

Instructions regarding War Diaries and Intelligence Summaries are contained in F.S. Regs., Part II. and the Staff Manual respectively. Title pages will be prepared in manuscript.

Hour, Date, Place	Summary of Events and Information	Remarks and references to Appendices
May 18th ROMARIN 9 a.m.	Routine duties including burial of interment & Brennus Shain and supervision of sudenation of sick and wounded.	Ref Map. Sheet 36 Scale — 1/40,000
11.30 a.m.	Visits made to 143rd Bgde in connection with Bgde higher in various matters concerning expediting forms and use of personnel. Loan collected today from 2nd S.A. Sg Amb.	
	One mot. Cycle collected today from 2nd S.A. Sg Amb. Weather again hot and roads very muddy	
May 19th ROMARIN	Uneventful day of routine duties. 1500 personalin and 2000 civil. refugees healed into Toulon and distributed today. Weather: dull. Some rain — road very slushy.	Do
May 20th ROMARIN 9.00 a.m.	Officer visiting Dressing Station and Entraining evacuation of sick and wounded. Went to Halgin, 4 me Bgde for Conversation with Brigadier Major.	Do
2.30 p.m.	Visited area in rear of 143 Bgde trenches with view to selecting better route of evacuation in case of action. Weather: again warm and bright.	
May 21st ROMARIN	Routine duties. Visited officers' DDgms in afternoon re schemes. Weather warm and bright.	Do

WAR DIARY
or
INTELLIGENCE SUMMARY.
(Erase heading not required.)

Army Form C. 2118.

Hour, Date, Place	Summary of Events and Information	Remarks and references to Appendices
MAY 22nd KOMARIN	9am Inspected dressing station and saw wounded evacuated.	Ref Map Sheet 36 Scale - 1/40,000
	10am Attended Conference of Brigadier and Regimental Officers at Hd.qrs. of 145 Brigade.	
	Another Small bullet (287) of wrappers boiled milk solution and instructed to machine gun section of bands.	
	Four mules added to strength today to replace his teams draught horses deficient.	
	Weather warmer tonight from storm.	
MAY 23rd KOMARIN	9.0 Went morning visit to dressing station to (admission of evacuation of sick & wounded	Do
	10.45 pm Saw an enemy aeroplane at Komapnatio weather warm and bright.	
MAY 24. KOMARIN	11 a.m. Visited A.D.M.S. visited and inspected sick & wounded station and trans- port.	Do
	Otherwise day of routine duties. Weather again very warm.	
MAY 25th KOMARIN	11.30 Visit & inspection by D.D.M.S. 2nd Army. am H.D.Army No 7049 transferred to Vety. Hosp.	Do
	6 pm attended office of A.D.M.S. (S.M.D) for consultation re rendered one hereinafter Krupfe mlk solution & proceed 6 3/4% sugar & g.
	10 pm Weather warm & bright.	

Army Form C. 2118.

WAR DIARY
or
INTELLIGENCE SUMMARY.
(Erase heading not required.)

Instructions regarding War Diaries and Intelligence Summaries are contained in F.S. Regs., Part II. and the Staff Manual respectively. Title pages will be prepared in manuscript.

Hour, Date, Place	Summary of Events and Information	Remarks and references to Appendices
May 26th ROMARIN	9am Attended Evacuation of Sick & Wounded. 2pm Visited the 19th Fd. Amb. for inspection of Transport. Trenches still very hot and wounded exceedingly heavy.	Ref Map. Sheet. 36 Scale 1/40,000
May 27th ROMARIN	9am Visited Dressing Station and supervised evacuation of sick & wounded) 10.30 am our men engaged in relieving duties, and a Champ at Champ at Scheme for evacuation of wounded from new Regimental aid posts with special reference to route to be employed. 3pm Inspection of Transport. 6pm Received urgent message to send all available Ambulance wagons to NIEPPE where a serious accident had occurred — a Subaltern & Aeroplane — resulting in some 7 persons (1 Officer) being killed & severely wounded. Weather — bright & hot — wind and moved dust about & to the enemy.	Do
May 28th ROMARIN	9am Went to evening Station & supervised of Convoy of wounded. 2pm Went to A.D.M.S. Office to meet new Sanitary P.M.O. Weather bright & pleasant.	Do

WAR DIARY or INTELLIGENCE SUMMARY.

Army Form C. 2118.

(Erase heading not required.)

Hour, Date, Place	Summary of Events and Information	Remarks and references to Appendices
May 29th ROMARIN 9 A.M.	Issued orders to each station & various duties.	
10 A.M.	Attended weekly conference of Brigadier & O.C.'s at headqrs. 145th Inf Bgde.	Ref Map Sheet 36. 1/40,000
12 noon	Visited headquarters 1/2 & 2/2 Co R.E. to discuss Ermelenham and progress of Nymenhof and posts in front.	
	Weather again bright becoming cold in evening.	
May 30th ROMARIN	Routine duties.	
	3rd Church Parade to-day. The Chaplains being unable to arrange service for this event.	
11 A.M.	3rd S.W.A.D & M.O. called and made inspection of Nieuwsphaegen, Nieuwhof Lines and Creek and Wounded Dressing Station.	Do..
	The 7th Officers visited each home lines. One heavy draught horse suffering from Conjunc Haemonhagica died to-day. No. 7029.	
	Weather: Bright and dry; much dust; cold in evening.	
May 31st ROMARIN	Routine duties.	
	300th day of Mobilization	
	Weather: Warm and bright; roads very dusty.	

Army Form C. 2118.

WAR DIARY
or
INTELLIGENCE SUMMARY.
(Erase heading not required.)

Instructions regarding War Diaries and Intelligence Summaries are contained in F.S. Regs., Part II and the Staff Manual respectively. Title pages will be prepared in manuscript.

Hour, Date, Place	Summary of Events and Information	Remarks and references to Appendices
	On this front the situation and general disposition of troops have not changed during the month. 941 Sick and 285 Wounded have passed through this Field Ambulance during the month. Note Special Chart attached. (App.1.) [The infectious cases are included amongst the general Sick.]	App. 1.

Joseph Young Lieut Ambulance RAMC
O.C. Field Ambulance
3rd (H.C.) Division

(73989) W4141—463. 400,000. 9/14. H.&J.Ltd. Forms/C. 2118/10.

1/3rd South. Mallard ?.C. — may 1918

The block has been detached & filed under "Khatta" "Attalopse" 17(c)

121/5930

48th Division

1/3 S.M. Field Ambulance

Vol IV

12/5930

June 1915

Army Form C. 2118.

WAR DIARY
or
INTELLIGENCE SUMMARY.
(Erase heading not required.)

Instructions regarding War Diaries and Intelligence Summaries are contained in F.S. Regs., Part II. and the Staff Manual respectively. Title pages will be prepared in manuscript.

Hour, Date, Place		Summary of Events and Information	Remarks and references to Appendices
JUNE 1st ROMARIN	9 a.m.	Visited Dressing Station and Supervised evacuation of sick and wounded.	Ref. Map. Sheet 36 1:40,000
	10 a.m.	General inspection of Headquarters, transport etc.	
	11.30 a.m.	Visit from D.A.D.M.S.	
		Remainder of day engaged in routine duties.	
		Weather: bright and warm.	
JUNE 2nd ROMARIN	9 a.m.	A larger number of wounded than usual evacuated this morning :20 cases.	Do
		Convoy of 4 ambulances for wounded alone.	
		Evacuation by motor convoy re-commenced today.	
	12 Noon	Visit from A.D.M.S.	
	2.30 p.m.	Conference in office of A.D.M.S. of O.C.s Field Ambulances and regimental M.Os.	
		Weather: still warm: roads very dusty.	
JUNE 3rd ROMARIN	9 a.m.	Visited Dressing Station and Supervised Evacuation of sick and wounded.	Do
	10 a.m.	Inspection billets of Div. Signal Co and R.E.	
	2 p.m.	Transfer of Major MOXEY and Capt. WILLIAMSON to Advanced Dressing Station and of Capt. HERAPATH to Headquarters Dressing Station ROMARIN.	
		1 NCO and 7 men as reinforcement arrived from Rest Station.	
		Weather: warm: roads dusty.	
JUNE 4th ROMARIN		An uneventful day of routine duties.	Do
		Weather: warm and bright after a chill morning.	

WAR DIARY or INTELLIGENCE SUMMARY

Army Form C. 2118.

(Erase heading not required.)

Instructions regarding War Diaries and Intelligence Summaries are contained in F.S. Regs., Part II. and the Staff Manual respectively. Title pages will be prepared in manuscript.

Hour, Date, Place		Summary of Events and Information	Remarks and references to Appendices
JUNE 5th ROMARIN	9 a.m. 11 a.m.	Practised men on application of respirators and smoke helmets under Drawing station. Col. SKINNER D.D.M.S. 3rd Corps called and inspected Sick and remodelled Drawing station and Head quarters. ROMARIN informed that about Brigade Conferences held on Saturdays have been abandoned. Weather very warm.	Ref Map Sheet 36 1 to 40,000 App. No 1.
JUNE 6th ROMARIN	9 a.m. 9.30 a.m. 10.30 "	Further practice on use of respirators at 9 relief parade. Went to Drawing station — tried to new Lathes etc. — known and working perfectly. This district subjected to considerable shelling in afternoon & our Engineers having this morning successfully blown up a mine in the German trench. In expectation of this bombardment church bands were being cancelled. Weather very warm.	Ref Map Sheet 36 30
JUNE 7th ROMARIN		An uneventful day of routine duties. Weather very warm.	
JUNE 8th ROMARIN	9 a.m. 1 p.m. 3 p.m.	} usual routine duties. Visited and inspected billets + horse-lines of 5 Glos + Berks Bn. Weather — hot + sultry with big thunderstorm + slight rain in afternoon.	30

Army Form C. 2118.

WAR DIARY
or
INTELLIGENCE SUMMARY.
(Erase heading not required.)

Instructions regarding War Diaries and Intelligence Summaries are contained in F.S. Regs., Part II. and the Staff Manual respectively. Title pages will be prepared in manuscript.

Hour, Date, Place		Summary of Events and Information	Remarks and references to Appendices
JUNE 9th ROMARIN	9am - 1pm	General routine duties.	
	2.30pm	Attended weekly Conference at Office of A.D.M.S. Weather - warm followed by thunderstorm & some rain in evening.	Ref Map Sheet 36 1:40,000
JUNE 10th ROMARIN	9am	Usual routine duties	
	12.30pm	Motored to BAILLEUL to attend experiments being carried out this a.m. by Capt the Wands and respirators against effects of Chlorine Gas. Experiments entirely successful.	DO
JUNE 11th ROMARIN		An uneventful day of ordinary routine duties.	DO
JUNE 12th ROMARIN	11am	After usual morning routine went to seek Provincial Drainage Station and superintend excavation of three roads to LA CRECHE and inspected Sanitary arrangements of Div Ammun Col. (46th Div)	Ref Map Sheet 5a HAZEBROUCK 1:100,000
	2.30	Saw Sports for the men of this unit. Weather warm and pleasant.	
JUNE 13th ROMARIN	9am	Church Services: for Non Conformists by Chaplain Meek and for Roman Catholics by R.C.Chaplain Father Purbic.	Ref Map Sheet 36
	10.30	Visited men stationed in "Huts", PLOEGSTEERT WOODS and surroundings	1:40,000

Army Form C. 2118.

WAR DIARY
or
INTELLIGENCE SUMMARY.
(Erase heading not required.)

Instructions regarding War Diaries and Intelligence Summaries are contained in F. S. Regs., Part II. and the Staff Manual respectively. Title pages will be prepared in manuscript.

Hour, Date, Place	Summary of Events and Information	Remarks and references to Appendices
JUNE 13th (continued) ROMARIN	3 p.m. Advanced Dressing Station now in Tavern of Courbichon Aine. Held competition for best ground and best style Officers Charger. Heavy draught pair horses, mules; Ambulance wagons and all other vehicles - also saddlery & harness. Competition judged by Col. HARRIS D.S.O; A.D.V.S, assisted by Capt STANLEY A.S.C. and Lieut HEATH A.V.S. Frontier. Warm & dry; cold in evening.	Ref Map Sheet No 36 1-40,000
JUNE 14th ROMARIN.	11:45 Inspection of front and of sick and wounded Dressing Station by the G.O.C 48th Division. Accompanied by A.D.M.S and D.A.D.M.S Frontier. again fine and dry.	Do
JUNE 15th ROMARIN.	Routine duties. Frontier: warm and dry.	Do
JUNE 16th ROMARIN.	Major MOXEY & Bro Hunt took over duties of R.M.O. 7th Worcesters vice Major ADDENBROOKE on leave. Ino Conference at Office of A.D.M.S today, that Officer having gone on leave. Frontier. again much warmer.	Do
JUNE 17th ROMARIN	Routine duties: Weather fine.	Do

WAR DIARY
or
INTELLIGENCE SUMMARY.
(Erase heading not required.)

Army Form C. 2118.

Hour, Date, Place	Summary of Events and Information	Remarks and references to Appendices
JUNE 18th ROMARIN.	Routine duties. No incident of consequence. Weather: cold, frost last noth in evening.	Ref Map Sheet no 3a 1" = 40,000
JUNE 19th ROMARIN.	9am Routine visit to each mounted Aid Post. 11am Visit to "Hole" in PLOEGSTEERT to inspect progress of construction of Advanced Dressing Station. 4pm Visit from D.A.D.M.S. Weather: warm and pleasant.	
JUNE 20th ROMARIN	To Church Parade today — Chaplain MEEK having gone away on 6 days leave. Collected one Furlois Ambulance carriage at BAILLEUL today. Weather: warm & pleasant.	D.D
JUNE 21st ROMARIN	9am Another routine visit to dressing station, visited PLOEGSTEERT Woods & again inspected construction of Advanced Dressing Station. Major MOXEY left to-day on leave for England. Weather: warm and pleasant.	D.D
JUNE 22nd ROMARIN 9am	Rode to PETIT POINT with reference to a Railway water shelter town J but none. 11am Col SKINNER called on visit of inspection. 12 noon. The DADMS do do. Weather: still warm and pleasant.	D.D

Army Form C. 2118.

WAR DIARY
or
INTELLIGENCE SUMMARY.
(Erase heading not required.)

Instructions regarding War Diaries and Intelligence Summaries are contained in F. S. Regs., Part II. and the Staff Manual respectively. Title pages will be prepared in manuscript.

Hour, Date, Place	Summary of Events and Information	Remarks and references to Appendices
JUNE 23rd 10 A.M.	Visit to "Huts" in PLOEGSTEERT WOODS.	Ref. Map Sheet 36 1 in. = 1 m.
ROMARIN. 12 noon	The A.D.M.S. called to see me with reference to various matters connected with the unit.	
2.30 p.m.	Weekly conference at office of A.E.M.S. resumed.	
	"All leave cancelled" order issued today.	
	Weather however, quite pleasant.	
JUNE 24th 10 A.M.	Rode to Headquarters of 144th Bde. for conference with the Brigadier General of that Bde.	0 0
11.30 A.M.	Called at office of A.D.M.S. who verbally informed that my head Q.me. with the 143rd Bde. on the nights of the 25th - 26th inst.; also that the 38th 3rd Aust. would take over from me on the 25th inst.	
ROMARIN 2 p.m.	The O.C. 38th 3rd Aust. called to inspect the Dressing Station and to accept information re methods of working.	0 0
5 p.m.	Lieut MILNE 38th 3rd Aust. arrived for instruction and to take over the various places now occupied by my unit.	
	Weather dull.	
JUNE 25th 10 A.M.	Visited Field Cashier at NIEPPE to draw cash for payment of men.	
ROMARIN. 11.30 A.M.	Col. SKINNER and Major CHISHOLM (D.A.D.M.S.) Canadians. called on route of inspection to dressing station in the Canadian area on the coast.	

WAR DIARY
or
INTELLIGENCE SUMMARY.

(Erase heading not required.)

Army Form C. 2118.

Instructions regarding War Diaries and Intelligence Summaries are contained in F.S. Regs., Part II. and the Staff Manual respectively. Title pages will be prepared in manuscript.

Hour, Date, Place	Summary of Events and Information	Remarks and references to Appendices
JUNE 25th. Cont'd. ROMARIN 3 p.m. 8 p.m.	to take over from The 38th Fd. Amb. One Section of the 38th Fd. Amb. arrived to take over dressing station. The A.D.M.S. 12th Divn. (Col. WILSON) met the D.A.D.M.S. called to see me with reference to methods and routes of evacuation with special reference to PLOEGSTEERT WOODS. A day in which every one was busy preparing to move.	Ref. Map Sheet 36 1:40,000
LE FERME DELPORTE BAILLEUL 10.30 p.m.	Fell in and marched independently by Brigade, via BAILLEUL to a farm (le FERME DELPORTE) about 2 miles S. of BAILLEUL. Weather dull all day; later thunderstorm and heavy rain; march was done without rain.	Ref. Map. HAZEBROUCK 6 a 1:100,000
JUNE 26th. 1.30 a.m. LE FERME DELPORTE 11 a.m. 9.30	Arrived at the FERME DELPORTE where we billeted. Scavenging parade to clean up billets and surroundings generally. Fell in and marched in rear of 143rd Bde. via OULTERSTEENE to VIEUX BERQUIN where we billeted. Weather steward full moon.	Ref. Map. ID –
JUNE 27th. VIEUX BERQUIN 11 a.m.	Church parade.	

Army Form C. 2118.

WAR DIARY
or
INTELLIGENCE SUMMARY.
(Erase heading not required.)

Instructions regarding War Diaries and Intelligence Summaries are contained in F.S. Regs., Part II. and the Staff Manual respectively. Title pages will be prepared in manuscript.

Hour, Date, Place	Summary of Events and Information	Remarks and references to Appendices
JUNE 27th VIEUX BERQUIN	8.45 p.m. Fell in to march in rear of 143rd Bde. and marched via MERVILLE and ST. VENANT to HAM en ARTOIS about 2 miles N.W. of the town of LILLERS. Weather unsettled: thunder & some rain: much colder: from for the most part observed.	Ref Map HAZEBROUCK 5A 1 - 100,000
JUNE 28th HAM en ARTOIS	5 a.m. Arrived at HAM en ARTOIS where we bivouacked. 5 p.m. Fell in again & fell in and marched with the 143rd Bde. via LILLERS and BURBURE to AUCHELL.	Do
AUCHELL	9.30 p.m. Arrived AUCHELL; Headquarters of bn and Sech. Hospital at the Hotel de Ville. Transport lines and camps in field ¼ mile distant. Weather - dull.	Do
JUNE 29th AUCHELL	Day of routine duties arranging Hospital taken over by "B" Section and the officers of that Section and improving Camp arrangements generally also 5 p.m. Attended Conference with Brigadier General 143rd Bde at the CHATEAU - LOZINGHEM. Subject of discussion "March Discipline." Major MOXEY informed mild from Leave. Weather: fair, colder.	Do

Army Form C. 2118.

WAR DIARY
or
INTELLIGENCE SUMMARY.
(Erase heading not required.)

Instructions regarding War Diaries and Intelligence Summaries are contained in F.S. Regs., Part II. and the Staff Manual respectively. Title pages will be prepared in manuscript.

Hour, Date, Place	Summary of Events and Information	Remarks and references to Appendices
JUNE 30th. RUCHELL	Routine duties, midweek inspection of Billets and Camps with Major Morey (Sanitary Officer) and Capt McKinnon (Camp Commdt).	Ref. Map HAZEBROUCK 5 F 1 - 100,000
4 P.M.	The A.D.M.S. called to inspect buildings and arrangements generally. Generally fine & no rain.	
	The General Situation on our Front remained for the most part unchanged — the only alterations being the dis-position of the units.	
	A number of cases of both neck and hand wounded that will be this field Ambulance shews a marked diminution as compared with the previous month. Vide separate chart attached hereto.	John Grant Lieut Colonel R.A.M.C. 3rd South Midland Field Ambulance 48th Division July 1st 1915

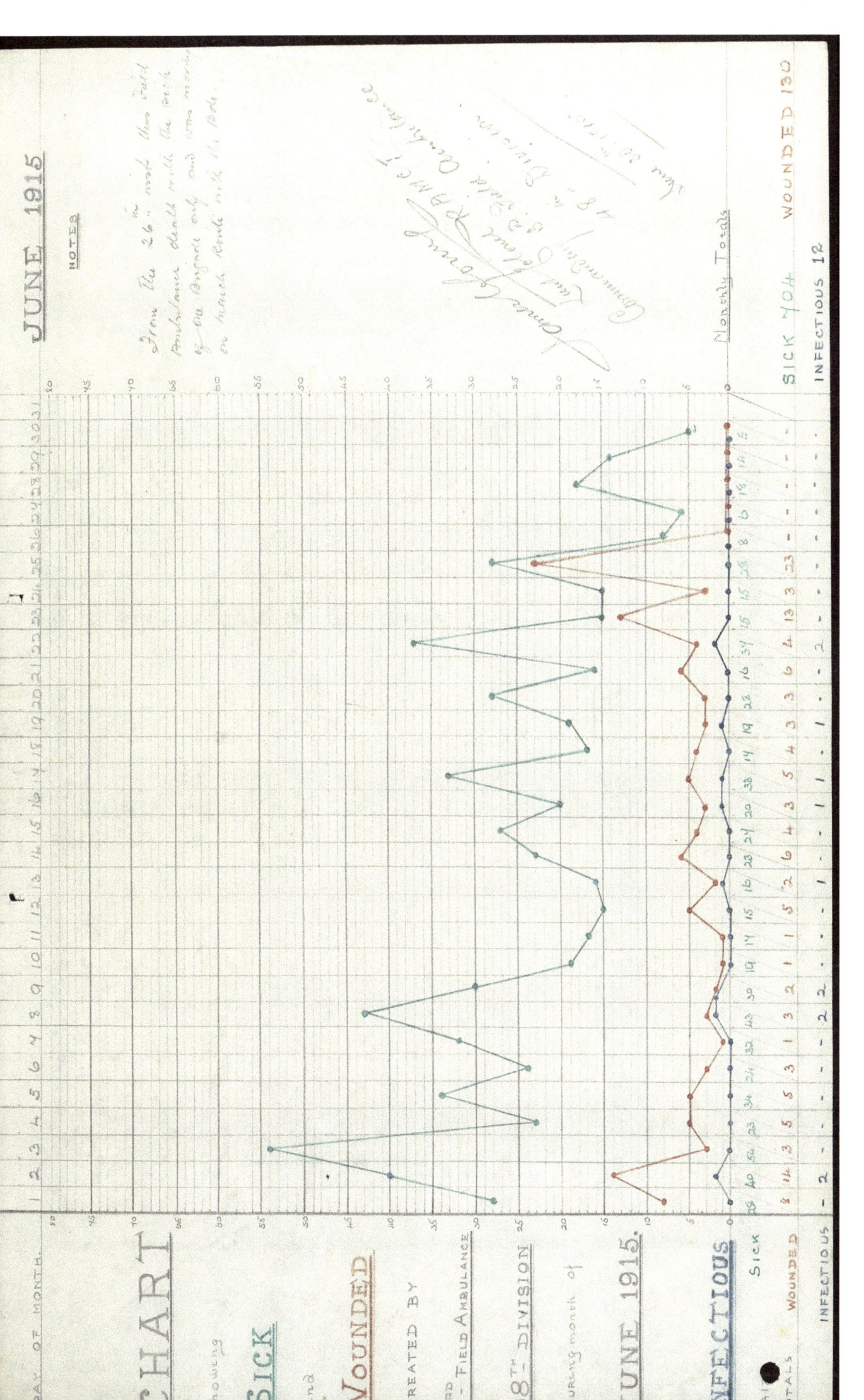

"C" Form (Duplicate). Army Form C. 2123.
MESSAGES AND SIGNALS.

ZNE
Pte Bailey

RM
2/6/15

Handed in at 145 Brigade Office 9. .m. Received 9.9 .m.

TO 3rd SM FIELD AMBULANCE

Sender's Number: BM 44
Day of Month: 2
AAA

The Bde conference usually held on Saturday have been cancelled

FROM PLACE & TIME 145 BDE 8.55 pm

121/6243

48th Division

121/6243

1/3 S.M. Field Ambulance

MV

July 15

Army Form C. 2118.

WAR DIARY
OR
INTELLIGENCE SUMMARY.
(Erase heading not required.)

Instructions regarding War Diaries and Intelligence Summaries are contained in F.S. Regs., Part II. and the Staff Manual respectively. Title pages will be prepared in manuscript.

Hour, Date, Place	Summary of Events and Information	Remarks and references to Appendices
JULY 1st 9 a.m. AUCHELL	Routine duties of Inspection of Sick Station, Examination of points and Registration of Evacuation.	Reference map N.W. EUROPE Sheet 1 in parts 4 Scale 1/40.000.
2.30 p.m.	Inspection of horses in full rub with picketing pegs feed bags &c. Weather fine.	
JULY 2nd 9 a.m. AUCHELL	Inspection of Barrack rooms and Camps and hospital lines. Routine duties at Sick Station.	
3–6 p.m.	Stood by in anticipation of visit of inspection by General Sir Douglas HAIG. At 6 p.m. received information that the General was not visiting this area to-day. Weather fine.	50
JULY 3rd 9 a.m. AUCHELL	Routine duties at Sick Station.	
10.30 a.m.	Accompanied Sick Convoy to LILLERS: visited No 4 C.C.S. and had interview with O.C. to obtain information with reference to evacuation of the Sick from this unit. Have had few cases of late, through an error in our instructions from A.D.M.S. to No. 6 C.C.S. and this area are now reverted as a result of this interview.	50
4.30 p.m.	General Sir DOUGLAS HAIG visited the Headquarters work station of this unit.	
5 p.m.	A.D.M.S. 48th Divn called. Weather beautiful warm.	60
JULY 4th 9 a.m. AUCHELL 11. Noon	Routine duties. Church Parade. Visit to Office of A.D.M.S. LILLERS – Weather beautiful warm.	

WAR DIARY
or
INTELLIGENCE SUMMARY.
(Erase heading not required.)

Army Form C. 2118.

Instructions regarding War Diaries and Intelligence Summaries are contained in F. S. Regs., Part II. and the Staff Manual respectively. Title pages will be prepared in manuscript.

Hour, Date, Place		Summary of Events and Information	Remarks and references to Appendices
JULY 5th AUCHELL	9 a.m.	Routine duties	Reference Maps
	11 "	Visit from A.D.M.S.	N.W. EUROPE
	11.30	" Officer Commanding motor Ambulance Convoy.	Sheet 1 and parts of 4.
	12.30	" A.P.M. 48th Division with reference to civil cellos in area of	Scale 1/250,000
		Goumier (The Hôtel de Ville) occupied by this Unit. These had been	
		reported by me to the A.P.M. as having been used by some of the Unit	
		stationed there and as being in a highly insanitary condition.	
		Weather dull & too warm.	
JULY 6th AUCHELL	9 a.m.	Routine duties with no incident of note.	Do
	2 p.m.	Lieut TRENCH O/C motor Ambulance depôt at Norrent called to see me with	
		reference to certain matters connected with motor ambulances and attached	
		personnel.	
		Weather bright warm becoming sultry with slight thunder showers in evening	
JULY 7th AUCHELL	9 a.m.	Routine duties and otherwise a day without incident.	Do
	8 a.m.	Weather: dull. Some rain in evening	
JULY 8th AUCHELL	9 a.m.	Routine duties.	Do
	4 p.m.	Capt HERAPATH attended (as per orders to that effect) Divisional	
		Medical Parade.	
		Weather: dull.	
JULY 9th AUCHELL	9 a.m.	A day of routine duties with no incident of note.	Do
	8 a.m.	Weather dull	

(73989) W4141—463. 400,000. 9/14. H.&J.Ltd. Forms/C. 2118/10.

Army Form C. 2118.

WAR DIARY
or
INTELLIGENCE SUMMARY.
(Erase heading not required.)

Instructions regarding War Diaries and Intelligence Summaries are contained in F.S. Regs., Part II. and the Staff Manual respectively. Title pages will be prepared in manuscript.

Hour, Date, Place	Summary of Events and Information	Remarks and references to Appendices
JULY 10th AUCHELL	9 a.m. Routine duties 5pm. Visited French Military Infection Hospital here: Saw number of cases of Cerebro-spinal fever and Enteric. Weather: fine	Reference Map N.W. EUROPE Sheet 1 and part of 4 Scale 1:250,000
JULY 11th AUCHELL	9 a.m. Routine duties 11.30 a.m. Church Parade 3 p.m. India Highland C.C.S. BILLERS to see case of acute appendicitis and ambulance certain by no to operation (immediate) a few nights ago. Patient doing well. Weather: fine	
July 12th AUCHELL	Routine duties 11 a.m. Visit of D.D.M.S. and D.O. Sanitary Section with reference to come points connected with Sanitation. 10 p.m. "Black" Brigade moving from AUCHEL. I sent a motor ambulance under Capt Scott Williamson to deal with sick. Weather fine	
July 13th AUCHELL	10 a.m. Visited the Séminaire "RJ PETIT AUCHELLOIS" to investigation of case of Gonorrhoea alleged to have been contracted there Remainder of day Routine duties. Weather: fine	

WAR DIARY
or
INTELLIGENCE SUMMARY
(Erase heading not required.)

Army Form C. 2118.

Instructions regarding War Diaries and Intelligence Summaries are contained in F.S. Regs., Part II. and the Staff Manual respectively. Title pages will be prepared in manuscript.

Hour, Date, Place	Summary of Events and Information	Remarks and references to Appendices
JULY 14th AUCHELL	9 a.m. Routine duties	Reference Map N.W. EUROPE Sheet 1 and part of 4. Scale 1:200,000
	10.30 a.m. Visit of A.D.M.S. with instructions to send officer to examine horses at "Au Petit Auchell" upon whom I detailed Johnson and whom I had arranged to be at the Sectional 11 a.m.	
	11 a.m. Inspected horses and found few to make necessary arrangements and report result.	
	3 p.m. Despatched to Ordnance all huts over established (12 in accn) and with verbal instructions from A.D.M.S. also 3 builder wagons.	
	Weather dull heavy rain at night	
JULY 15th AUCHELL	9 a.m. Routine duties. Section officers engaged in re-packing Equipment consequent upon order to return 16 ASC & builder wagons. Weather fine & warm	00
JULY 16th AUCHELL	Routine duties; no incident of importance	00
	Weather wet & cloudless	
JULY 17th AUCHELL	Empty our Sick Cases admitted to Hospital during past 24 hours mostly cases of conjest'd consequent upon return of drivers to area after a few days in trenches. Weather dull & showery becoming very cold in evening	00

(73989) W4141—463. 400,000. 9/14. H.&J.Ltd. Forms/C. 2118/10.

Army Form C. 2118.

WAR DIARY
or
INTELLIGENCE SUMMARY.
(Erase heading not required.)

Instructions regarding War Diaries and Intelligence Summaries are contained in F. S. Regs., Part II. and the Staff Manual respectively. Title pages will be prepared in manuscript.

Hour, Date, Place	Summary of Events and Information	Remarks and references to Appendices
July 18th AUCHELL 11.30 am	Church Parade to Divine Service. Routine duties. Weather fair, warm & still.	Reference Map. N W EUROPE Sheet 1 out-put of 4. Scale 1/250,000 OD
July 19th AUCHELL	No incident of importance to record today. Weather apparently fair.	
July 20th AUCHELL 10.30 am	All motor ambulances left under care of Lieut Smyth to report to O.C. Div Supply Column.	
9.30 pm	All sections busy packing wagon preparing to move. "C" Section and all transport to LILLERS Station.	
12 mid.	"A" + "B" Sections marched to LILLERS Station for entraining. Weather fine.	
July 21st LILLERS 3 am	Train entraining whole of med. unit & transport left LILLERS Station.	DO
DOULLENS 8 am	Arrived DOULLENS.	Reference Map. AMIENS Set B. Sheet 12 Scale 1/50,000
9.30	Left Amiens for MONDICOURT.	
10.20 am	Arrived MONDICOURT.	
MONDICOURT 11.0 am	Left MONDICOURT by march route.	
COIGNEUX 1 pm	Arrived COIGNEUX where we bivouaced in field near road. Weather fine.	
July 22nd 10 am	Officer with A.D.M.S. visited HEBUTERNE where I established an Advanced Dressing Station; also SAILLY-au-BOIS where a Second Dress. Station was established. Weather dull. very wet night.	DO

(73989) W4141—463. 400,000. 9/14. H.&J.Ltd. Forms/C. 2118/10.

WAR DIARY
or
INTELLIGENCE SUMMARY.
(Erase heading not required.)

Army Form C. 2118.

Instructions regarding War Diaries and Intelligence Summaries are contained in F.S. Regs., Part II. and the Staff Manual respectively. Title pages will be prepared in manuscript.

Hour, Date, Place	Summary of Events and Information	Remarks and references to Appendices
JULY 23rd COIGNEUX	10 a.m. Visited Divisional Station at SAILLY AU BOIS and arranged details with OC Remainder of day spent in arranging details in Camp Frattin during with me interior	Reference Map AMIENS Set. B Sheet 12 Scale 1:100,000
JULY 24th COIGNEUX	10 a.m. The D.D.M.S (IV Corps 3rd Army) and A.D.M.S (4th Div) called and inspected Divn site Sailly & where Advt Officers inspected Divisional Station. thence to HEBUTERNE to inspect Advanced Dressing Station: also visited Trenches and inspected sanitary conditions there. 3 p.m. Took Capt Newbold to C.C.S BEAUVAL as he had been ill and required a temperature for some days. Frattin unsettled	
JULY 25th COIGNEUX	9.30 a.m. Church Parade for Divine Service 10 a.m. Rode to SAILLY to inspect Divisional Station and arrangements for providing baths for troops where the Officer in Charge had instituted 11.30 Visited A.D.M.S to interview with reference to requirements to above 12 noon Visited VAUCHELLES as required of A.D.M.S. to endeavour to find a place suitable for obtaining out personnel of my kind on a Field Amb 1 p.m. Returned to Office of A.D.M. S. & wrote report of result of enquiries 2.30 pm The A.D.M.S called and together we returned to VAUCHELLES to him to inspect buildings selected by me and reported upon to him 5 p.m Visited French Divisional Post Station at COUIN Majr Murray evacuated to C.C.S today & Church & school bys strength of unit Frattin unsettled: continues	

(73989) W4141—463. 400,000. 9/14. H.&J.Ltd. Forms/C. 2118/10.

WAR DIARY
or
INTELLIGENCE SUMMARY.
(Erase heading not required.)

Army Form C. 2118.

Hour, Date, Place	Summary of Events and Information	Remarks and references to Appendices
JULY 26th COIGNEUX.	10 a.m. Accompanied by A.D.M.S. visited Dressing Station at SAILLY and inspected proposed site of huts etc.	Reference Map AMIENS, Ser. B. Sheet 12. Scale 1/80,000
	11.30 a.m. Rode to HEBUTERNE to inspect Dressing Station there: also to inspect site for A.D.S. in the Keep.	
	Received orders to move by march route to ST-LEGER on the aftn. noon of the 27th and to VAUCHELLES on the following day. Weather unsettled. rain at night.	
JULY 27th COIGNEUX.	9.30 a.m. Rode to SAILLY and inspected Dressing Station and Baths.	do
ST-LEGER	3 p.m. Unit paraded and moved by march route to ST-LEGER where we 4 p.m. occupied billets in Lons Dolmen & CARON Farm. & Trenches. Very unsettled: Thunder showers/rain in afternoon.	
JULY 28th ST-LEGER	7 a.m. Despatched orderly with instructions to Lieut. Drake to take over Anbulce. of Reg. Med. Off. of 1/14 Ontario Balln. vice Majr Swinnerton, at 9 a.m.	
	9 a.m. Unit paraded and marched via AUTHIE to VAUCHELLES where	
VAUCHELLES	12 noon we occupied the CHATEAU-VAUCHELLES and Dependances.	
	Visit of A.D.M.S.	
	4.30 p.m. Visit of A.D.V.S. who inspected horses. Weather: fine milk occasional showers.	
JULY 29th VAUCHELLES	10 a.m. Visit of A.D.M.S. whom I afterwards accompanied to SAILLY for inspection of Dressing Station & Bath House: ad we took 50 men who were now accupying huts. Weather: forence fine after many hrs.	do

Army Form C. 2118.

WAR DIARY
or
INTELLIGENCE SUMMARY.
(Erase heading not required.)

Instructions regarding War Diaries and Intelligence Summaries are contained in F. S. Regs., Part II. and the Staff Manual respectively. Title pages will be prepared in manuscript.

Hour, Date, Place	Summary of Events and Information	Remarks and references to Appendices
JULY 30th VAUCHELLES 10 a.m.	Visit of A.D.M.S.	Reference Map
6 p.m.	" D.A.D.M.S. with verbal instructions re inoculation - antityphoid - of	AMIENS
	30 men of 5th R. War. Regt. who are to be sent here in the morning	5F. R. Sheet 12.
7 p.m.	The Rev. H. R. Bernard C.F. (C.g.S.) temporary attached joined this unit today	Scale $\frac{1}{80,000}$
	Weather: fine; warm	
JULY 31st	Routine duties;	
VAUCHELLES 12 noon	Visit from Col. SWAN D.D.M.S. (IV Corps)	
	from of R. Warwick Regiment failed to turn up for inoculation	
	Weather: fine; warm.	
"	Considerable change in distribution of Hosp. having taken	Appendix 1.
	place during the month. Were motor ambulances also redistribution	Sick Chart.
	of sections of the various Field Ambulances of this Division	
	From the 1st to the 19th inclusive this unit dealt only with	
	the sick of the 143rd Batt: since then the unit has formed	
	Advanced Dressing Stations only.	

James Young
Lieut Col RAMC
Comm'g 3rd Field Amb.

(73989) W4141—463. 400,000. 9/14. H.&J.Ltd. Forms/C. 2118/10.

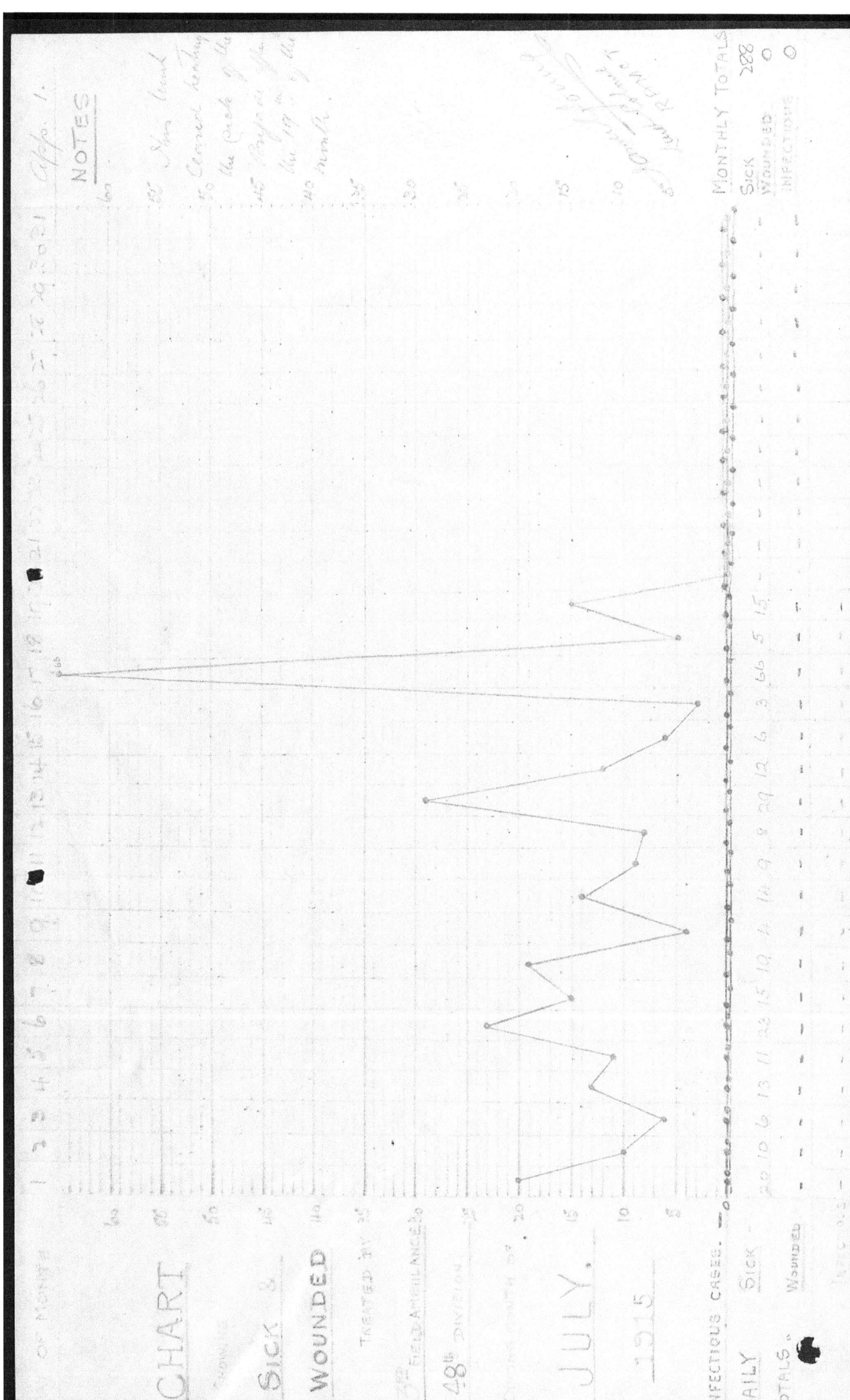

48th Division

121/6598

WAR DIARY
FOR 1st to 31st AUGUST 1915

1/3rd South Midland Field Ambulance.
Vol VI

[signature]

LIEUT. COL. R.A.M.C.T.
COMMANDING 1/3RD SOUTH MIDLAND FIELD AMBULANCE

121/6598

August 1915

WAR DIARY or INTELLIGENCE SUMMARY

Army Form C. 2118.

(Erase heading not required.)

Instructions regarding War Diaries and Intelligence Summaries are contained in F. S. Regs., Part II. and the Staff Manual respectively. Title pages will be prepared in manuscript.

Hour, Date, Place		Summary of Events and Information	Remarks and references to Appendices
VAUCHELLES AUG. 1st 1915	10 a.m.	The A.D.M.S. accompanied by D.A.D.M.S. and Lieut. Col. Henshaw 1st, 2nd Fld. 48th Division visited my headquarters with information that as the 1st, 3rd Fld. now nearing a Divisional Rest Station at SARTON had to evacuate that village. I went to proposed to take over with my hand the duties of Divl. Rest Stn.	Reference Map AMIENS Ser B : Sheet 12 Scale 1 – 80,000
	11.30 a.m.	Visited SAILLY au BOIS where I had established a Dressing Station and Divisional Baths under Capt. Scott-Williamson. On the previous day 690 men and 9 officers had been dealt with at the Baths. Lieut. Dacre acting (informally) R.M.O. with the ½ Oxfords. Health : fine : warm.	Do
VAUCHELLES AUG. 2nd		Routine duties : no incident to record. Health : very stormy : heavy rain storm : thunder.	
VAUCHELLES AUG. 3rd	10 a.m. 12 noon	Visited Dressing Stations at SAILLY au BOIS and HEBUTERNE. The A.D.M.S. visited my headquarters. Health : very unsettled : heavy rainstorms at intervals.	Do
VAUCHELLES AUG. 4th		Routine duties ; no incident to record Health unsettled	Do
VAUCHELLES AUG. 5th	10 a.m. 10.15 12 noon 1 p.m. 3 p.m.	The A. and Q.M.G. accompanied by D.A.Q.M.G. called with instructions for me to find billets for prolonged stay of half a Battalion in this village. Visited and inspected Dressing Station and Baths at SAILLY au BOIS. The A.D.M.S. visited headquarters at VAUCHELLES Lieut. ALLISON R.A.M.C. (Temp. Lieut.) reported for duty with this unit. A.D.M.S. again called to take in Chatillon (Ambulance) to DOULLENS for purpose of purchasing eatables required for Baths at SAILLY. Health still very unsettled.	Do

(9 29 6) W 4141—463 100,000 9/14 H W V   Forms/C. 2118/10

Army Form C. 2118.

WAR DIARY
or
INTELLIGENCE SUMMARY.
(Erase heading not required.)

Instructions regarding War Diaries and Intelligence Summaries are contained in F.S. Regs., Part II. and the Staff Manual respectively. Title pages will be prepared in manuscript.

Hour, Date, Place		Summary of Events and Information	Remarks and references to Appendices
VAUCHELLES AUG. 6th 1915	10.30 a.m.	Today opened Divisional Rest Station at CHATEAU VAUCHELLES and took over 81 patients from the 1st Field Ambulance at SARTON.	Reference Map AMIENS Sct B Sheet 12 Scale 1 = 80000
	at 3 p.m.	24 others were received from 2nd Fd Amb at LOUVENCOURT. Patients accommodated in huts in orchard of Chateau. The village school.	
		Now utilised as Office Dispensary and Pack Store.	
		Lieut ALLISON employed today in taking samples of water drawn from the numerous wells in the village.	
	2 p.m.	Having since the 29th ult employed a number of men in the fields to avoid the farmers and proprietors of land in the ingathering of the crops, I visited the various workers.	
		Health very unsettled. Some rain.	
VAUCHELLES AUG. 7th	10 a.m.	Visited office of A.D.M.S. at BUS-LES-ARTS.	Do
	12 noon	The A.D.M.S. the A.P.M. D.H.Q. M.D.S. Q.M.G. called with reference to billeting half (Ambulance) Staff in VAUCHELLES reported to them action already taken and that all billets had been obtained.	
	2 p.m.	Arrival of Half (Ambulance) Party. Lieut ALLISON again employed taking samples of water.	
		Health unsettled some rain	
VAUCHELLES AUG. 8th	7.30 a.m.	Communion Service (C of E) held in Barn for men of Unit.	Do
	10.30 "	Visit of A.D.M.S.	
	11.30 "	Divine Service for men of Field Ambulance and patients.	
	3 p.m.	Visited men at work in the fields.	
		Weather fair	

Army Form C. 2118.

WAR DIARY
or
INTELLIGENCE SUMMARY.
(Erase heading not required.)

Instructions regarding War Diaries and Intelligence Summaries are contained in F. S. Regs., Part II. and the Staff Manual respectively. Title pages will be prepared in manuscript.

Hour, Date, Place		Summary of Events and Information	Remarks and references to Appendices
VAUCHELLES AUG. 9th	11 am	Visited Dressing Station at SAILLY au BOIS. The A.D.M.S. also came. Afterwards accompanied him to Advanced Dressing Station HEBUTERNE	Reference Map AMIENS Set B : sheet 12 Scale 1 – 80,000
	2.30 pm	Visited men at rest in tents.	
	8 pm	Very heavy thunderstorm accompanied by most vivid lightning and very heavy rain. Casted over an hour. Weather very unsettled.	Do
VAUCHELLES AUG. 10th		Issued routine orders in morning	
	2 pm	visited "hospitals" at work in fields	
	4"	The A.D.M.S visited the Divisional Rest Station.	
		The Rev. Burrows C.F. left today for duty at ST. OMER. Weather: bright sunshine. No rain.	
VAUCHELLES AUG. 11th	10 am	Visit from the A.D.M.S. Recommended him for patients in Div. Rest Stn. now very crowded, and today some new Bell tents arrived which should improve matters. Weather: fine	Do
VAUCHELLES AUG. 12th	10 am	Visited DOULLENS with Telegurbs to purchase of ordinary "wachers" for Baths at SAILLY. Remainder of day routine duties. Weather fine	Do
VAUCHELLES AUG. 13th		Routine duties in morning	Do
	3 pm	Accompanied the A.D.M.S to COUIN to inspect Baths and methods of treatment. Cenches inspected by French Ambulance there. Lieut HARTY nephew went for duty today. Weather fine	

Army Form C. 2118.

WAR DIARY
or
INTELLIGENCE SUMMARY.
(Erase heading not required.)

Instructions regarding War Diaries and Intelligence Summaries are contained in F.S. Regs., Part II. and the Staff Manual respectively. Title pages will be prepared in manuscript.

Hour, Date, Place		Summary of Events and Information	Remarks and references to Appendices
VAUCHELLES AUG 14th	3pm	Visited Machine Gun Co: over 170 patients in their First Station today. Visited Dressing Station at SAILLY-Laurent-BOIS. Weather: Excellent: rain in the evening.	Reference Map AMIENS Set B : Sheet 12 Scale 1 - 80,000
VAUCHELLES AUG 15th	10.15 10.30	Church Parade. The A.D.m.S. called. Remainder of day routine duties. Weather: very unsettled: some heavy rain storms.	Do
VAUCHELLES AUG 16th	10.0 11.0 3.30pm	A.D.M.S. called. Accompanied Major Richey R.F.C. to LOUVENCOURT. Found him making arrangements for burial of one of his sergeants accidentally killed last evening. Met officers of R.F.C. at AUTHIE. Accompanied him to COUIN to inspect Baths of French Ambulance there, with view to ascertaining whether arrangements in this Division. Weather: fair.	Do
VAUCHELLES AUG 17th	7.45 9.30am 3.30pm	Dispersal of field rations. Went round all Medical Cases in First Station will return from. A.D.M.D. called. Visited probable (available sites for Baths for Battalions) Orders and precautions. Weather: rain in the whole morning. Weather unsettled and cold for season of year.	Do
VAUCHELLES AUG 18th	7.45am 9.20 6.30pm	Dispersal of field rations. Went round (compared cases in First Station all medical. Hourly Weather.) The O.D.M.S. Vick Corps called and inspected First Station.	Do

Forms/C. 2118/10

Army Form C. 2118.

WAR DIARY
or
INTELLIGENCE SUMMARY.
(Erase heading not required.)

Instructions regarding War Diaries and Intelligence Summaries are contained in F. S. Regs., Part II. and the Staff Manual respectively. Title pages will be prepared in manuscript.

Hour, Date, Place	Summary of Events and Information	Remarks and references to Appendices
VAUCHELLES Aug. 19th	7.30 am Arranged for despatch of field returns. 9.30 Visited and examined "Otter" cases with Lieut ALLISON. 11.30 Visited workers in fields. 12.40 Had from Divisional Sanitary Officer. Visited Burying Station at BAIZY. 3 pm Heathens more killed; no news today	Reference Map AMIENS Set B Sheet 12 Scale 1 - 80,000
VAUCHELLES Aug. 20th	9.30 Visited and examined medical cases with Capt. HERBPATH 12 noon The A.D.M.S. called and inspected Rest Station. Weather: fine	Do
VAUCHELLES Aug. 21st	9.30 Visited and examined surgical cases with Lieut. HARTY. Remainder of day routine duties.	Do
VAUCHELLES Aug. 22nd	Usual routine morning duties. 11.30 am Church Parade Divine service held by the Rev. Canon WELCHMAN C.F. 12 noon Communion Service. 3 pm Officer of Mobile Laboratory called to investigate cases of so called "Trench Fever". 3.45 pm A.D.M.S. talk Divisional Sanitary Officer and his patients on "Flies" called to investigate causes and breeding places of these pests. Weather: fine	Do

Army Form C. 2118.

WAR DIARY
or
INTELLIGENCE SUMMARY.
(Erase heading not required.)

Instructions regarding War Diaries and Intelligence Summaries are contained in F.S. Regs, Part II. and the Staff Manual respectively. Title pages will be prepared in manuscript.

Hour, Date, Place	Summary of Events and Information	Remarks and references to Appendices
VAUCHELLES AUG. 23rd	10 a.m. A.D.C. went round Cubic. Visited reconnaissance by the ADC — the various Detachments in the Village with a view to ascertaining their Sanitary Condition and water supply. Especially that used for drinking. The various "Syphos" which as a fortnight refreshment supplied to troops in these places. 3 p.m. Visited Dressing Station at SAILLY au BOIS. Weather: warm and fine; bright sunshine.	Reference Map AMIENS Ser: B : Sheet 12 Scale 1 - 80,000
VAUCHELLES AUG. 24th	3 a.m. Major GREEN returned from leave. 9:30 Visited wounded men on D.R.S. 12 noon. The A.D.M.S. called with instructions to act to BEAUVAL to light small hospital marquees. 2 p.m. Lieut HERAPATH journeyed to BEAUVAL and collected three marquees. Weather: very fine and warm.	Do
VAUCHELLES AUG. 25th	8:30 a.m. Lieut. HARTY proceeded to BUS for duty as member of Board of Officers to investigate billeting facilities of various villages in the Division. Ordinary routine duties today. Weather: fine, warm, bright sunshine.	Do
VAUCHELLES AUG. 26th	10:15 After usual routine duties. Visited Dressing Station at SAILLY au BOIS and 11:30 the A.D.M.S. visited the HEBUTERNE 4:30 p.m. The A.D.M.S. visited the D.R.S. 6-10 p.m. The Band of the 5th R. Surrey Regt played in the Orchard for the troops 9:30 Sgt Major ... from the Base joined the Unit. Weather: warm bright sunshine	Do

(9 29 6) W 4141—463 100,000 9/14 H W V Forms/C. 2118/10

Army Form C. 2118.

WAR DIARY
or
INTELLIGENCE SUMMARY.
(Erase heading not required.)

Instructions regarding War Diaries and Intelligence Summaries are contained in F.S. Regs., Part II. and the Staff Manual respectively. Title pages will be prepared in manuscript.

Hour, Date, Place	Summary of Events and Information	Remarks and references to Appendices
VAUCHELLES AUG. 27th	Routine of ordinary duties, nothing unusual to record. Weather: delightful, warm & pleasant.	Reference Map AMIENS Ser B. Sheet 12 Scale 1 – 80,000
VAUCHELLES AUG. 28th 10 AM	A.D.M.S. visited Buth, Roy. Station and examined a number of patients.	
10.45	D.M.S. in D. Army (Surgeon General TREHERNE) with A.D.M.S. 4th Corps visited and inspected Div. Rest Stn.	Do
3/T.	Col. NEWSHOLME; Col KENWOOD and Capt CORNWATH visited and inspected the D.R.S.	
	Weather: fine & warm; thunderstorm & rain at night.	
VAUCHELLES AUG 29th 10AM	Journeyed to LOUVENCOURT to interview Col ROBERTS of the 48th Division Front with reference to Lorries attached to my Unit.	Do
11.30	Church Parade: Divine Service by the Rev. Canon WELCHMAN C.F.	
2.30 pm	A.D.M.S. called to take me to AUTHIEULE to inspect Barton Ambulance for use at Baths at Dressing Station SAILLY.	
	Weather: fine & warm; rain at night.	
VAUCHELLES AUG 30th 11.30	Routine duties. Rev. H.A. MEEK C.F. left this morning for C.C.S. – Sent down sick.	
3.30	A.D.M.S. called with reference to colour markings and instructions to local personnel by Column vehicles.	
	Weather: unsettled.	
VAUCHELLES AUG 31st 10.30	Proceeded to AMIENS to purchase 3 Lorries and other articles required for use at Baths and D.R.S.	
	Weather: unsettled.	

WAR DIARY

FOR

SEPTEMBER

1915.

1/3rd South Midland Field Ambulance

Army Form C. 2118.

WAR DIARY
or
INTELLIGENCE SUMMARY.
(Erase heading not required.)

Instructions regarding War Diaries and Intelligence Summaries are contained in F. S. Regs., Part II. and the Staff Manual respectively. Title pages will be prepared in manuscript.

Hour, Date, Place 1915		Summary of Events and Information	Remarks and references to Appendices
VAUCHELLES Sept. 1st		The A.D.M.S. visited the Divisional Rest Station this morning. No other incident to record. Routine duties. Weather unsettled. Some rain during previous night.	Reference Map FRANCE Sheet 57 D Scale 1:40,000
Do Sept 2nd	10am	Rode m motor ambulance div'l taking patients & staff at AUTHIE. ST LEGER, COIGNEUX and SAILLY AU BOIS visiting the Dressing Station and Billets at Col moved village.	
	5.30pm - 6.30pm	No 9 S.C. M.T. Pierrot Troop gave an entertainment to the patients in the Div. Rest Station.	Do
		Pte HERMAN of this unit whilst on duty at the Baths at Authie, during Stand To HEBUTERNE sustained a gunshot wound of abdomen and was conveyed to 2nd S.C. Amb. He was found on opening the abdomen to have a gunshot perforation on posterior wall of Stomach. Operation performed in 2nd Fd Amb. Weather — bad — cold and altogether miserable.	
Do Sept 3rd	10am	Having received no official information that Pte HERMAN 3 had been evacuated to C.C.S. I proceeded to BEUVAL for the purpose of visiting him but found on arrival there that I had been misinformed	Do
	3pm	Capt GUISE and other representative of the British Red Cross Society and the D.R.S. a visit with a view to providing certain articles for the comfort of the patients. Weather — again wet and miserable.	

Army Form C. 2118.

WAR DIARY
or
INTELLIGENCE SUMMARY.
(Erase heading not required.)

Hour, Date, Place		Summary of Events and Information	Remarks and references to Appendices
VAUCHELLES			Reference Map
Sept 4th	9.30 am	Visited the 2nd Fd. Amb. at LOUVENCOURT and saw Pte HERMANS	FRANCE
		Remainder of day routine duties.	Sheet 57 D
		Weather: Dull cold, but fine on the whole.	Scale 1: 40,000
Do Sept 5th	10 am	Motored to SAILLY via ACHIEUX and COURCELLES. From SAILLY walked to HEBUTERNE to visit Advanced Dressing Station and Bathe. Returned to SAILLY and inspected Baths and Dressing Station there.	
		LIEUT. HARTY engaged in matters of Billeting Board to report on accommodation of village of VAUCHELLES.	Do
		Weather: Dull but mostly (?settled).	
Do Sept 6th	10.30 am	The A.D.M.S. called and approved palatio on D.R.S.	
	11.30 am	The A.D.V.S. called with reference to unsuitable riding horse.	
		LIEUT. HARTY engaged on matters of Billeting Board to report on accommodation of village of COURCELLES.	Do
		LIEUT. ROE returned from leave. Lieut. and Q.M. HILL proceeded on leave.	
		Weather much finer, warm, bright sunshine.	
Do Sept 7th	10 am	A.D.M.S. called. Motor Ambulance Workshops Unit attached to this unit today. Rev. HINGLEY C.F. (Presbyterian) attached for temporary duty with this unit. LIEUT. MOORE R.A.M.C.T. detailed this S.O. Runt for duty today. Weather: Warm, pleasant.	Do

WAR DIARY
or
INTELLIGENCE SUMMARY.
(Erase heading not required.)

Army Form C. 2118.

Instructions regarding War Diaries and Intelligence Summaries are contained in F.S. Regs., Part II. and the Staff Manual respectively. Title pages will be prepared in manuscript.

Hour, Date, Place		Summary of Events and Information	Remarks and references to Appendices
VAUCHELLES Sept. 6th	10.30	Lieut. ALLISON having this day left the unit for duty with the 6th R. War. Regt. Lieut HARTY proceeded for duty at Dressing Station SAILLY.	Reference Map FRANCE Sheet 57 D Scale 1:40,000
	10 a.m.	Motored to COUIN & met Bolla Rally occupied by French Cavalry, whilst guarding a decreen by the G.O.C. 145th Bde. I had placed in charge a corporal and three privates.	
	12 noon	The A.D.M.S visited the Dressing Station and inspected some patients. Weather - beautiful, warm, bright sunshine.	
VAUCHELLES Sept 9th	9.30 a.m.	Scanned medical carts with Capt. HERAPATH this morning. Weather very beautiful, warm, bright sunshine.	Do
VAUCHELLES Sept 10th	9.30 a.m.	Scanned surgical cars with Major GREEN.	
	11 a.m.	A.D.M.S visited A.R.S. Weather fine, cold in evening	Do
VAUCHELLES Sept 11th	10 a.m. 5 p.m.	Visited Dressing Station & Baths at SAILLY au BOIS. Left by motor for BOULOGNE to proceed to England on leave having received from Lynn to return on service grounds affairs. Major GREEN took over command of Unit in my absence. Weather fine.	Do

Army Form C. 2118.

WAR DIARY
or
INTELLIGENCE SUMMARY.
(Erase heading not required.)

Instructions regarding War Diaries and Intelligence Summaries are contained in F.S. Regs., Part II. and the Staff Manual respectively. Title pages will be prepared in manuscript.

Hour, Date, Place		Summary of Events and Information	Remarks and references to Appendices
VAUCHELLES Sept. 12"	3 pm	Quarli maski returned from leave. Divine Service. Quarli maski admitted to 2/1 S.D. Amb. injured through fall from horse. Weather fine.	Reference Map FRANCE Sheet 57 D Scale 1:40,000
VAUCHELLES Sept. 13"		Routine duties. Weather fine.	
VAUCHELLES Sept. 14"	11 AM	D.A.D.M.S. called with instructions to draw up scheme for evacuating wounded in event of advance. Scheme submitted. All leave stopped. Weather hot & cold.	Do
VAUCHELLES Sept. 15"	10 AM	Major GREEN visited D.A.D.M.S. with reference to Scheme. also visited B.S.S. at SAILLY and BALLS as COUIN. Scheme for Balls at Headqrs. approved. Weather fine.	Do
VAUCHELLES Sept. 16"		Major GREEN visited Dressing Stations at SAILLY and HEBUTERNE. Quarli maski returned to duty from 2/1 S.D. Amb. Weather fine.	Do
VAUCHELLES Sept. 17"	9.30 a.m. 3 pm	Major GREEN examined patients with Lieuts ROE and MOORE. Visited Dressing Station at SAILLY. Weather fine.	Do

(9 29 6) W 4141—463 100,000 9/14 H W V   Forms/C. 2118/10

Army Form C. 2118.

WAR DIARY
or
INTELLIGENCE SUMMARY.
(Erase heading not required.)

Instructions regarding War Diaries and Intelligence Summaries are contained in F.S. Regs., Part II. and the Staff Manual respectively. Title pages will be prepared in manuscript.

Hour, Date, Place	Summary of Events and Information	Remarks and references to Appendices
VAUCHELLES Sept 18"	Routine duties weather - fine	Reference Map FRANCE Sheet 57 D. Scale 1-40000
VAUCHELLES Sept 19" 10am 3pm	Major GREEN inspected Stone Carts with Lieut MOORE. Divine Service. Weather very hot.	
VAUCHELLES Sept 20" 11am	Major GREEN visited SAILLY and BOITONS at COUIN, then WADMS office. Weather fine	Do
VAUCHELLES Sept 21" 3pm	Routine duties in morning. Baths at COUIN taken on by 15th Fd Amb. The ADMS called at Headquarters and discussed scheme for evacuation of wounded with Major GREEN. Weather fine	
VAUCHELLES Sept 22"	Acting in accordance with instructions from ADMS, commenced evacuation of all patients from Divisional Rest Station. Major GREEN visited HEBUTERNE Dressing Station. Weather very fine	Do
VAUCHELLES Sept 23"	Completed evacuation of patients from DRS and rearranged Hospital for admission of wounded. Weather: Heavy thunderstorm in evening.	
VAUCHELLES Sept 24" 9.30	Visited offices of ADMS and later Dressing Station at SAILLY. Baths completed at Headquarters. Weather: wet	Do

Army Form C. 2118.

WAR DIARY
or
INTELLIGENCE SUMMARY.
(Erase heading not required.)

Instructions regarding War Diaries and Intelligence Summaries are contained in F.S. Regs., Part II. and the Staff Manual respectively. Title pages will be prepared in manuscript.

Hour, Date, Place	Summary of Events and Information	Remarks and references to Appendices
VAUCHELLES Sept 25.	Routine duties. Weather: very wet.	Reference Map FRANCE Sheet 57 D Scale 1: 40,000
VAUCHELLES Sept 26. 10 am	Visited SAILLY and HEBUTERNE with A.D.M.S.; inspected 2 proposed bivouac.	
3 pm	Pantagrum. Divine Service. Weather: very wet.	
VAUCHELLES Sept 27. 3.30	Routine duties. Visit from D.A.D.M.S. VIIth Corps. Weather: cold, dull day; no rain.	Do
VAUCHELLES Sept 28. 11 am	Routine duties. A.D.M.S. called. Weather: very cold: snow at night.	
VAUCHELLES Sept 29. 10 am 3 pm	Visited SAILLY in morning. Afterwards proceeded to DOULLENS to interview Sub Prefect with reference to one being School room which was granted on condition that another room was found for use of School & this was done. Weather: cold and dull.	
VAUCHELLES Sept 30.	Routine duties. Weather: cold & dull; no rain.	

CONFIDENTIAL

1211 4496

48th Division

WAR DIARY.

October 1915.

1/3rd South Midland Field Ambulance
R.A.M.C. (T.)

Oct 1915

Army Form C. 2118.

WAR DIARY
or
INTELLIGENCE SUMMARY.
(Erase heading not required.)

Instructions regarding War Diaries and Intelligence Summaries are contained in F. S. Regs., Part II. and the Staff Manual respectively. Title pages will be prepared in manuscript.

Hour, Date, Place		Summary of Events and Information	Remarks and references to Appendices
VAUCHELLES Oct 1st	10.30 a.m.	Returned from leave today. General routine work. Weather fine, cold.	Reference Map FRANCE LENS - Sheet 11 Scale 1/100,000
VAUCHELLES Oct 2nd	11.30	A.D.M.S. called with information that as matters appeared to have quietened down on this front he would probably give two beds again to a D.R.S. Weather fine, cold.	Do
VAUCHELLES Oct 3rd	12 noon	Routine duties. The A.D.M.S. called with information that he was issuing orders for Dressing Stations and Baths at HEBUTERNE and SAILLY au BOIS to be handed over by us to the 2nd Field Amb. (S.M.) and that my Unit should reopen as a D.T.R.S.	
	3 pm	Church Parade: Divine Service by Canon WELCHMAN C.F. Today in reply to Confidential letter from A.D.M.S. I recommended Capt. Maj. Jas. DAVIS and Staff. Sergt. Jas. CREESE for special mention — in dispatches. Weather fine, fine autumnal.	
VAUCHELLES Oct 4th		Orders for handing our Dressing Stations at HEBUTERNE and SAILLY having been received I issued instructions to the O.i.C. this Stations to be prepared to hand over tomorrow and arranged with O.C. 2nd Fd Amb. accordingly.	Do

Army Form C. 2118.

WAR DIARY
or
INTELLIGENCE SUMMARY.

(Erase heading not required.)

Instructions regarding War Diaries and Intelligence Summaries are contained in F.S. Regs., Part II. and the Staff Manual, respectively. Title pages will be prepared in manuscript.

Hour, Date, Place		Summary of Events and Information	Remarks and references to Appendices
VAUCHELLES Oct 4th (cont)		Major GREEN and Artificers engaged in repairing billets for additional officers and men — The Coffin & the billets at Lens.	Reference Map FRANCE LENS – Sheet 11 Scale 100,000
	4 pm	Major WALSH D.A. & Q.M.G. called with reference to A.F. B213. Promotion of Lieuts HARTY, SMYTHE and DACRE to Captains in Gazette of Oct 2nd afternoon in todays "TIMES" and other newspapers. Weather: fine	
VAUCHELLES Oct 5th	10.30 am	The A.D.M.S. called to discuss various points in connection with the charge of duties.	Do
	3 pm	Capt WILLIAMSON and party from SAILLY arrived and reported having handed over Dressing Station and Baths there to officers of 2nd 29 Mid.	
	4 pm	Capt SMYTHE and party from HEBUTERNE arrived and reported having handed over Dressing Station & Baths there to officer of 2nd 29 Mid. Weather: very wet: both parties on above arrived soaked and mud covered.	
VAUCHELLES Oct 6th		Today all officers busily engaged in getting rooms cleaned and made habitable for the men & to see there arrival yesterday have been accommodated in tents. The travelling Incinerator having arrived in VAUCHELLES Capt MOORE was appointed to take medical charge of Same hopes as they have no M.O. Weather: fine: mud still plentiful.	Do

… Army Form C. 2118.

WAR DIARY
or
INTELLIGENCE SUMMARY.
(Erase heading not required.)

Hour, Date, Place	Summary of Events and Information	Remarks and references to Appendices
VAUCHELLES Oct 7th	Routine duties:- An acknowledgement of service on been founded cards was to-day received by the following officers and N.C.O's:- Capts. WILLIAMSON and SMYTHE Sergt Major DAVIS and Staff Sergt CREESE. who was expressed in the following terms :- "48th (South Midland) Division ON ACTIVE SERVICE (Name of Officer or N.C.O.) 3rd S.M. Field Ambulance. Your Commanding Officer and Brigade Commander have informed me that you have distinguished yourself by your conduct in the Field. I have read their report with much pleasure. R. Fanshawe Major General Commanding 48th (S.M.) Division" Weather fine, Autumnal.	Reference Map FRANCE LENS - Sheet 11 Scale 1/100,000

Army Form C. 2118.

WAR DIARY
or
INTELLIGENCE SUMMARY.
(Erase heading not required.)

Instructions regarding War Diaries and Intelligence Summaries are contained in F.S. Regs., Part II. and the Staff Manual respectively. Title pages will be prepared in manuscript.

Hour, Date, Place	Summary of Events and Information	Remarks and references to Appendices
VAUCHELLES Oct 8"	9.30 a.m. Rode to SARTON - to Field Cashier. Day of routine duties in office. Camps and Billets. Weather fine: a bright autumnal day.	Reference Map FRANCE LENS - Sheet 11 Scale 1/100,000
VAUCHELLES Oct 9"	Routine duties. Weather; fine.	
VAUCHELLES Oct 10"	Leave being again been opened Capt WILLIAMSON left today on 8 days leave. 8.30 a.m. Inspected the morning Parade. 10.30 a.m. Church Parade: Divine Service by the Rev. MAUDE-ROXBY. Weather: a perfect autumn day, bright sunshine.	Do
VAUCHELLES Oct 11"	8.30 a.m. "A" & "C" Sections - route march via RAINCHEVAL and MARIEUX. "B" Section being Section on duty at Divn. R.L. Stn. Routine duties. Weather: dull: some rain in "evening".	Do
VAUCHELLES Oct 12"	The A.D.M.S. called my attention to the fact that I must now open out my D.R.S. to full number of 200 patients and to keep patients for 10 days if necessary. My forecast now nevertheless were to accommodate not more than 100 patients and to retain no more for a longer period than 7 days. Weather: dull.	Do

Forms/C. 2118/10

Army Form C. 2118.

WAR DIARY
or
INTELLIGENCE SUMMARY.
(Erase heading not required.)

Instructions regarding War Diaries and Intelligence Summaries are contained in F. S. Regs., Part II. and the Staff Manual respectively. Title pages will be prepared in manuscript.

Hour, Date, Place		Summary of Events and Information	Remarks and references to Appendices
VAUCHELLES Oct. 13th		Routine duties; no special incident. Capt SMYTHE detailed for duty with the 1/4th R. Berks Regt. Vice Capt BEAN the M.O. of that Regt. on 8 days leave.	Reference Map FRANCE LENS - Sheet 11 Scale 1:100,000
	3. p.m.	Capt SMYTHE reported to O.C. of the Regt at HEBUTERNE.	
		Supply motor ambulance to convey civilian (suffering from Enteric fever) from COIGNEUX to hospital at DOULLENS. Weather: Unsettled. Some rain in forenoon.	Do
VAUCHELLES Oct. 14th	8.30 a.m.	Inspected clothing of men for whom new clothing had been demanded by O.C's sections.	
		Lieut & Q.M. WOODS. H.W. left on 4 days leave. Weather: dull.	
VAUCHELLES Oct. 15th	4.p.m.	Routine duties, inspection of billets etc. Major WALSH D.A.V. Q.M.G. called with reference to arranging for billeting a Field Co. R.E. (36th Divn) in this village. Visited & selected Coi-milk. Unit officer. Weather: dull	Do
VAUCHELLES Oct. 16th	6.p.m.	Capt DACRE detailed for duty with 3rd R SUSSEX REGT. during temporary absence on sick leave of Capt WAUGH. Meeting of Officers to discuss matters affecting the comfort and well being of men in billets for the winter. Weather: Dull.	Do

(9 29 6) W 4141—463 100,000 9/14 H W V Forms/C. 2118/10

Army Form C. 2118.

WAR DIARY
or
INTELLIGENCE SUMMARY.
(Erase heading not required.)

Instructions regarding War Diaries and Intelligence Summaries are contained in F.S. Regs., Part II. and the Staff Manual respectively. Title pages will be prepared in manuscript.

Hour, Date, Place	Summary of Events and Information	Remarks and references to Appendices
VAUCHELLES Oct 17" 10.30 am	Church Parade: Service conducted by the Rev. Mauge Revd C.F.	Reference Map FRANCE LENS - Sheet 11 Scale 1/100,000
11.30 am	The A.D.V.S. called and inspected horses. Weather dull.	
VAUCHELLES Oct 18" 8.30 am	Accompanied by Major WALSH D.A.A.+Q.M.G. and Capt. OATWAY 121st 3rd Co. R.E. 36th Division went round village to select site for Camp for their Company.	Do
12 noon	A.D.M.S. called. Several lorries of artillery had for a couple of hours thro' the town. Weather: dull + much colder.	
VAUCHELLES Oct 19:	Hon. Lieut. + Q.M. WOODS MILL returned from leave today. Weather: dull + cold	Do
VAUCHELLES Oct 20"	Routine duties. Weather: dull + cold.	Do
VAUCHELLES Oct 21st 3.30 pm	Colonel BOYCE A.A.+Q.M.G. and Major WALSH D.A.A.+Q.M.G. called and inspected the D.R.S. Baths, Pack stores etc. Weather: dull + cold. Some rain thro' night.	Do

Army Form C. 2118.

WAR DIARY
or
INTELLIGENCE SUMMARY.

(Erase heading not required.)

Instructions regarding War Diaries and Intelligence Summaries are contained in F.S. Regs., Part II. and the Staff Manual respectively. Title pages will be prepared in manuscript.

Hour, Date, Place	Summary of Events and Information	Remarks and references to Appendices
VAUCHELLES Oct 22"d	Revd R.B. ROE and Capt. MOORE left today on detached duty & take over temporarily medical charge of the 48 Div Amm. Col. and 1/4 Glos. Regt. respectively. CAPT. SMYTHE returned from detached duty with the 4" R. Berks Regt. Weather cold day	Reference Map FRANCE LENS - Sheet 11 Scale 100,000
VAUCHELLES Oct 23"d 8.45" a.m.	The G.O.C. of the 48 Division General FANSHAWE called and inspected the D.R.S, Baths, Office, Dispensary & Pack Store	Do
11 a.m.	The A.D.M.S. called. discussed the question of lighting & heating the patients tents and marquees. Weather getting much colder	
VAUCHELLES Oct 24" 10.30 a	"A" Section took over duties of D.R.S. from "B" Section today. Church Parade. Divine Service & Rev. Maurice Roby C.F. Weather dull & cold.	Do
VAUCHELLES Oct 25"	The Rev. HELM C.F rejoined the 5" Glos. Regt. from this F.A. for duty. Visit of H.M. KING GEORGE and other distinguished personages to this front. Weather Cold - now wet and disagreeable.	Do

WAR DIARY
or
INTELLIGENCE SUMMARY.
(Erase heading not required.)

Army Form C. 2118.

Hour, Date, Place	Summary of Events and Information	Remarks and references to Appendices
VAUCHELLES Oct 26th	5:30 a.m. M CHAILLOU - Stopford. Left on 8 days' leave. Routine duties. Weather fine but cold.	Reference Map FRANCE LENS – Sheet 11 Scale 1/100,000
VAUCHELLES Oct 27th	9:30 a.m. Proc. to LOUVENCOURT to interview Col. ROBERTS. O.C. TRAIN. Remainder of day routine duties. Weather dull, cold & raw.	Do
VAUCHELLES Oct 28th	10:30 a.m. Capt. HERAPATH proceed to BUS as member of Medical Board. Routine duties. Weather a wet miserable day; mud everywhere.	Do
VAUCHELLES Oct 29th	Routine duties. 3 p.m. A.D.M.S. called to discuss flooring for Marquees. Weather dull. Cold & raw.	Do
VAUCHELLES Oct 30th	8:30 a.m. Capt. HERAPATH left on 8 days' leave. Lieut ROE returned from attached duty with the 48th Div. Amm. Col. 3 p.m. Major DANIELSON called to see the proprietor of CHATEAU VAUCHELLES with a view to coming to an agreement with him for looking over part of orchard for one no wagon lines for this unit. We are unable to do this. Weather cold & raw.	Do
VAUCHELLES Oct 31st	10:30 a.m. Church Parade. Divine Service held by Rev. Monde-Ronsby. Capt. MOORE rejoined unit from detached duty with the 1/4 Glos Regt. Weather cold, raw, wet.	Do

James Jones
Lieut Colonel R.A.M.C.T.
Commanding 2nd South Midlands Field Amb.

48th Division

CONFIDENTIAL.

121/7637

WAR DIARY.

NOVEMBER 1915.

1/3rd South Midland Field Ambulance.
48th Division.

Vol VIII

1/21/7637

Nov 1915

Army Form C. 2118.

Instructions regarding War Diaries and Intelligence
Summaries are contained in F.S. Regs., Part II.
and the Staff Manual respectively. Title pages
will be prepared in manuscript.

WAR DIARY
or
INTELLIGENCE SUMMARY.
(Erase heading not required.)

Hour, Date, Place	Summary of Events and Information	Remarks and references to Appendices
VAUCHELLES NOV. 1st	The first day of a new month finds this Unit comparatively exhausted as in the beginning of the previous month. The men are all comfortably quartered in billets. Teams do — every endeavour having been made on the part of their officers to make the men as comfortable as possible. Captains commanding have been provided with (and seats fitted up, ablution sheds, urinals and latrines constructed for each section. The comfort of the patients in the Divisional Rest Station has also been for general care; improvements in lighting & heating of the marquee & rooms in which the patients are, have been made and generally their comfort & welfare have been improved. A new dressing room and steam disinfector have been constructed at the Bath and the bathing of the patients, the men of my own Unit and the troops in the Village generally has been carried out altogether more satisfactorily and in greater comfort. Weather: wet, cold and raw.	Reference Map FRANCE LENS — Sheet 11 Scale 1 = 100,000
VAUCHELLES NOV 2nd	9am. At the 9 o'clock parade I made a short address to the men in the course of taking official farewell of Regt. Sergt. S. Davis who has been attached to the Unit on Sup Sergt. Instructor for 7½ years and who leaves the Unit today to report to the A Base IV Division for duty with No. 12 Field Ambulance. Capt. Moore proceeded for detached duty with the Bucks Battalion. Weather: most unpleasant wet and raw every where.	Do

Army Form C. 2118.

WAR DIARY
or
INTELLIGENCE SUMMARY.
(Erase heading not required.)

Instructions regarding War Diaries and Intelligence Summaries are contained in F.S. Regs., Part II. and the Staff Manual respectively. Title pages will be prepared in manuscript.

Hour, Date, Place		Summary of Events and Information	Remarks and references to Appendices
VAUCHELLES Nov 3rd	11 am	A.D.M.S. called with instructions that on the 1st S.M. Field Ambulance had now over 100 cases of Scabies to deal with I must be prepared to take a considerable greater number of Cases into the D.R.S. Today M. EMAILLOU Interpreter returned from leave. Weather - dry & fine	Reference Map FRANCE LENS - Sheet 11. Scale 1 = 100,000
VAUCHELLES Nov 4th	8.30 am	Lieut ROE proceeded for temporary duty with 17th R.Morc. Regt. In the evening I received a memo from the A.D.M.S. instructing me to submit the names of two additional M.O.'s & men for leave. "the G.O.C. having awarded 2 of the 3 R.A.M.C. this leave to you" Went for good arrangements at VAUCHELLES. Weather: cold & fine	Do
VAUCHELLES Nov 5th		Routine duties. Capt. SMYTHE proceeded for temporary duty with the 1/6 Gloster's. Weather: fine; frost at night	Do
VAUCHELLES Nov 6th	9 am	Visited South Midland Casualty Clearing Station at AMIENS. Weather: fine; cold	Do
VAUCHELLES Nov 7th	10.30 am	Church Parade: service by Rev. MAUDE-ROXBY C.F. (C.J.E.) Weather: fine; cold.	Do

Army Form C. 2118.

WAR DIARY
or
INTELLIGENCE SUMMARY.
(Erase heading not required.)

Instructions regarding War Diaries and Intelligence Summaries are contained in F. S. Regs., Part II. and the Staff Manual respectively. Title pages will be prepared in manuscript.

Hour, Date, Place		Summary of Events and Information	Remarks and references to Appendices
VAUCHELLES Nov. 8th	11 a.m.	The A.D.V.S. called with reference to outbreak of skin disease in one or two horses – suspected mange. Weather: Fine Autumn day.	Reference Map FRANCE LENS – Sheet 11 Scale 1 – 100,000
VAUCHELLES Nov. 9th		No incident of note. Weather: fine mild night when heavy rain fell.	Do
VAUCHELLES Nov. 10th	4.30 p.m.	The Rev. H.A. MEEK 4th Class Chaplain reported the need for the Base. Attended lecture by Colonel ALEXIS THOMSON on War Surgery of Abdominal wounds, at 2nd F.A. Amb., LOUVENCOURT. Weather: heavy rain at intervals with occasional gleams of sunshine.	Do
VAUCHELLES Nov. 11th	2 p.m.	Routine duties. Officers representative of British Red Cross Society called with view to obtaining certain articles for use of patients in D.R.S. Offer gratefully accepted. Weather: dull & wet; very heavy rain at night; mud plentiful.	Do
VAUCHELLES Nov. 12th	11 a.m.	D.A.D.M.S. called. Capt. MOORE returned from temporary duty with the Bucks Batt'n. Ox. L.I. for duty with the Unit. Weather: wet & stormy.	Do

Army Form C. 2118.

WAR DIARY
or
INTELLIGENCE SUMMARY.
(Erase heading not required.)

Instructions regarding War Diaries and Intelligence Summaries are contained in F.S. Regs., Part II. and the Staff Manual respectively. Title pages will be prepared in manuscript.

Hour, Date, Place	Summary of Events and Information	Remarks and references to Appendices
VAUCHELLES Nov. 13" 8.30 a.m.	Capt HARTY proceeded to MARIEUX to see professionally the G.O.C. VII.º Corps (General SNOW).	Reference Map FRANCE LENS – Sheet 11 Scale 1 – 100,000
2.30 p.m.	Attended lecture at the Recreation Room BUS on "Smoke Helmets" and "Poison Gases" by Capt HARTLEY; A.D.M.S provided. Weather fine.	Do
VAUCHELLES Nov. 14. 10.30 a.m.	Church Parade; Cy. E. Service by the Rev. ROXBY. C.F. A.D.M.S. called & inspected D.R.S.: was specially interested in a brick fireplace constructed to heat hospital marquee.	
4 p.m.	Major DANIELSON and Capt WILLIAMSON (from Scottish called with reference to making arrangements for payment for use of orchard now occupied by D.R.S. They interviewed M. GOSSELIN	
7.30 p.m.	Proceeded at Lecture in the Canteen Recreation Room given by the Rev. H.R. McGRK C.F. on "The Australian Bush"; Revº Colonie inaugurating a course of popular lectures for the N.C.O's & men arranged during the winter months while we are (Phil Stationary. Weather fine	
VAUCHELLES Nov. 15.	Rev HINGLEY C.F. attached for duty with 2ⁿᵈ ɪˢᵗ Aus. Lieut. R.B. ROE returned to duty with the ɪˢᵗ Aus. from leave. On duty with the 1/5 "R. Warc. Regt. Weather: a slight fall of snow had taken place during the night; ground (slightly) covered.	Do

Forms/C. 2118/10

WAR DIARY
or
INTELLIGENCE SUMMARY.
(Erase heading not required.)

Army Form C. 2118.

Instructions regarding War Diaries and Intelligence Summaries are contained in F. S. Regs., Part II. and the Staff Manual respectively. Title pages will be prepared in manuscript.

Hour, Date, Place	Summary of Events and Information	Remarks and references to Appendices
VAUCHELLES Nov 16th	Routine duties. Forwarded to A.D.M.S. recommendation of promotion of Staff Sergt. S. Crewe to rank of Sergt. Major. Late promotion approved by A.D.M.S. Weather: a heavy fall of snow had occurred during the night at 7 a.m. snow still falling: ground covered some 6-7 inches deep.	Reference Map FRANCE LENS - Sheet 11 Scale 1-100,000
VAUCHELLES Nov 17th	Staff Sergt. Crewe promoted to Sergt. Major. Routine duties. Weather: mainly sharp frost at night.	Do
VAUCHELLES Nov 18th 9 a.s. 3.30 pm	A.D.M.S. called & inspected D.R.S.: discussed question of heating & lighting. D.D.M.S. VIIth Corps called and inspected D.R.S. Weather: frost in morning; thaw set in later in day.	Do
VAUCHELLES Nov 19th 10 am 2.30 pm	By appointment met Col. ROBERTS 48th Div. Supply Column met him, Major CRAIG Office 121st Field Co. R.E. (36th Div.) and Major OCCLESTON 5th Entrenching Bn. with a view to re-adjusting billets and providing accommodation for 1 Off. & 10 Other Ranks of 121st F.A. Co. Pte RICKARDS left today for England in accordance from Army Council - for Employment on Government work at NOTTHAM CHEMICAL WORKS BRISTOL. Weather: cold & windy.	Do

WAR DIARY
or
INTELLIGENCE SUMMARY.
(Erase heading not required.)

Army Form C. 2118.

Instructions regarding War Diaries and Intelligence Summaries are contained in F.S. Regs., Part II. and the Staff Manual respectively. Title pages will be prepared in manuscript.

Hour, Date, Place	Summary of Events and Information	Remarks and references to Appendices
VAUCHELLES Nov. 20. 9.30 a.m.	Lieut R.B. ROE left for detached duty with 1/8. R. Warwicks.	Reference Map FRANCE LENS — Sheet 11 Scale 1 — 100,000
12. noon	A.D.M.S. & the G.O.C. 46. Division visited the D.R.S. noted the general view of clearing the latter, the Steam Disinfector conducted by and in use of the Field Ambulance.	
4 p.m.	Lieut R.I. DACRE left on 8 days leave of absence.	
"	Major DANEELSON and Capt. WILLIAMSON of the LONDON SCOTTISH interviewed M. GOSSELIN the proprietor of the Chateau VAUCHELLES for hire of Orchard in use of D.R.S.	
8 p.m.	Dined with the G.O.C. at his headquarters.	
	Weather: cold snow, slight frost at night.	
VAUCHELLES Nov 21st	10.30 a.m. C of E Service & Rev. ROXBY. C.F.	as
	11.30 a.m. Non Conformist Service & Rev. H.P. MEEK. C.F.	
	Weather: raw & windy — dry.	
VAUCHELLES Nov 22nd	1 p.m. A.D.M.S. visited the D.R.S	as
	D.M.S. III Army (Surgeon General TREHERNE) called and inspected the D.R.S.	
4 p.m.	A.A. & Q.M.G & D.A.A. & Q.M.G. called with reference to Police arrangements of the Village	
	Weather: dry hot raw — cold.	

WAR DIARY
or
INTELLIGENCE SUMMARY.
(Erase heading not required.)

Army Form C. 2118.

Hour, Date, Place	Summary of Events and Information	Remarks and references to Appendices
VAUCHELLES Nov 23rd 12:30 pm	Major SUMMERHAYES and an Officer of the 4th OXFORDS called to see Bolsho & Dimenfacts which is proposed to enrollent in Random changeover for use of that kind. Weather: dull & cold.	Reference Maps FRANCE LENS - Sheet 11 Scale 1:100,000
VAUCHELLES Nov 24th 5pm	Capt MOORE returned from detached duty. Present at meeting of so called "South Midland Mechanical Society" at headquarters of 2nd S.M. and LOUVENCOURT where Capt DALE opened a discussion on "Some trades of Sanitary Interest". Weather: cold & raw.	Do
VAUCHELLES Nov 25th 11:30 am	A.D.M.S. called. Capt SMYTHE returned from detached duty. Weather: mild and glorious and note considerable crunching of the road. Very cold at night.	Do
VAUCHELLES Nov 26th	No incidents to report; routine duties only. Weather: much colder; some snow fell in evening & from from frost at night.	Do
VAUCHELLES Nov 27th	Routine duties. Weather: very cold; sharp frost.	Do

WAR DIARY or INTELLIGENCE SUMMARY

Army Form C. 2118.

(Erase heading not required.)

Hour, Date, Place	Summary of Events and Information	Remarks and references to Appendices
VAUCHELLES Nov 28. 10.30am	C. of E. Service by the Rev. ROXBY C.F.	Reference Map FRANCE LENS — Sheet 11 Scale 1 - 100,000
11.30	Non conformist service by the Rev. H.P. MEEN C.F.	
3.30pm	Capt CHANDLER called with instructions to submit by 6pm on the 29 inst. a report with plans for accommodating and subsisting 10 officers + 500 men in close billets in this village in case of emergency.	
6pm	Paid a visit to the man i/c the band re "Army Historical Association of Bristol"; in connection with a weekly lecture arranged for a Committee of N.C.Os, men. The lecture was given in the newly re-erected marquee. Weather: very severe frost.	Do
VAUCHELLES Nov 29.	Capt DABRE returned from leave. Lieut ROE returned from detached duty with 18 "Horwichs". Sat in report & plans for above billetting arrangements to Div. Weather: thaw set in in morning; heavy rain all day.	Do
6pm		
VAUCHELLES Nov 30.	Three officers and 6 N.C.Os. of the 97th Field Amb. 30 Div. attached today for instructional purposes.	Do
11am	D.A.D.M.S. called regarding us to submit 6-A.D.M.S. duty a scheme for instruction alone - 5 days course	
12.30pm	The A.P.M. 46 Div. called with reference to police arrangements this village. Weather: heavier; again much milder.	

121/793

WAR DIARY.

OF

1/3RD S.M. FIELD AMBULANCE - 48TH DIVISION.

FOR

THE MONTH OF DECEMBER 1915.

Vol IX

Dec 1915

WAR DIARY
or
INTELLIGENCE SUMMARY
(Erase heading not required.)

Army Form C. 2118.

Hour, Date, Place	Summary of Events and Information	Remarks and references to Appendices
VAUCHELLES Dec. 1st	The first day of another month finds this Field Ambulance still stationed at VAUCHELLES and running the Divisional Rest Station. The average number of patients has somewhat increased and the incidence of colder weather has necessitated certain changes in the internal management. Huts have been constructed into which 40 patients have been transferred from small hospital marquees can be accommodated with greater comfort. The muddy condition of the orchard and surroundings has necessitated the making of wood fire which prevent the infirmaries have been made in tending out the pontage of fuel and inadequate supply of stones while leave much to be desired in this direction. Experiments have been made with fuel (pieces in the cars) erection of brick kitchen ovens and an endeavour has been made in this way to minimise the shortage of fuel difficulty. A number of steps and other appliances have also been made for use in messrooms etc. With the exception of a brief visit from the A.D.M.S. no incident of note to record today. The three officers of the 97th 2nd Ambulance attached for instruction visited the Dressing Station of the 2nd F.M. 2/2 Field at SAILLY LORAY. *hcallun* Miller Lieut Col	Reference Map FRANCE – LENS Sheet – 11 Scale – 1:100,000

Army Form C. 2118.

WAR DIARY
or
INTELLIGENCE SUMMARY.
(Erase heading not required.)

Instructions regarding War Diaries and Intelligence Summaries are contained in F. S. Regs., Part II. and the Staff Manual respectively. Title pages will be prepared in manuscript.

Hour, Date, Place		Summary of Events and Information	Remarks and references to Appendices
VAUCHELLES Dec 2nd	11 am	The G.O.C. 48th Div. paid a short visit to the D.R.S. today. The three officers of the 97 & 98 Ambs. temporarily attached received instruction in the various administrative duties of a Field Ambulance. Weather: mild and moist.	Reference Map FRANCE – LENS Sheet – 11 Scale – 1:100.000
VAUCHELLES Dec 3rd		Routine duties: no medical record. Weather: milder, wet; mud plentiful	Do
VAUCHELLES Dec 4th		Lieut R.B. ROE proceeded on 14 days leave on re-engaging in temporary effrts R.A.M.C. MAJOR BARON 48' Div. Supply Column called with reference to re-inforcements in men of mechanical transport attacked. Weather: a wet and boisterous day. Wind and rain.	Do
VAUCHELLES Dec 5th	10 am	Church of England Service conducted by the Rev. STREATFIELD C.F. in absence on leave of Rev. MAUDE-ROXBY.	
	11:30 am	Non Conformist Service conducted by Rev H.A. MEEK C.F.	
	3 pm	CAPT. CHANDLER R.A.M.C. Staff called with reference to accommodation available for billeting troops in this village. Capt SMYTHE attached to 1/1 mounted for temporary duty vice Capt SHERIDAN on sick leave.	
	6 pm	attended Concert given by Bandsmen in the Canteen Recreation marquee. Weather: wet and stormy	
VAUCHELLES Dec 6th		Memo from A.D.M.S. to inform me that Capt. HARTY had been appointed for special work at Base in connection with diseases of the Ear, Throat & Nose.	Do
	3 pm	A.D.M.S. Called. Weather: Mild. Some rain.	

WAR DIARY or INTELLIGENCE SUMMARY

Army Form C. 2118.

(Erase heading not required.)

Hour, Date, Place		Summary of Events and Information	Remarks and references to Appendices
VAUCHELLES Dec 7th	11.30	Three Officers and 6 N.C.O's temporarily attached from the 97th Field Amb. left this morning to rejoin their unit. Weather - fine in morning; very wet afternoon & evening.	Reference Map FRANCE - LENS Sheet 11 Scale - 1:100,000
VAUCHELLES Dec 8th	9.0 a.m.	Three more Officers & 6 NCOs of 97th Fd. Amb. arrived today for instruction - 8 days course.	
	10 a.m.	Rode to Divisional Headquarters BUS where I saw the A.A & Q.M.G. & when I handed report on water supply of VAUCHELLES.	
	12 noon	A.D.M.S. called.	
	4.30 pm	Attended meeting of Medical Officers at LOUVENCOURT - the Hangers of 2nd & 3rd Amb. at which Capt McLEOD of the mobile laboratory read a paper on "Albuminuria and Nephritis". The paper was followed by a discussion. Today there are 150 patients on the D.R.S. 70 having been admitted during the last two days. Coal is now very scarce & notwithstanding the weather is now mild again otherwise the patients in the huts marquees must suffer from the want of fuel. On account of the much, much work is being done to improve way in the making of roads from the huts and barns in which the patients are accommodated.	
VAUCHELLES Dec 9th		Routine duties today Weather: mild; wet	Do
VAUCHELLES Dec 10th		Routine duties. Weather fine very mild.	Do

Army Form C. 2118.

WAR DIARY
or
INTELLIGENCE SUMMARY.
(Erase heading not required.)

Instructions regarding War Diaries and Intelligence Summaries are contained in F.S. Regs., Part II. and the Staff Manual respectively. Title pages will be prepared in manuscript.

Hour, Date, Place		Summary of Events and Information	Remarks and references to Appendices
VAUCHELLES Dec. 11th	10 am	Rode to SARTON to draw money from Field Cashier. Rev. ROXBY returned from leave. Weather: high wind: some rain.	Reference Map FRANCE – LENS Sheet 11. Scale – 1:100,000
VAUCHELLES Dec. 12th	10 am	Called on Col. ROBERTS H.Qrs. Div. Train with reference to replacing former Corporal STRIDE attached to my train, whose work and conduct are unsatisfactory. Divisional Church service conducted by Revs. ROXBY & MEEK C. of E. Weather: mild.	Do
VAUCHELLES Dec. 13th	noon	Word from A.D.M.S.	
	4 pm	Capt. HERAPATH proceeded for temporary detached duty until 12th 34. And to relieve Capt. BOWATER of that unit on Special leave. Capts HARTY and MOORE proceeded on 8 days leave. Col. SMYTH-OSBOURNE A.A.Q.M.G. visited the D.R.S. and inspected Billets, also infected practice site and expressed pleasure & much interest in all arrangements. Weather: fine: sunshine.	Do
VAUCHELLES Dec 14th	9.30 am	Had to investigate case of Corpl STRIDE today. As he is today leaving this unit to rejoin Highd. Div. Train. I recommended him to O.C. that unit to take steps at the draft mills.	
	3.30 pm	The D.D.M.S. 1st Army called and inspected D.R.S. and especially the Disinfector. Three Officers & 6 N.C.Os. 97, 3rd And. reported here accrued and referred Weather: delightful frost day	

Forms/C. 2118/10

WAR DIARY or INTELLIGENCE SUMMARY.

Army Form C. 2118.

(Erase heading not required.)

Place	Date	Hour	Summary of Events and Information	Remarks and references to Appendices
VAUCHELLES	Dec 15	11.30 a.m.	Lieut BATEMAN and 6 N.C.O.s of the 97th Field Ambulance arrived for course of instruction.	Reference Map FRANCE – LENS Sheet No 11 Scale 1:100,000
		2 p.m.	Two officers of 13 R.C. arrived for purpose of inspecting D.R.S. with view to providing comforts for patients.	
		3 "	Major HAYES Commanding 97th Field Amb. called to inspect D.R.S. and to obtain information.	
		7 "	Capt. HERAPATH returned to unit from temporary duty at LA HAYE FERME the Evening Station of the 1/1 S.M. Field Amb., Capt. SMYTHE relieved from duty with 1/9 R Provincials taking his place. Weather: raw & cold.	
Do	" 16	11 a.m.	A.D.M.S. called with instructions that he proposed sending this Unit to take over Divisional Stations at SAILLY au BOIS and HEBUTERNE again in the beginning of January.	Do
		12 noon	Lieut HEATHCOTE of the 97th Fd. Amb. arrived for temporary attachment to this Unit for instruction. Weather: raw & cold. Cameron	
Do	" 17		Perkins Rubie: A Continental edition of a Lady paper published included (16th) announces the new Advent of Sir John FRENCH as Commander in Chief of the British Army at the Front. Sir Douglas HAIG to be his successor. Weather: raw & cold. Cameron	Do
Do	" 18	11 a.m.	D.A.D.M.S. and Capt DALE called. The latter made suggestion for slight improvement in connection with Disinfector. Weather: milder.	Do
Do	" 19	10.30 a.m.	Church Service held by Rev. M.M. ROXBY C.F. C.T.F. to Non Conformist Service held today.	Do
		4 p.m.	Capt HERAPATH took over duties at LE HAYE FERME from Capt SMYTHE who proceeded for temporary duty with 1/4 R. Bicker Regt. Weather: fine & mild.	

Army Form C. 2118.

WAR DIARY
or
INTELLIGENCE SUMMARY.
(Erase heading not required.)

Instructions regarding War Diaries and Intelligence Summaries are contained in F.S. Regs., Part II. and the Staff Manual respectively. Title pages will be prepared in manuscript.

Place	Date	Hour	Summary of Events and Information	Remarks and references to Appendices
VAUCHELLES	Dec. 20	2 p.m.	Proceeded, accompanied by the Quarter Master, to BEAUQUESNE to interview the Supply Officer there with reference to drawing Medical Comforts. Having received the necessary orders we proceeded to CANAPLES to draw Medical Comfort stores. Weather: mild.	Reference map. FRANCE - LENS Sheet No 11 Scale 1 - 100,000
Do.	" 21st	10 a.m.	Despatched the two attached Officers to SAILLY and HEBUTERNE to see the Dressing Station there. Above officers rejoined their unit - Dec 97th, 2d Arch - on completion of errand of instruction.	
		6 p.m.	Capt ROE returned from 14 days leave. Weather: wet: mild.	
Do.	" 22nd	10.30 a.m	Self, O.C. 48 Division (General FANSHAWE) visited and inspected the D.R.S. Weather: mild: wet.	Do
Do.	" 23rd	11 a.m	R.D.M.S. accompanied by the A.A. Q.M.G. and Capt DALE called this morning. The first named to see case of alleged trench foot. Major GREEN and Lieut WOODS-HILL engaged today in making a [survey] of the village to prepare by furnishing a report on the accommodation of troops in billets. Capt MOORE returned from 8 days leave. Weather: mild: wet.	Do
Do.	" 24th	5 p.m.	Sent Capt ROE to relieve Capt HERAPATH at LA HAYE FERME.	
		6 "	Accompanied by other officers I attended the Serjts. Mess where the Sergts. were holding Christmas festivities. Weather: mild: fresh at intervals.	Do
Do. (Christmas Day)	" 25	7 a.m. 8.45 9 a.m. 12 noon 1 p.m.	Communion Services by Rev H. Manser ROXBY and Rev HAMMER. Inspection parade. Contract Service for C. of E. and Nm conformists both chaplains officiating. Patients dinners having been served I visited all [wards?] & Marquees and offered the [season?] greetings to the patients Visited 'B' Section who were letting their Christmas festivities in the Canadian Recreation marquee.	Do

WAR DIARY or INTELLIGENCE SUMMARY

Army Form C. 2118.

Place	Date	Hour	Summary of Events and Information	Remarks and references to Appendices
VAUCHELLES	Dec. 25 (contd)	1:30 pm	Received the following telegram from the A.D.M.S. "General FANSHAWE wishes best wishes for Christmas to all ranks R.A.M.C. and Please convey to ranks (Revere before their speedy recovery) A.D.M."	Reference Map FRANCE – LENS Sheet No 11 Scale 1 – 100,000
		2:30 pm	Again visited the ranks and conveyed to the patients, who appeared much gratified, the General's good wishes. Caused the first paragraph of the telegram having reference R.A.M.C. to be included in my "Daily Orders".	
		3 pm	General FANSHAWE himself drove up to the Headquarters to offer personally the seasons greetings. Attended the tea & concert given by "B" Section in connection with their Christmas festivities. Weather unsettled. mild: some rain.	
Do.	"26"	9 am	C. of E. Service conducted by Rev. H. MOUDE-ROXBY.	Do
		5 pm	Visited "A" & "C" Sections who were holding their Christmas festivities. "B" Section being busy in their relief at the D.R.S. Weather mild.	
Do.	"27"		Lieut. v OM WOODS-HILL engaged in making survey of the cellars with accommodation available in case of shelling – with a view to reporting on same. Today received HM THE KING'S Christmas message to the troops. Weather mild seeming cold in the evening.	Do
Do.	"28"	9 am	An urgent message was received to send an officer to No.8 Flying Squadron ground at MARIEUX which I was informed an aeroplane accident had occurred. Capt. ROE proceeded there immediately where he found Sr. observer Lieut. ALCHIN R.F.A. attached R.F.C. had sustained a fracture of the skull, the pilot escaped unhurt.	Do
		2:30 pm	Attended office of A.D.M.S. with Cols BARLING & HOPKINS when the A.D. informed me that the G.O.C. of the Division had forwarded a Cup to be competed for by teams of the various units in the Division at Association Football. The R.A.M.C. to be represented by a combined team selected from the three field ambulances and Sanitary Section.	
		2:30	Entertainment provided by men of this unit to patients in D.R.S. and the children of the village – the latter being also provided with a supply of sweets.	

Army Form C. 2118.

WAR DIARY
or
INTELLIGENCE SUMMARY.
(Erase heading not required.)

Instructions regarding War Diaries and Intelligence Summaries are contained in F. S. Regs., Part II. and the Staff Manual respectively. Title pages will be prepared in manuscript.

Place	Date	Hour	Summary of Events and Information	Remarks and references to Appendices
VAUCHELLES	Dec. 28	6.30 p.m.	Attended "A" Section entertainment in the Cinema Recreation room. Trenches mud.	Reference Map FRANCE - LENS Sheet No 11 Scale 1:100,000
Do.	"29"	11.30 am	Visited No 19. C.C.S. at DOULLENS, borrowed and afterwards drew supply of petrol for use of motor Ambulances at the 48th Div. Supply Column.	
		2.30 - 4 pm	The recently formed Divisional Band visited VAUCHELLES and played a selection of music in front of the Mairie; much enjoyed by patients, troops & villagers.	
"		8.30	Visited Cinema recreation room and exhibited toys to winners of Chess & Whist Competitions which have been held during the past few months. Trenches mud: fine. Routine duties for the most part.	
Do	"30"		Attended Series of short football matches which had been arranged between teams from 1st, 2nd, & 3rd Field Ambulances for purpose of selecting team for the General's Cup. R.D.M.S. & officers of the other Ambulances also present. Received instructions from A.D.M.S. to take over dressing station at SAILLY & HEBUTERNE on Jany 3rd in relief of 2nd Field Ambulance. Trenches: fine.	Do.
		2.30 pm		
Do	"31st"	9. am	Inspected parade.	
		10.30	Had men not January inoculated and those in-oculated only once paraded and addressed them on the value of inoculation estopedially to these colour Statches & other troops of convincing nature will in view to personally them to undergo the operation. There not inoculated in this unit very few the percentage! Inoculated they 100% of Officers & 97½% of men. During the past few days the Matrons list has been carried out & the V.O. amongst the horses of my unit in common with others in the Division; no positive result has been obtained in any case so far. Trenches: still : some rain.	Do.

48th Division

1/3rd S.M. 2nd Anzac

Sam

Vol No X

F/24/11

Jan 1916

Army Form C. 2118.

WAR DIARY
or
INTELLIGENCE SUMMARY.
(Erase heading not required.)

Instructions regarding War Diaries and Intelligence Summaries are contained in F. S. Regs., Part II and the Staff Manual respectively. Title pages will be prepared in manuscript.

3rd SOUTH MIDLAND FD. AMBULANCE
No. ....
-1 FEB 1916
R.A.M.C.T.

Place	Date	Hour	Summary of Events and Information	Remarks and references to Appendices
VAUCHELLES LES AUTHIE	JANY 1st		The first day of a New Year finds no change in the General situation on this Front and no change in the position or duties of this unit. The weather cleared the past month has been on the whole mild and the fall excessively heavy falls of rain — more especially during the latter half of the month. The Sickness rate has been by no means high the Casualties comparitively few. A small number of "Trench Foot" cases and a few "frostbite" cases have passed through the Div: Rest Station but in neither instance has the number been great. That might be normally expected. The morning of today was occupied by the completion of numerous "returns" of which one to had to be dealt with besides a considerable amount of General Correspondence. In the afternoon Col. SHAH D.D.M.S. VII Corps & Major BROWN D.D.M.S. called but did not inspect D.R.S. Today Sir John French's "Despatch" was published and the following officers of this field Ambul. meet had the honour of being mentioned. Lieut Colonel James Young T.D. M.D. Capt. G. Scott Williamson Capt. H. S. D. Scoggie also St. Sergh. J. Davis. Late Sergh Major.	Ref MAP FRANCE LENS 11 Scale 1 - 100,000
Do	JANY 2nd	9 a.m.	Weather: Jan: mild. Church Parade. Service held by the Rev Moude Roxby. Weather: not stormy.	
Do	JANY 3rd	12 noon 2 p.m. 3.25	Today the C.O. proceeded for 8 days leave, his duties during his absence being carried out by Ma[jor] T.A. GREEN. Work over Dressing Stations at SAILLY & HEBUTERNE from 2nd 24 Amb. "B" (Queens) under Capt HERAPATH with Capt SMYTHE and ROE proceeded to these duties. Capt ROE taking charge of ADS at HEBUTERNE. Weather fine high wind Patients - sitting up Cases Evacuated to C.C.S by Light Railway: Supplied Evacuating Off for 1st + 3rd F.As	6

Wt. W10791/1773 500,000 1/15 D.D. & L. A.D.S.S./Forms/C. 2118.

Army Form C. 2118.

WAR DIARY
or
INTELLIGENCE SUMMARY.
(Erase heading not required.)

Instructions regarding War Diaries and Intelligence Summaries are contained in F. S. Regs., Part II. and the Staff Manual respectively. Title pages will be prepared in manuscript.

Place	Date 1916	Hour	Summary of Events and Information	Remarks and references to Appendices
VAUCHELLES LES AUTHIE	Jany 4th	12 noon	A.D.M.S. called. Lieut WOODS HILL etc. looked to attend Divisional Tom on 4" x 5" mile. Routine duties. Weather: fine, mild.	Ref. Map FRANCE LENS.11 Scale 1/100,000
Do	Jany 5th	11 a.m.	Divisional Tour (early) motor. Charge of A.P./Q.M.G. visited and inspected the D.R.S. A.D.M.S. also present. Joined Lieut FAIRFAX attached for duty. Capt SMYTHE returned from detached duty with 1/4 R. Berks Regt. Weather: fine	Do
Do	Jany 6th	10 a.m.	Major GREEN acting C.O. visited SAILLY & inspected Dressing Station. Weather: fine	
Do	Jany 7th		Routine duties Weather: wet & stormy	
Do	Jany 8th	2.30 p.m.	Had to send special motor ambulance to COURCELLES to convey two Civilians Typhoid cases to Hospital AMIENS. Weather: unsettled.	Do
Do	Jany 9th	9 a.m. 11	Church Parade; Service held by Rev Meek. C.F. A.D.M.S. called. Weather: fine	
Do	Jany 10th	10 a.m.	Major GREEN being C.O. visited SAILLY and inspected Dressing Station & Baths. New Officers baths working satisfactorily. Weather: fine	New
Do	Jany 11th	12.30 p.m. 2 p.m.	A.D.M.S called. The R.A.M.C. Association football team played Divisional Cavalry team in the first round of the "Danzlowe" Cup and were defeated by 1 goal to nil. Weather: fine in morning – wet afternoon –	

Army Form C. 2118.

WAR DIARY
or
INTELLIGENCE SUMMARY.
(Erase heading not required.)

Instructions regarding War Diaries and Intelligence Summaries are contained in F. S. Regs., Part II. and the Staff Manual respectively. Title pages will be prepared in manuscript.

Place	Date 1916	Hour	Summary of Events and Information	Remarks and references to Appendices
VAUCHELLES LES AUTHIE	Jany 12	6.30 p.m.	Routine work. Lieut Colonel J. YOUNG returned from 8 days leave. Weather: dull	Ref. Map FRANCE LENS – 11 Scale 1/100,000
Do	Jany 13	2 p.m.	Visited Divisional Station at SAILLY au BUTERNE Weather: stormy; heavy rain at intervals.	
Do	Jany 14	2.30 p.m.	Attended Headquarters of VII th Corps at MARIEUX to hear an address on the administrative arrangements at the recent attack on the enemy trenches at LOOS. Weather: stormy: some rain.	
Do	Jany 15		Routine duties; nothing special to record. Weather: fair	
Do	Jany 16	9 a.m.	Church Parade. Routine duties. Weather: fine	
Do	Jany 17	11 a.m.	Received a visit from M. LEGRANDE French Liaison Officer VII Corps. with reference to billeting claims in part of M. GOSSELIN the proprietor of the Chateau & Grounds occupied by D.R.S.	
		2.30 p.m.	Visited Divisional Station at SAILLY and inspected dressing station, baths & new disinfector in course of construction. Capt G. SCOTT WILLIAMSON proceeded to England on 8 days leave. Weather: fine morning: wet & stormy in afternoon.	
Do	Jany 18	11 a.m.	D.A.D.M.S. called.	
		3.30 p.m.	A.A.Q.M.G. 48th Divn and A.A.& Q.M.G's 66th & 67th Divisions & the D.D.M.S. VII Corps visited and inspected the D.R.S and new disinfector in Baths, Disinfector, Pack Store, Field Kitchens etc. Weather: fine in morning, became wet later.	

WAR DIARY or INTELLIGENCE SUMMARY

Army Form C. 2118

Place	Date 1916	Hour	Summary of Events and Information	Remarks and references to Appendices
VAUCHELLES LES AUTHIE	JANY 19th		Today Capt. ROE returned to Headquarters for 48 hours not being relieved by Capt SMYTHE. Capt ROE was suffering from effects of chill prev., a shell having burst in roadway near him, another in the roof of the dressing station whilst a third struck the chimney of the house adj'ing his billet. He was none the less weather, no settled fine in morning; some rain later.	Ref. Maps FRANCE 1/40,000 Scale 1/40,000
DO	JANY 20	12 noon	Inspected Chemist with view to reviewing its capacity for reception of wounded in case of necessity in order that I might submit a report of all accommodation available for wounded in the village.	
		4 p.m.	Capt McLEOD Mobile Laboratory Collect with reference to result of his analysis of a number of specimens of urine taken from the men of this unit for the purpose of investigation with reference to prevalence of Albuminuria. He reports amongst troops in the trenches and there was excellent units-living water have enjoyed much from the conditions generally. Of 700 specimens taken from this unit 173 have been found to show albumen in both new were entrenched footballers & players while in a third there was a trace of albumen found. In the 173 former cases directed generally with obvious cause, whilst in playing any available opportunity for Conference put (suffering from more or less peroxidant R.E.D. ache for the past three months. Capt McLEOD interviewed the men & took another specimen from each. Weather: unsettled; some rain.	
DO	JANY 21st	9 a.m.	At 9 o'clock parage I made an inspection of all (mostly black eye goggles).	
		12.45 p.m.	The R.A. + Q.M.G. called to inform me that I must make arrangements for billeting 514 men & 3 officers arriving at VAUCHELLES this evening to remain until the following morning.	
		2.30 p.m.	Capt ROE returned to duty at HEBUTERNE relieving Capt SMYTHE (who returned) to SAILLY.	DO
		9.30 p.m.	Accompanied the R.A. + Q.M.G. + Capt LEA 48. Divl Staff to VAUCHELLES station to meet the 3 officers & 514 men referred to in paragraph 2 of to-day's diary. Three officers were perfectly satisfied with the arrangements I had made for the comfort & billeting of the men on their arrival. Weather: unsettled; some rain.	

WAR DIARY
or
INTELLIGENCE SUMMARY
(Erase heading not required.)

Army Form C. 2118

Place	Date 1916	Hour	Summary of Events and Information	Remarks and references to Appendices
VAUCHELLES LES AUTHIE	JANY 22nd	10 am	Had all Officers & men paraded who arrived last night. Paraded & handed them over to their respective Officers & Guides of their regiments to march them to their respective Batts. Routine duties in office afterwards. Weather: unsettled; fine in morning; rain later.	Ref: Map FRANCE LENS - 11 Scale 1/100,000
Do	JANY 23	9 am	Church Parade. Weather: unsettled. Cold. Rain.	
Do	JANY 24	2-30 pm	Went to Bussey Station at SAILLY, inspected Baths and progress made with construction of Disinfector. Weather - unsettled; cold rain.	
Do	JANY 25		Selected Lieut FAIRFAX to proceed to SAILLY in order that he may report at D.S. FONQUEVILLERS at 9 o'clock on the morning of the 26th to relieve an officer of the 143rd Bde - Recalled Capt SMYTHE from SAILLY. Weather: unsettled	Do
Do	JANY 26	10.30 am	Rode to LOUVENCOURT to attend Conference of Med. Officers just back with reference to some recent Gas attacks. a Gas Expert attended & gave considerable information of intrinsic value.	Do
		5 pm	Lieut FAIRFAX returned from duty with the 143rd Bde. Proceeded to SAILLY for duty at the D.S. Capt SMYTHE remaining for duty at the D.R.S. Weather: fine; mild.	
Do	JANY 27	3 pm	Rode to LOUVENCOURT to attend Medical Conference at which Lt Col FITZGERALD CO. No 12 Fd. Amb. gave an account of his experiences in dealing with large numbers of wounded 2/Lt. at the 2nd Battle of YPRES. Capt DACRE rejoined the Unit after nearly 6 months detached duty with the 1/5 R Sussex Regt. One NCO & 11 men joined from Wycombe - re-inforcements from the Base - Weather: fine, mild.	Do

Army Form C. 2118

WAR DIARY
or
INTELLIGENCE SUMMARY
(Erase heading not required.)

Place	Date 1916	Hour	Summary of Events and Information	Remarks and references to Appendices
VAUCHELLES LES AUTHIE	JANY 28th	9 a.m.	At the 9 o'clock parade this morning I inspected Ororta Helmets & Goggles. Men forming up informed – found yesterday examined for scabies. No cases discovered in the draft though it has been found that amongst the reinforcements who have joined other units a considerable number of men have been affected with this disease.	Ref Map FRANCE LENS 11 Scale 1/100,000
		10 "		
		4 p.m.	D.D.M.S. and D.A.D.M.S. VIIth Corps called. Capt. WILLIAMSON returned from leave – weather fine; mild.	
Do	JANY 29th	10 a.m.	Rode to office of A.D.M.S. at BUS. Informed me that it was probable I might have to move from VAUCHELLES to BERTRANCOURT. Visited the latter village in company with Capt. BECKTON D.A.D.M.S. 48th Divn and inspected No 11 Fd Amb. with a view of necessary of taking over from them in the event of my having to move.	Do
		3 p.m.	Visited SAPLEY & HEBUTERNE and made certain arrangements at these two Fd stations for reception of any unusual number of casualties in anticipation of a "little affair" against the enemy contemplated by certain regiments of this division during the night. weather: fine/ cold/ colder.	
Do	JANY 30th	9 a.m.	Church Parade.	Do
		10 a.m.	Capt. CLARKE Adjt 48th Divn Supply Train Asked Capt LEA of the 48 Divn Staff called with reference to finding accommodation for 1st S.M. Fd Amb in the village; it is contemplated moving this unit from its present quarters at ARQUEVES. The "little affair" contemplated informed the enemy during the night came I hardly ming to a clause must what prevented: Confined is a severe bombardment of the enemy trenches by our Artillery. weather: Colder clear most all day.	
Do	JANY 31st	10 a.m.	The Officer of the R.E. VIIth Corps called for information regarding water supply of VAUCHELLES.	Do
		3 p.m.	A.D. to S. visited the D.R.S. weather: fine colder	

signed Lt. COLONEL
COMDG. 3rd. STH. MID. FD. AMBULANCE.

AF—C2118.

WAR DIARY.

OF

1/3rd South Midland Field Ambulance.

for

February 1916.

Vol XII

CONFIDENTIAL

WAR DIARY
or
INTELLIGENCE SUMMARY

(Erase heading not required.)

Army Form C. 2118

Place	Date 1916	Hour	Summary of Events and Information	Remarks and references to Appendices
VAUCHELLES au AUTHIE	Feb 1.		Routine Duties. Prepare plans of the wider Supply of village for use of C.R.E. VIIth Corps. Weather – a beautiful spring-like day.	
"	Feb 2.		In the morning received instructions from A.D.M.S. that in view of the approaching move of the 1/1st S.m. Fd Amb I was to prepare to receive from that unit some 60 patients suffering from Scabies or later in the afternoon I admitted 58 patients from 1/1st S.m. Fd Amb. Weather fine.	
"	Feb 3.		Opened out a Sick Station, as distinct from the D.R.S. of the Division at Coudo, with 2 motor ambulances, & for more cell avenues which have not already passed through a field ambulance, of for the collection of sick from certain areas east of the VIIth Corps. Also took over the collection of sick previously collected by the 1/1st S.m. Fd Amb. Weather – Colder – Sharp frost. Sergt FENEMORE made Cook left Unit to rejoin headquarters.	
	Feb 4.		Capt SMYTHE detailed to attend XIR of VIIth Corps via Major BROWNE D.S.O. on leave. Weather – rough & troublesome.	
	Feb 5.		Routine Duties. Major GREEN returned from leave. Weather much colder.	
	Feb 6.		Church Parade 9 a.m. Routine Duties. Weather wet – prevail.	

WAR DIARY or INTELLIGENCE SUMMARY

Army Form C. 2118

Place	Date 1916	Hour	Summary of Events and Information	Remarks and references to Appendices
VAUCHELLES to AUTHIE	Feb 7		Routine duties. In the afternoon an Officer from the Base Paymasters Office called to give instructions in matters concerning pay & allied duties. He expressed himself as quite satisfied with the methods adopted by this unit. Weather fine in morning. Snowing wet & boisterous	
	Feb 8		Routine duties. A.D.M.S. called in morning. Weather fine in morning; cold; some rain in afternoon	
	Feb 9		In afternoon attended Conference at Office of A.D.M.S. to receive instructions re impending move of Unit. Weather: windy. Some Snow.	
	Feb 10		Major Snow & the Interpreter proceeded to SOUASTRE x to consult with Officers of Divisional & 144th Brigade Staff re billeting the Ambulance in that Autre village. The Advanced dressing stations of the units at SAILLY au BOIS ⊕ + HEBUTERNE ⊙ were handed over to 1/6 S. Mid. Fd Amb. + B Section of this Ambulance took over the Advanced Dressing Station at FONQUEVILLERS ✱ + CHATEAU L'HAIE. Capt Monfelt with B Section (less 6 Othr.ranks) to FONQUEVILLERS + Revd Fairfax + 6 men to CHATEAU L'HAIE. Weather fair. Cold	x FRANCE S.P. D.22. + 57. J 18 ⊕ 57 K.9.15. ✱ 57 E.27 ⊙ 57 J.6.
	Feb 11		Non" Chaudeau - the Interpreter- proceeded on leave. routine duties. Received orders to send a Section to open a Dressing Station at SOUASTRE with an advanced dressing station at BIENVILLERS x	x 57 E.2.18.

Army Form C. 2118

WAR DIARY
or
INTELLIGENCE SUMMARY
(Erase heading not required.)

Instructions regarding War Diaries and Intelligence Summaries are contained in F. S. Regs., Part II. and the Staff Manual respectively. Title Pages will be prepared in manuscript.

Place	Date 1916	Hour	Summary of Events and Information	Remarks and references to Appendices
VAUCHELLES & AUTHIE	Feb 12	1 pm	C. Section under the Command of Capt Scott Williamson (with him Capt Dexer) marched out to open dressing station at SOUASTRE. Cold wet day	
	Feb 13		Church parade 9 a.m. Routine duties. Weather unsettled	
	Feb 14	a.m.	A.D.M.S. called & informed Lt Col Young that he had been appointed A.D.M.S. 61st Division (formed from 2nd line of our 48th Division). In the afternoon Lt Col Young was ordered by wire to report to "War Office" forthwith. Capt Scott Williamson proceeded to BIENVILLERS + HANNESCAMP the 14th for Portgate. In the afternoon took over that part of the front with the Brigade major of the 144th Half Brigade. He afterwards supplied an Advanced Dressing Station with 1 officer + 12 other ranks at BIENVILLERS. 4 of whom would in rotation man Regimental Reinforce Regimental Aid Post personnel at HANNESCAMP	M.O. × FRANCE 57 E. 10
	Feb 15		Lt Col Young, T.D., proceeded to England at 1:30 p.m. and was shewer of B the charge of the unit. Major Jaquer temporary took over the Command of the unit. The A.D.M.S. agreed to the suggestion of Capt. Scott Williamson in BIENVILLERS + HANNESCAMP & Capt Dexer + 12 other ranks proceeded in the afternoon to the former place. wet rainy bad town weather.	
	Feb 16		Visited SOUASTRE in morning that a Conference c Capt Williamson & Heneford. Must arrange for accommodation of remainder of Ambulance here A.D.M.S. D.A.+D.M.O. Here arrange to number of patients in D.R.S. in last 3 days. large increase in number of patients in D.R.S. in last 3 days. weather stormy & torrential rain.	
	Feb 17		Capt. Smyth proceeded on leave. A working party of 3 NCOs + 12 men of the 36th Division who attached to us for rations. A fine cold day	

Army Form C. 2118

WAR DIARY
or
INTELLIGENCE SUMMARY
(Erase heading not required.)

Instructions regarding War Diaries and Intelligence Summaries are contained in F. S. Regs., Part II. and the Staff Manual respectively. Title Pages will be prepared in manuscript.

Place	Date 1916	Hour	Summary of Events and Information	Remarks and references to Appendices
VAUCHELLES to AUTHIE	Feb 18		Routine Duties. Visited SOUASTRE in Evening to discuss accommodation here. 2 Engs Welshmen. As it is not very satisfactory. Weather very wet + boisterous	
	Feb 19		Received Orders from the A.D.M.S. re new arrangements of the work of the Ambulances. We give up the Divisional Rest Station + proceed to Field Ambulance work to SOUASTRE. We also have to treat all the Scabies of the Division. During the day dispatched all the "Rest Station" Scabies cases to SOUASTRE. Also removed certain stores here. Weather fine	
	Feb 20.		Closed the D.R.S. at 12 noon + in the afternoon despatched the patient (64) to the / 2nd S.M. Fd Amb. at SARTON. In the Evening received orders to proceed on 21st to SOUASTRE. A fine spring like day	
	Feb 21.		Morning spent in packing up. At 1:30 p.m. paraded + marched out of VAUCHELLES + arrived at SOUASTRE at 4 p.m. Lt Bruce RAWE (T.O.) (Mr. TORONTO) reported for duty with the Field Ambulance Two horses broken on the Strengths A cold fine day	
SOUASTRE	Feb 22		Routine duties. A.D.M.S. called in morning from Chateau (Infanterie) returned from leave. Cold wintery weather	
	Feb 23		Routine duties. A.D.M.S. called. Transfered present arrangements + proposed Divisional Weather - Cold, wet, + snow at night	
	Feb 24		Routine duties. Shower baths for Scabies cases completed + isolation treatment commenced. A cold frosty day. Commenced to transfer cases to D.R.S. at SARTON.* *Annex Sg. Ten will relieve the congestion in the Dressing Station which has been acute for last 20 + 3 days 4.11.18

Army Form C. 2118

WAR DIARY
or
INTELLIGENCE SUMMARY
(Erase heading not required.)

Instructions regarding War Diaries and Intelligence Summaries are contained in F. S. Regs., Part II. and the Staff Manual respectively. Title Pages will be prepared in manuscript.

Place	Date 1916	Hour	Summary of Events and Information	Remarks and references to Appendices
SOUASTRE	Feb 25		A heavy fall of Snow during the night accompanied by high wind has made the road almost impassable, transport vehicles falling about very different. Four motor Ambulances put out of action, had to be dug out. Routine duties but everything quiet	
	Feb 26		Routine duties. The Snow Storm having ceased, patients fit for light duty & men of the unit busy occupied in clearing Snow from the street of our section of the village. Weather milder in the Evening	
	Feb 27		Capt Smythe returned from leave. DADMS called in afternoon - Routine duties. Weather. Short thaw followed by frost more Snow during Early morning	
	Feb 28		Routine duties. ADMS called in morning inspecting arrangements. Weather. Thaw again set in & temperature is again higher	
	Feb 29		Routine duties. Nothing of importance occurred Weather mild & some rain	

1875 Wt. W593/826 1,000,000 4/15 J.B.C. & A. A.D.S.S./Forms/C. 2118.

WAR DIARY
or
INTELLIGENCE SUMMARY

(Erase heading not required.)

Army Form C. 2118

Place	Date	Hour	Summary of Events and Information	Remarks and references to Appendices
VAUCHELLES & AUTHIE			Short Summary of the work of the Unit while in Charge of the D.R.S., 48th Division. The Divisional Rest Station was opened at VAUCHELLES lu AUTHIE * on Aug 6. 1915 and closed on Feb 20. 1916. ※ Note During that time 3,355 R&R + 201 wounded were admitted; Of these 3300 R&R + 200 wounded belonged to the 48th Division, and 55 R&R - 1 wounded belonged to other Divisions. The way in which they were disposed of is shown in the difference table. The Cases as a whole were of the usual type — innumerable diseases, Influenza, Bronchitis, Rheumatism, 'Trench Fever'; Conditions attributable to Exposure to Cold wet in the trenches, Shell Shock (shewn as wounded). The length of time during which patients were kept in the D.R.S., varied at different times from 7 days to 10-3 weeks. Two to some extent regulated by holding influenza cases. From August to the middle of November, the patients were housed in marquees + Bell Tents in an orchard. Some also were accommodated in a large barn. At the latter date the marquees + tents were found to be very unsatisfactory on account of the rain & mud, and two 'Armstrong' huts were issued to us. These were supplemented by three other huts built by men of the unit out of material supplied by the R.E.s; + by utilising the village school room. Hot Shower baths & a fumigator were erected by men of the unit and proved very valuable. All patients were (both Eng.)	Note Frames 57 I 32. 33

Army Form C. 2118

WAR DIARY
or
INTELLIGENCE SUMMARY
(Erase heading not required.)

Place	Date	Hour	Summary of Events and Information	Remarks and references to Appendices
VAUCHELLES to AUTHIE			Prompted bathed on admission and their clothes were fumigated. The blankets of all patients, who were discharged, were fumigated before being re-issued	

Month	Admitted			To July			To C.C.S.	
	Sick	Wounded		Sick	Wounded		Sick	Wounded
August 1915 (6th-31st)	581	35		262	12		145	20
September 1915	454	26		389	10		121	16
October "	343	18		204	5		124	12
November "	506	13		279	8		237	6
December "	533	22		335	7		170	10
January 1916	557	53		367	20		173	28
February " (1 to 20th)	381	34		347	32		107	10
Totals	3,355	201		2,183	94		1,077	102

J. Green
MAJOR R.A.M.C.
O.C. 2/1st STH. MID. FLD. AMBULANCE.

Army Form C. 2118.

WAR DIARY.

For month of March 1916

1/3rd South Midland Field Ambulance
R A M C (T F)

CONFIDENTIAL
March/16

J.O.C. Green Major RAMC-TF
Cmdg 1/3rd S.M. Fld Amb

1/3 S M Fd Amb
Vol XIII
48

WAR DIARY or INTELLIGENCE SUMMARY

Army Form C. 2118

Place	Date 1916	Hour	Summary of Events and Information	Remarks and references to Appendices
SOUASTRE	March 1	10 a.m.	A.D.M.S. called at 10 a.m. Afterwards went with the Divisional Claims Officer the Interpreter to interview Mons GOSSELIN of VAUCHELLES AUTHIE with reference to an Extension claim for damages against this unit while in occupation of his property from Aug 3rd 1915 – Feb 21st 1916. Each item had to be taken separately and the work was not finished until evening. A fine day but very muddy roads. Evacuated A.D.S. at BIENVILLERS au BOIS, village being removed from 48th Division Area. 6th Divn. retained to SOUASTRE. Routine duties. Some rain. Weather dull.	
"	March 2		Routine duties. Weather dull.	
"	March 3		Owing to the impending move of the 1/1st South Midland Field Ambulance of VAUCHELLES, were instructed to receive all the sick & wounded from the front lines by the 48th Division until further notice. Weather dull. Some rain.	
"	March 4		Heavy snow fall commenced in the night & continued more or less all day. The road to FONQUEVILLERS became impassable and one motor ambulance had to be dug out of it. Arranged to fetch urgent cases from A.D.S. at BATTERIES by horse ambulance yesterday. Received orders to disinfect Coleus Sisting up Cases A.C.S. by train from VAUCHELLES to AUTHIE. But concerned and anything o/c the storm. Lieut FAIRFAX sent to assist Capt HERRPATH at FONQUEVILLERS till Doctor posted to La HAIE.	
"	March 5		a few hours out on Fatigue Parties from the Units were employed in clearing snow from the roads & freeing ditches in order to let the water run away. With afternoon the Divisional Claims Officer called at Blair Jour Fermin of VAUCHELLES Divisional Claims Officer Frost at night.	
"	March 6		A mild sunshine morning. In afternoon visited FONQUEVILLERS & inspected A.D.S., Baths, Routine Duties in morning & Sanitary Station which is being formed there. On return Fonquillers men wild furnish Sanitary Station which is being formed there. Weather very severe. A keen frost all called at LA HAIE inspected arrangement there. Weather very severe. A keen frost night during the night & morning.	

WAR DIARY or INTELLIGENCE SUMMARY

Army Form C. 2118

Place	Date 1916	Hour	Summary of Events and Information	Remarks and references to Appendices
SOUASTRE	March 7		Routine duties. In the afternoon received orders to be prepared to evacuate the Horse lines & all billets north of the SOUASTRE – BIENVILLERS road as that part of village was being shelled. Weather cold. Snow at night.	
	March 8		Routine inspection duties & billets. Prepared to use in the morning. ADMS called. Sergt Kent Brooks came up to report for temporary duty with the Ambulance. Weather fine. Slight frost at night.	
	March 9		Routine duties during the morning. The Town Major called & we were busy all the day with the HEBU – BIENVILLERS Road Thoroughfare. We chose same to put with more than half of available accommodation + town Baths re. Weather frost morning but snow at night.	
	March 10		In the morning went with ADMS and D.D.S. re accommodation at SOUASTRE & after consultation with Capt Bing Murison re where we transport the Field Quarters of the Ambulance to & ____ the Chateau at COUIN & it were possible to move it there. In the afternoon rode over to COUIN to inspect Chateau. Weather heavy snow during the morning. Wet & muddy during the evening.	*France 5T J.K.
	March 11		A Section under command of Lt Smythe proceeded to the Chateau Beam COUIN at 11am. C Section with Capt Wakeman (in Command) (Capt Roy remained in A/D's SOUASTRE) where the Quarters of the Division will continue to be situated. There is accommodation for 50 patients at SOUASTRE in case of necessity (in addition to the Cadre ass'y in the event of COUIN in the meanwhile forming everything ready for 100 patients if it were thought that he always there out. Weather fine, but cold. Temp: C Smith Ranke sent to Officer Hospital - Sick -	

WAR DIARY or INTELLIGENCE SUMMARY

Army Form C. 2118

Place	Date 1916	Hour	Summary of Events and Information	Remarks and references to Appendices
COUIN	March 12		Commenced taking in cases at COUIN at 9 am. Evacuated all cases (except Scabies) from SOUASTRE during the morning. The DDMS 10th Corps ADMS called at 1.30 pm. Weather gloomy but evening around the Hospital.	
	March 13		Routine duties in morning. Visited SOUASTRE in afternoon. Weather fine evening. Conference at ADMS office BUS.	
	March 14		Routine duties all day. At 7 pm during heavy shelling of FONQUEVILLERS, a 4.5" shell struck the ADS. Here & completely wrecked the officers mess. Fortunately everybody had time to take underground cover save one of the ambulance was hurt. A rather busy night at that Bearer officers until 1.30 am as instructions received devoid to 2 Bearer orderlies for permanent duty at BAYENCOURT & arrange for the daily visit of the MO at LA HAIE Khedome place.	
	March 15		Spent the morning in a visit to all Subdivisions at each of which I inspected arrangements at GAVENCOURT, FONQUEVILLERS, LAHAIE & SOUASTRE. At FONQUEVILLERS found the Sadlers busy repairing the damage to the previous night. Work was also being done on the underground shelter with the Sucrier Road to make it MDS & in a new communication trench to an MO Artillery Dugout which has been given time. The later will accommodate 24 lying down cases. In the afternoon the ADMS & RA & Bund called & informed me that we should soon have to train and of Chaulnes to into huts. Weather still fine but a little colder	

WAR DIARY or INTELLIGENCE SUMMARY

Army Form C. 2118

(Erase heading not required.)

Instructions regarding War Diaries and Intelligence Summaries are contained in F. S. Regs., Part II. and the Staff Manual respectively. Title Pages will be prepared in manuscript.

Place	Date 1916	Hour	Summary of Events and Information	Remarks and references to Appendices
COUIN	March 16		In morning visited ADMS at his Office. General routine duties during rest of day. Weather fine	
"	March 17		Routine duties. Today went to hospital site in huts. Weather - fine	
"	March 18		ADMS called. Routine duties. Commenced sandbagging from of A.D.S. forewheelers. Capt Hemphill came down from ADS for 24 hours. Weather. Rainfall fine but a shower fram in afternoon.	
"	March 19		9 am Church Parade. Map writing R.O. 48th Division called re measures all ranks in huts for occupation by the Ambulance. Weather fine.	
"	March 20		Commenced attending to hospital huts for housing ranks. Weather fine. DADMS called. ADMS & DA+DMS.	
"	March 21		Routine duties & attending to alterations in huts to weather showers.	
"	March 22		ADMS & DA+DMS called. Inspected our new horse lines site. Weather showery	
"	March 23		A bombing attack took place during night - carried out by troops on our sector of the Divisional line - met with some success. On arrival Enemy fire at 2.a.m. started at 6.30. The first wounded reported that he first wounded reached him at 8.30 am. Total number 1 Officer, 18 Other ranks. the Ambulance at 5.30 at this last at 8.30 am. Weather fine	
"	March 24		Sue to leave Chateau today but heavy snowfall in night made huts unfit from Genl officer asked permission to remain another day. Alteration to huts have not progressed very rapidly	

WAR DIARY
or
INTELLIGENCE SUMMARY

Army Form C. 2118

(Erase heading not required.)

Instructions regarding War Diaries and Intelligence Summaries are contained in F. S. Regs, Part II. and the Staff Manual respectively. Title Pages will be prepared in manuscript.

Place	Date 1916	Hour	Summary of Events and Information	Remarks and references to Appendices
BEVIN	Mar 25.		Paymaster had G.I. 2 hut fit for patients (bunks floors etc.) and in the afternoon transferred the patients to them. 26 others on the floor of nurses waterproof Camp had been laid. Weather Severe Frost in night followed by rain & thaw	
	Mar 26.	9 am	Office & Inspection work. 10 am Visited our Stations at BAYENCOURT. LA HAIE. FONQUEVILLERS & SOUASTRE. Weather wet & cold	
	Mar 27	10 am	A.D.M.S. Called. Temp R.S. Queen Rawa left the unit on being posted as M.O. to 1st Glouch Regt	
		2.30 pm	Attended weekly Conference at A.D.M.S.'s Office. Weather wet & cold	
	Mar 28	9 am	Office work & Inspection. 11 am went to Advanced Depot for Med Stores at BEAUVAL. Weather fine but cold	
	Mar 29		Routine duties & Inspection. Weather Cold. Heavy Snow in afternoon	
	Mar 30		Attended A.D.M.S's Office at 9.30 am. O.C. 1/1 Fd Ambulance also present. Received orders to remove C Section from SOUASTRE tomorrow as the 1/1 st Amb. are moving into that place. Section for-units will remain at SOUASTRE the headed by 1/1 st Amb. Affls: visited SOUASTRE & gave necessary instruction for the change. Weather fine & warmer than for some time	
	Mar 31	am	Office duties & Inspection of all huts & Hospital tents. In afternoon saw Sanitary Officer re Incinerator & in afternoon to send over a Horsefall Incinerator. C Section returned to Head Quarters from SOUASTRE. Weather fine but warm	

Jaquer Majr RAMC
O.C. 1/3 South Midland Field Ambulance

April 1916

CONFIDENTIAL

484

COMMITTEE FOR THE
MEDICAL HISTORY OF THE WAR
Date

WAR DIARY.

OF

1/3RD SOUTH MIDLAND FIELD AMBULANCE

FOR

APRIL. 1916.

Vol XIV

LaGuen Major R.A.M.C.T.
Comdg 1/3rd S.M. Fld. Amb:

WAR DIARY or INTELLIGENCE SUMMARY

Army Form C. 2118

Place	Date 1916	Hour	Summary of Events and Information	Remarks and references to Appendices
COIGN	Apr 1		Routine duties + Inspection — weather fine TSOATH	
	Apr 2.16		Routine duties + inspections. Arranged with OC M.S. hut at Coub for Exchange of Collecting area in accordance with instructions from ADMS. We now take in wounded from Rugby Sector of the front +the 1/1st from the left sector. The personnel at the advanced dressing station remain the same pending the completion of underground dressing station of FONQUIVILLERS. Capt Kempel of my Unit. Weather — Glorious	
	Apr 3	9.30 am	GOC Division inspected the hospital. At 11.30 am attended a GOC Conference near SAILLY. At 2.30 pm attended weekly conference at ADMS Office. Glorious hot day	
	Apr 4		Routine duties — very cold day but fine	
	Apr 5		" "	
	Apr 6		Routine duties in morning. At 8.30 pm the Germans made an attack on BUCQUOY on our right near troops Royal Irish. but did not penetrate. Rain in the night	
	Apr 7		ADMS + DADMS called. Chaplain Canon Welldon returned from leave. Weather fine. Capt Dalbon presented on leave	
	Apr 8		Routine duties — weather fine	
	Apr 9		Men of Unit attended the Divisional Church Parade at 11.30 am. ADMS called — weather fine	
	Apr 10		We have had a busy night. A new trench was dug in front of HÉBUTERNE + as a result of this we admitted 26 casualties in 24 hours. In afternoon visited ADMS at his Office chiefly. Sent Lt ROE, RAMC (TC) for temp duty with the 1/4 Gloster Battalion — weather fine	

WAR DIARY
or
INTELLIGENCE SUMMARY

(Erase heading not required.)

Army Form C. 2118

Place	Date 1916	Hour	Summary of Events and Information	Remarks and references to Appendices
COUIN	Apr 11		In the morning trailed the advanced dressing station at FONQUIVILLERS. In the afternoon attended G.O.C. Conference at School of Instruction. Weather - appealingly cold & wet	
	Apr 12		Routine duties at Hd Qrs. Lt FAIRLEY RAMC (T.C.) reported for duty. Wet weather continued	
	Apr 13		Routine duties at Hd Qrs. Allowed Lt FAIRFAX & Chaplain MEEK forwarded to Hd Qnl on special leave. Weather fine	
	Apr 14		Surgeon Gen'l O'Keefe D.M.S. 4th Army + Col Wilson DDMS 8th Corps inspected the Hospital + advanced dressing station during the morning. In the afternoon attended G.O.C. Conference. A wet day	
	Apr 15		Routine duties at Hd Qrs. Weather fine	
	Apr 16		9 am Church parade for Brigade + patients at Hospital Ground. Canon Wilkinson officiating. Routine duties. Weather fine	
	Apr 17		am. visited O.P.S. at FONQUIVILLERS where I found the convalescence ward temporary Rehn factory. Lt Glanville RAMC(T.C.) reported for duty. Weather. Wet - cold + boisterous	
	Apr 18		am. An officer of the "Graves Commission" called + along with the mayor of COUIN trailed the Site of the proposed new Cemetery with the final alignment the Ambulance + approved of it. In the afternoon attended G.O.C. Conference at Hd Qrs. Weather - very wet	
	Apr 19		Routine duties - Weather wet	
	Apr 20		Routine duties. Capt Drew returned from leave - wet day	
	Apr 21		Good Friday. Men of unit attended Service at 10 am. In afternoon attended GOC Conference. Rain in morning. Rain afternoon & night.	

WAR DIARY or INTELLIGENCE SUMMARY

Army Form C. 2118

(Erase heading not required.)

Instructions regarding War Diaries and Intelligence Summaries are contained in F. S. Regs., Part II. and the Staff Manual respectively. Title Pages will be prepared in manuscript.

Place	Date 1916	Hour	Summary of Events and Information	Remarks and references to Appendices
COUIN	Apr 22		Routine duties – weather – wet –	
	Apr 23		Easter Sunday. Divine Service (Canon Welchman officiating) at 9 am for personnel of fankards. Lt FAIRFAX returned from leave. Lt CLANVILLE left for being posted to the 32nd Division RAMC (TC). weather – fine	
	Apr 24	am	Routine duties. In afternoon attended a tactical exercise presided over by G.O.C.; weather fine	
	25		" " " " " "	
	26		Routine duties " " " "	
	27	am	Visited FONQUIVILLERS & found that the Underground dressing station was unfit for use. It is arranged that we change over A.D.S. with 11th Sn 7th Corps on the 30th inst – we go to HEBUTERNE. – weather fine	
	28	"	am Visited ADMS at his Office. Routine duties – weather fine	
	29	"	A.D.M.S. called. During morning received orders from ADMS cancelling for present move until further orders – weather fine	
	30	"	9 am Church parade (Canon Welchman officiating) 10 am ADMS called 11 am to see Hopedale Hospital – weather – Heavy rain storm in afternoon – otherwise fine	

Army Form C. 2118

WAR DIARY
or
INTELLIGENCE SUMMARY
(Erase heading not required.)

Instructions regarding War Diaries and Intelligence Summaries are contained in F.S. Regs., Part II. and the Staff Manual respectively. Title Pages will be prepared in manuscript.

Place	Date	Hour	Summary of Events and Information	Remarks and references to Appendices
COUIN	Apr 1916		The usual duties connected with the work of a Field Ambulance open for the reception of sick & wounded from the front line have been carried out during the month. At the Advanced Dressing Station at FONQUEVILLERS Baths, fumigation of clothes & the distribution of clean underclothing to the troops has been undertaken. In addition fumigations during 96 hours for 48 hrs. down cases numerous Sitting Cases have been completed and conveyed up to the Dressing Station in the village by Communication Trenches. The damage caused by the Explosion of a Shell in the Dressing Station last month has also been repaired & the front of the building protected by Sandbags. At the Head Quarters at COUIN Huts for Orderlies have been erected, windows for Orderlies & personnel have been provided with bombproof floors, windows for Orderlies having been made of a Shone ball & triangular construction. An operating room has been built & a small ward for 6 severe cases can be kept for several days is in process of Construction. During the whole of the month has been carried out by the personnel of the Unit. A summary of the number of Cases admitted to the Ambulance, with detail of their disposal is appended.	

J.A.Green Major R.A.M.C.
O.C. 1/3 South Midland Field Amb.

30/4/16

WAR DIARY or INTELLIGENCE SUMMARY

Army Form C. 2118

1/3RD South Midland Field Ambulance
Summary of Daily State of Sick and Wounded
APRIL 1916.

DATE	REMAINED		ADMITTED		DISCHARGED TO DUTY		TRANSFERRED TO DIV. REST STN		EVACUATED TO C.C.S.		DIED		REMAINING	
	Sick	Wounded	Sick	Wounded	Sick	Wounded	Sick	Wounded	Sick	Wounded	Sick	Wounded	Sick	Wounded
1	97	3	53	15	8	—	21	1	7	6	—	2	76*	9
2	76	9	38	6	3	—	25	3	5	6	—	1	81	5
3	81	5	19	7	3	—	30	1	3	3	—	1	59	7
4	59	7	26	11	2	—	12	1	6	8	—	—	65	9
5	65	9	20	2	2	—	20	6	2	3	—	—	61	2
6	61	2	24	1	5	—	15	—	5	2	—	—	60	1
7	60	1	20	1	—	—	18	—	3	1	—	—	59	1
8	59	1	26	1	8	—	14	—	11	—	—	—	52	2
9	52	2	33	3	4	—	19	1	7	1	—	—	55	3
10	55	3	20	27	2	—	13	—	7	23	—	1	53	6
11	53	6	30	3	1	—	10	3	10	1	—	1	62	4
12	62	4	34	8	7	—	2	2	6	2	—	1	81	7
13	81	7	27	1	6	—	33	5	6	—	—	—	63	3
14	63	3	24	21	2	—	16	—	12	4	—	—	57	20
15	57	20	30	—	4	—	9	13	14	4	—	—	60	3
16	60	3	23	9	1	—	4	1	4	6	—	—	74	5
17	74	5	32	5	8	1	16	3	7	3	—	—	75	3
18	75	3	29	4	5	—	16	—	9	4	—	—	74	3
19	74	3	15	4	1	—	10	2	12	—	—	—	66	5
20	66	5	37	3	4	—	23	1	3	—	—	—	73	7
21	73	7	25	1	6	—	20	4	5	2	—	1	67	1
22	67	1	23	7	—	—	23	—	9	3	—	—	58	5
23	58	5	31	11	—	—	8	4	6	9	—	—	75	3
24	75	3	21	12	8	1	29	1	8	6	—	—	51	7
25	51	7	34	7	3	2	14	4	13	6	—	—	55	2
26	55	2	29	—	4	—	8	1	3	—	—	—	69	1
27	69	1	24	—	4	—	18	1	20	—	—	—	51	—
28	51	—	40	9	—	—	16	—	5	8	—	—	70	1
29	70	1	24	4	3	—	23	—	13	2	—	—	55	3
30	55	3	19	8	2	—	10	2	11	7	—	—	51	2

* 38 "Scabies" Cases transferred to 1/1st S.M. Fld Amb.

SECRET

WM/15

A.F.C. 2118 — WAR DIARY.

1/3RD S.M. Fd Amb

MAY 1916.

J A Green
Major RAMC T
Cmdg 1/3rd S.M. Fd Amb.

COMMITTEE FOR THE
MEDICAL HISTORY OF THE WAR
Date 26 JUN. 1915

Army Form C. 2118

WAR DIARY
or
INTELLIGENCE SUMMARY
(Erase heading not required.)

Ref. Map LENS
1 – 100,000

Place	Date 1916	Hour	Summary of Events and Information	Remarks and references to Appendices
COUIN	May 1		Routine duties. Capt ROE (TC) left the unit on proceeding to the 29th CCS. Capt (TC) Smith left the unit on proceeding as M.O. 2nd Wores Bde RFA. weather fine	
	May 2		Routine duties. Capt Nevopath & 32 Other ranks of B section arrived at Head Quarters from FORQUEVILLERS. Capt Scott Williamson & 22 Other ranks left the DHQ & took over the A.D.S. at HEBUTERNE from the 1/1st S. Mid Fd Amb. Lt (TC) Fawley left the Unit for temporary duty as M.O. 1/5th Gloster Batt. weather fine	
	May 3		All Cases remaining in the 1/1 S.M. F.A. (including Scabies) were transferred to this Ambulance every 4th impending move of the former unit to BEAUVAL where the 144th Fd Amb are going into rest. fine day.	
	May 4		A busy day. From noon yesterday known wounded or received on transfer 175 Cases. The admissions were chiefly from 144th Bde which marched to BEAUVAL today. Capt Coupe of the unit was admitted to Hospital today suffering from German measles. weather fine	
	May 5		Routine duties. weather. Showers at night	
	May 6		" " weather fine	
	May 7		Proceeded on leave during Capt Scott Williamson in Command of the unit Capt Dakre relieve Capt Williamson at HEBUTERNE. weather showery field	
	May 8		Routine duties – weather fresh & showery	
	May 9		" " Capt Moore returned from leave. Weather. Wet all day	
	May 10		Capt Mayne proceeded to HEBUTERNE & Capt Dakre returned to Hd Qrs	
	" 11		Routine duties – weather fresh showery	

WAR DIARY or INTELLIGENCE SUMMARY

Army Form C. 2118

Place	Date 1916	Hour	Summary of Events and Information	Remarks and references to Appendices
COUIN	May 12		Routine duties. A.D.M.S. visited the unit. Large numbers of Pick today. Weather Cold fresh	
	May 13		Routine duties. Lt Fairly (T.C.) having returned to the Unit proceeded to HEBUTERNE for duty at the O.P.D.S. All Ghun Envelope letters having been censored according to orders from the 7th & 13th inst, a report was forwarded to the A.D.M.S to the effect that no illegal information has been detected in any of them	
	May 14		Routine duties. Weather Cold	
	" 15		" Major Ghun returned from leave. Weather Heavy rain	
	" 16		At 2.30 a.m. a heavy bombardment of a portion of our front gave rise to a large number of casualties chiefly of the 1/4th Royal Berks but also including a few of the 1/Bucks Batt. Wounded began to arrive at the A.D.S. HEBUTERNE at 3 a.m. 9 at the Hot Dép of the Ambulance at 6 a.m. One officer & 46 other ranks were evacuated to C.C.S. by the day & M.A.C. at 11 a.m. At 2.30 pm inspected transport & at 3 pm visited HEBUTERNE transferred A.D.S. & proposed baths there. Weather fine	
	17		Routine duties. Capt Williamson returned to A.D.S. HEBUTERNE & Lt Fairly returned to Hd Qts weather fine	
	18		Routine duties. The 145th Bgde (Inf.) marched to BEAUVAL, having been relieved by the 144th Inf Bgde. In afternoon visited the 29th C.C.S. at GEZAINCOURT. Weather showers	
	19		Routine duties. Weather fine	
	20		" Received report of Capt Moore on the work of men attached to the A.D.S. after the heavy bombardment of the 18th -	

WAR DIARY or INTELLIGENCE SUMMARY

Army Form C. 2118

Place	Date 1916	Hour	Summary of Events and Information	Remarks and references to Appendices
COUIN	May 20 (cont)		Church Parade. Capt Drene attached temporarily as M.O. to 1/s Warwicks. Weather Glorious	
	21	9 am	Church Parade. In afternoon visited O.C. 1/4th Royal Scots at BEAUVAL to get his confirmation of report of work of the Ambulance in morning 1/16th – that. Then to RECMENIL FARM and HEM to see O.C. advanced depot of Red Cross So ciety. Weather fine	
	22		Routine duties. Weather – much colder + some rain	
	23		" " Fine generally but some rain at night	
	24		" " very wet	
	25		" " "	
	26		" " Fine	
	27		" " Fine. Lieut Esher learnt to HEBUTERNE but they returned same evening	
	28		Church Parade 9 am. Capt Hope proceeded for a Course of Instruction to 4th Army Ambulance School Lt (T.P.) Fairley detached for duty with Entrenching Batt. at HONQUEVILLETTE. Stuffy – fume. rained night Weather –	
	29		Routine duties but busy on account of shortage of Officers. Capt Scott Williamson proceeded on Special leave. Weather: heavy rain at night. Lt. Fowler proceeded to A.D.S. HEBUTERNE	
	30		Routine duties – weather – wet + cool	
	31		" " in morning for D.M.S. 4th Army medical ambulance + universal certain armaments. weather fine.	

WAR DIARY or INTELLIGENCE SUMMARY

Army Form C. 2118

Place	Date	Hour	Summary of Events and Information	Remarks and references to Appendices
COVIN	10/16		Except on the 16th instant there have not been any large numbers of wounded admitted to the ambulance. On the other hand the number of sick admitted has frequently been above the average. This has been to a great extent due to the fact that Brigades have been very late into Rest Billets & sorting out their MER before proceeding on the march. The epidemic of German Measles which was prevalent at the beginning of the month is dying out. Apart from the treatment of the sick mounted the personnel of the Unit have been busily engaged in constructive work. The materials (of) which have been supplied by the Engineers. A small ward for (6) acute cases has been built & I have reorganised show & tea been furnished by the Red Cross recently. Work of knife & forceps. Bedding & the Ward fillings. Laws shows the 1 yr's work on experience has shown that in some cases "an emergency" develops so quickly that immediate operation in a Rest Ambulance must be resorted to if a man's life has to be saved. Two cases (one needing amputation just below the knee & the other requiring amputation thro' the lower end of the thigh) have been successfully treated in this ambulance. I am now both in England alive & well. Two large wood & timber canvas have also been built & 2 huts (wood) have been floored; & two other huts one for an officers' wash & the other for a pack also recently done are being regimed considered. A system of ventilating the wards from below without falling in the direct rays of the air has been introduced by hinging about 8 corrugated	

1875 Wt. W593/826 1,000,000 4/15 J.B.C. & A. A.D.S.S./Forms/C. 2118.

WAR DIARY
or
INTELLIGENCE SUMMARY
(Erase heading not required.)

Army Form C. 2118

Place	Date 1916	Hour	Summary of Events and Information	Remarks and references to Appendices
BUIN	May		so that they can be ranged or lowered at will. Stove kept alight are introduced into the side part of the hut at intervals and on the level of the ground. Cinder paths with a substratum of chalk & flints & reverse of the sides are being laid through the camp and are a great boon in wet weather. Attached is a daily list of patients admitted during the month shewing the manner in which they have been disposed of. J Agnew Major RAMC OC 1/3 South Midland Field Ambulance 48th Division	

1/3RD South Midland Field Ambulance

Summary of Daily State of Sick and Wounded - May 1916

DATE	REMAINING		ADMITTED		DISCHARGED TO DUTY		TRANSFERRED TO Divl REST STN		EVACUATED TO C.C. STN		DIED		REMAINED		REMARKS
	Sick	Wounded	Sick	Wounded	Sick	Wounded	Sick	Wounded	Sick	Wounded	Sick	Wounded	Sick	Wounded	
1	51	2	17	4	2	-	24	-	6	1	-	-	36	5	
2	36	5	14	3	6	-	10	2	3	3	-	-	31	3	
3	31	3	29	2	1	-	12	1	4	2	-	-	43	2	
4	43	2	110*	5	-	-	8	1	14	4	-	-	131	2	*Includes 27 Scabies cases and 26 other sick cases transferred from 1/1st S Mid Fd Amb
5	131	2	40	3	5	-	35	1	12	2	-	-	119	2	
6	119	2	39	5	9	-	24	-	10	3	-	-	117	3	
7	117	2	37	1	4	-	23	1	10	1	-	-	117	1	
8	117	1	42	1	10	-	18	-	13	1	-	-	117	1	
9	117	1	30	-	7	1	22	-	3	-	-	-	109	-	6 Dental cases transferred to 1/1st S Mid Fd Amb
10	109	-	22	2	8	-	23	-	6	-	-	-	94	2	
11	94	2	31	3	7	-	20	1	2	4	-	-	94	-	2 Dental cases transferred to 1/1st S Mid Fd Amb
12	94	-	41	2	10	-	20	-	6	-	-	-	99	2	
13	99	2	31	6	2	-	17	-	8	5	-	-	103	3	
14	103	3	30	1	9	-	24	-	2	1	-	-	99	3	
15	99	3	14	-	5	-	17	1	1	-	-	-	90	2	
16	90	2	28	47	6	1	12	-	5	47	-	-	95	1	
17	95	1	36	4	6	-	16	1	8	4	-	-	101	-	
18	101	-	31	3	7	-	18	-	3	3	-	-	104	-	
19	104	-	16	3	4	-	12	-	4	2	-	-	100	1	
20	100	1	26	1	1	-	22	-	1	2	-	-	102	-	
21	102	-	28	-	9	-	17	-	4	-	-	-	100	-	
22	100	-	21	2	4	-	12	-	4	-	-	-	101	2	
23	101	2	15	2	3	-	16	1	2	2	-	1	95	-	
24	95	-	31	1	3	-	11	-	2	-	-	-	110	1	
25	110	1	35	1	9	-	13	-	5	1	-	-	118	1	
26	118	1	37	3	8	-	13	-	4	1	-	-	130	3	
27	130	3	27	-	9	2	40	1	6	-	-	-	102	-	
28	102	-	22	5	12	-	22	-	2	2	-	-	88	3	
29	88	3	21	12	5	-	5	3	5	3	-	1	86	11	
30	86	11	25	5	6	1	16	6	4	-	-	-	85	9	
31	85	9	22	8	3	-	8	4	-	5	-	-	96	8	

Army Form C. 2118

WAR DIARY
or
INTELLIGENCE SUMMARY
(Erase heading not required.)

Instructions regarding War Diaries and Intelligence Summaries are contained in F.S. Regs., Part II. and the Staff Manual respectively. Title Pages will be prepared in manuscript.

Place	Date 1916	Hour	Summary of Events and Information	Remarks and references to Appendices
COUIN	June 1		Routine duties. A.D.M.S. called – Commenced arrangements for re-accomodation of Scabies Patient in This marked of present units. Capt Dagre relieved from temporary duty as M.O./S. Warwick & was sent for similar duty to 1/4 Glosters. weather – fine	
	2.		Routine duties. Allotted 2 horse ambulance to proceed with 144 "day" Bgde to BEAUVAL. One period up 17 cases on the march. weather fine	
	3.		Routine duties. A.D.M.S. called. Capt Moore returned from attending a course of instruction at Ecole pour Short "A" Army; & proceeded for duty to A.D.S. HEBUTERNE. weather fine	
	4.		Church parade 9am. Senfries pakents transferred from tents to huts in field adjoining the Ambulance compound. Capt Horsfall proceeded on leave & tempore relieved from A.D.S. for duty at Hd Qts. weather Showery.	
	5.		Routine duties " "	
	6.		" " fine weather	
	7.		" "	
	8.		A.D.M.S. called. Capt Scott Williamson returned from leave & proceeded to HEBUTERNE to relieve and connect there.	
	9.		Remainder of C Section proceeded to *HEBUTERNE. Owing to rearrangement of our line it has become necessary to find new accommodation for K. A.D.S. in HEBUTERNE. The line at present held by the division comprises Eg & H Sectors & extends from K.17 a.1.100, to K.23 d.3.4 * It has been decided to build 2 Elephant Huts – one at K.15.6.5.3. 2 other Mg 4 K.15.8.3.3. Each will be partitioned by a 6ft layer & Earth on top & which will be a bursting bay. Stop the two Elephant Huts will be connected by a 7:3m. French 911 deep & they will be entered by trenches from the village. The Grads' portion of H sector or the whole of G sector the the South of this A.D.S. to be which connecting the new Elephant Huts it is proposed to cut out & uphold several bays each capable of holding 3 stretcher. Have now got a large nerve dressing both for main dressing station & for A.D.S. & my section weather Showery.	*Trench map HEBUTERNE 1-20000

WAR DIARY or INTELLIGENCE SUMMARY

Army Form C. 2118

Place: COUIN

Date 1916	Hour	Summary of Events and Information	Remarks and references to Appendices

June 10. Routine duties. Weather wet & stormy.

11 9am Church Parade. Routine duties. In the afternoon went to Advanced depot of Red X Society to obtain fillings for an Officers went as I have received orders that I have to take over the Officers rest hostel in a few days. Weather fine.

12 Routine duties & busy with alterations & extension of hospital arrangement to provide accommodation & protect from rain. Admitted to hospital temporary sick off the strength. Weather – Cold – Heavy rain.

Horse lines removed & improved owing to bad condition of ground which will be repaired to protect from rain

13 A busy day at Head Quarters. Lage Gainsdale Flatfield have the care of in HEBUTERNE for the evacuation of the New A.D.S. which must be completed quickly. Received Red X their hospital equipment from the Red X Society for use in Officers rest. Weather very bad – Cold & pouring with rain.

14 Opened Officers Rest Hospital with accommodation for 9 Officers. The ward is a converted hut with accommodation for patients with one When the present arrangements are completed I shall be able to put up 40 or 50 lying down cases by arranging certain other huts now occupied in part by Scabies patients & further 120 cases could be accommodated. Brought the clocks one advanced 1 hour throughout the Army in FRANCE.
Weather – fine

15 Busy morning inside HEBUTERNE. Went over work on A.D.S. there. This is proceeding very well considering the shortage of labor. A small infantry fatigue is assisting the members of C Section with the work. O.C. A.D.S. suggests digging an evacuation trench out into the plain but it is doubtful if the labour can be found to complete it in time. Weather dull but fine.

16 Routine duties. Weather fine but cold –

WAR DIARY
or
INTELLIGENCE SUMMARY

(Erase heading not required.)

Army Form C. 2118

Place	Date 1916	Hour	Summary of Events and Information	Remarks and references to Appendices
COUIN	June 17		Routine duties. A.D.M.S. called. Fine day but cold. Capt Dale returned to unit from duty with 1/4 London.	
	June 18		Routine parade today owing to presence of WMR. In afternoon visited Advanced Dpt Red X Society to obtain further hospital extras in view of impending events. Weather fine.	
	19		Routine duties at HQtrs. Arranged with 143rd Brigade to have certain fields near HQS in HERUTERNE for Horse + sleeping accommodation (in tents) for personnel of unit. O.C. A.T.S. two obtained further help from Infantry + commenced digging an Evacuation trench from K.15 b.2.3. across the plain towards K.15.a.0.0.; with a view to an Evacuation route for the Evacuation of wounded down the valley Rd towards SAILLY.	X Trench map HERUTERNE 1:20000
	20		Routine duties. The Sergt Major instructed certain convalescent patients, who are being retained for duty in the event of active operations taking place, in the methods of loading + unloading ambulance wagons. A.D.M.S. called. Weather fine warm.	
	21		The G.O.C. Division inspected the camp + details of arrangement for the reception + treatment of the wounded in the near future. The Divisional Band played for the patients from 6 - 8 pm. Weather stormily fine.	
	22		A.D.M.S. called. Went to Advanced Stores to report return. Then to Trench Mortar School at VAUCHELLES to see if Lt Grice of my unit, who has been attached for some time, would be able to return to unit. Dr SPITERI Romé (T.C.) attached with unit this morning. Weather fine warm.	
	23		Routine duties in morning. In afternoon the new D.A.M.S. & H.G.R. (Col. Sermon) called + inspected ambulance. He approved of the arrangements. Heavy rain + close in morning, in afternoon a large thunderstorm broke over the district + rapidly flooded the camp. Commenced clearing out "sick" from the Ambulance.	

WAR DIARY or INTELLIGENCE SUMMARY

Army Form C. 2118

Place	Date 1916	Hour	Summary of Events and Information	Remarks and references to Appendices
COUIN	June 24		No sick admitted after 12 noon today – Except to the Officers Ward what still remains open – Lt SPITERI & 7 other Ranks were despatched to No 29 C.C.S. for temporary duty there. Bombardment commenced this morning. Made the first of the three day returns 'B' Admissions – Remaining' at noon today – Have to continue until further orders at 6 a.m.; noon; 9 p.m. weather. Strife rain during night. A.D.M.S. called – All sick cleared out of Ambulance – Very few casualties – Bombardment continues. Weather improving	
	June 26		Quiet day at 1st Dumplin & though Bombardment increase in severity there are still very few Casualties on our front. A.D.M.S. called. Heavy rain storms during day. Lt FAIRLEY Range (T.C) returned from sick leave duty. Still very quiet & few casualties. Bombardment continues - Heavy rain during last night & today	
	June 27			
	June 28		The wet weather still continues & is delaying operations. The Divisional Collecting Station at T.16d.81 (map) (5.7/5) opened at 12 noon. & Rest- 3 Motor Ambulances & 2 Horse Ambulances to Rendezvous there. The Ford Cars is returned at Head Quarters. All slightly wounded will be treated there & dispatches to C.C.S. by light railway from ACHEUX. We are to receive all lying down cases. Except Abdominal, Brain, & other very serious cases which go to the Operating Hospital in AUTHIE as long as they can deal with them.	
	June 29		A dull showery day. A.D.M.S. called – Few Casualties	

Army Form C. 2118

WAR DIARY
or
INTELLIGENCE SUMMARY
(Erase heading not required.)

Place	Date	Hour	Summary of Events and Information	Remarks and references to Appendices
COUIN	June 30 1916		A quiet day at Head Quarters. Heavy bombardment continue. Convoy received orders from M.D.M.S. to have 1 Section Complete ready to march at 8 a.m. Weather improving fine warning breeze. Relieve 7 horse Ambulances & 2 motor ambulances from the Breeching Station.

There has been a month's preparation. The head Quarters of the Ambulance at COUIN can now accommodate between 400 ~ 500 patients. The Advance dressing station at HERUTERRE is not so complete as one would have wished owing to lack of time for underground accommodation has been provided for about 80 lying down cases. In addition to 50 ~ 60 sitting up cases. Advanced post- staffed by R.A.M.C. orderlies have been arranged that both the Regimental Aid Post in Fort G & it Sectors & the A.D.S. the N.D.S. The Brigade Stretcher Bearers Aided in doing this work at the A.D.S. have been very arduous exhibit great credit on all who have participated in it.

The Casualties on our front during the bombardment have been very few, chiefly owing to the fact that the trenches have only been slightly held.

Appended is a summary of the day & list of her wounded during the month.

J.Aspen Major R.A.M.C.
O.C. 1/3 South Midland Field Ambulance
(48th Division) | |

Summary of Daily State of Sick and Wounded

JUNE 1916.

DATE	Remaining		Admitted		To C.C.S		To D.R.S		To Duty		Died		Remained	
	Sick	Wounded	Sick	Wounded	Sick	Wounded	Sick	Wounded	Sick	Wounded	Sick	Wounded	Sick	Wounded
1	96	8	43	2	2	–	–	–	6	2	–	–	131	8
2	131	8	31	3	3	–	30	6	22	–	–	–	107	5
3	107	5	15	3	4	2	10	1	6	–	–	–	102	5
4	102	5	21	12	5	8	25	2	9	–	–	1	84	6
5	84	6	14	2	6	1	7	2	3	1	–	–	82	4
6	82	4	6	1	–	–	9	1	5	–	–	–	74	4
7	74	4	13	12	3	12	11	1	9	–	–	–	64	3
8	64	3	12	3	1	2	10	–	3	–	–	–	62	4
9	62	4	10	4	1	5	9	–	2	–	–	–	60	3
10	60	3	22	–	1	–	10	2	4	–	–	–	67	1
11	67	1	14	1	4	1	5	–	–	–	–	–	72	1
12	72	1	15	4	–	3	10	–	–	–	–	–	77	2
13	77	2	39	–	2	–	16	1	1	–	–	–	97	1
14	97	1	35	3	5	3	16	–	11	–	1	–	99	1
15	99	1	27	–	5	–	16	–	3	–	–	–	102	1
16	102	1	28	7	5	6	–	–	4	–	–	–	121	2
17	121	2	27	4	11	4	24	–	2	–	–	1	111	1
18	111	1	42	1	15	1	18	1	3	–	–	–	117	–
19	117	–	21	3	12	3	–	–	12	–	–	–	114	–
20	114	–	21	3	9	1	–	–	16	–	–	1	110	1
21	110	1	19	1	21	1	–	–	9	1	–	–	99	–
22	99	–	18	5	10	5	–	–	13	–	–	–	94	–
23	94	–	60	5	66	5	–	–	3	–	1	–	84	–
24	84	–	17	3	30	3	–	–	34	–	–	–	37	–
*25	37	–	–	9	–	5	–	–	36	–	–	–	1	4
26	1	4	–	9	–	8	–	–	1	–	–	–	–	5
27	–	5	–	24	–	21	–	–	–	3	–	–	–	5
28	–	5	–	17	–	16	–	–	–	–	–	–	–	6
29	–	6	2	4	1	2	–	–	–	1	–	–	1	7
30	1	7	2	6	2	2	–	–	–	–	–	–	1	11

* no 'Sick' (Except Officers) admitted after this date

Major Lt. Colonel
COMDG. 1/3rd. 6TH. MID. FD. AMBULANCE.

No 1/3 7th Field Ambulance
WAR DIARY

FOR THE MONTH OF

JULY. 1916.

WAR DIARY or INTELLIGENCE SUMMARY

Army Form C. 2118

Place	Date 1916	Hour	Summary of Events and Information	Remarks and references to Appendices
COUIN	July 1st		The first day of the attack. Our Division, being in reserve, was split up to form reserve detachments to various parts of the VIIIth Corps area. At 9.40 am B Section under Capt Stempfil paraded and marched with the 145th Infantry Brigade to MAILLY-MAILLET. Stores they were collecting for the high. C Section under Capt Scott-Williamson, remained at Head Quarters COUIN. Two Bath's were billeted in the South by HEBUTERNE & hate orders not to attack. Consequently we had Companions for Casualties of our own. The 56th Division on our left, which attacked GOMMECOURT from the South, had large numbers of officers & men sent to about the Ambulance of that division which was opened near us. In the evening we advanced 76 horses of khakis wounded direct to our own Ambulance. At 3 pm received orders to send (unspotted) the M.O. of the 1/2nd Warwicks who were temporarily attached to the 4th Division & FAIRLEY to replace the M.O. Capt Kerr RAMEY M.O. tw Engineers found in for temporary duty. A fine warm day.	FRANCE LENS 11
	July 2nd		Early in morning the RAM's VIII Corps withdrew 5" motor ambulances from the 1/2nd's who got them, now unit to assist the SAME in evacuating willing cases as the Railway at ACHEUX was temporary over taxed. At same time received orders that we had to evacuate our own wounded to D.C.S. for absence of RAM's at MAILLY-MAILLET Arranged to rent "Setting Case" in the Sanitary Officers motor Lorry at 11.30 am. ADMS created a relief we transferred B Section to the CEMETERY at MAILLY-MAILLET with 16 additional Shelter beams. This section was going to open up an ADS at HANEL during the Evening in readiness for an attack by 143rd & 145th Inf. Brgde. This attack was countermanded at the last moment he progress has been effected on 8th Corps front. At 4.30 pm Supper for 7 kitchens college wealth two morrow.	
	July 3		A very quiet day at Head Quarters — with nothing doing on our front. The whole Division is being reassembled & B Section marched into Camp at 9.15 pm. A fine day	

Army Form C. 2118

WAR DIARY
or
INTELLIGENCE SUMMARY
(Erase heading not required.)

Instructions regarding War Diaries and Intelligence Summaries are contained in F. S. Regs., Part II. and the Staff Manual respectively. Title Pages will be prepared in manuscript.

Place	Date 1916	Hour	Summary of Events and Information	Remarks and references to Appendices
COUIN	July 4th		Another good day with nothing doing on our front. Lt Fairley rejoined on being relieved from the M/o Warwick Batt. A very heavy thunderstorm broke over the Camp during the afternoon & flooded our Camp. During the night a shell damaged no 3 or 4 Elephant huts in ADS. Anyone at HEBUTERNE but did not injure anyone though a lot of Equipment was destroyed. Weather fine.	
	July 5		A horse attached to Indian Cavt was killed at SAILLY. The afternoon — weather fine. Everything quiet.	
	July 6		A busy day. The Leave lorries are line held by 31st Div. which has been withdrawn & heavy shelling of OUINCAMPS was responsible for a number of casualties. Weather fine but clear.	
	July 7		Today commenced to take no sick are more. Lt FAIRFAX RAWE (T.C.) left on being transferred to the M/1st S.M. Fd Amb. Weather Pouring wet. Camp flooded.	
	July 8		Nothing of Importance. Weather fine	
	July 9		Church parade 9 a.m. ADMS called in Evening. Weather fine	
	10		Nothing of Importance. Weather fine	
	11		" " "	
	12		In afternoon attended Conference of O.Cs Fd Amb. at ADMS's Office. Weather fine but dull. Lt Fairley (T.C.) posted to temp. duty as MO 1/6 Warwicks.	
	13		The Division is on the move. Commenced packing up ready to move to our new ?	
	14		O.C. 129th Fd Amb & his 2nd in Command (36th Div) called. They took over from us tomorrow. Sent a Party of 1 Officer + 12 men to ADS HEBUTERNE. Capt Beale Kilvington this Section (Lieut 1 Officer + 12 Other Ranks) returned from HEBUTERNE. Lt STITERI & 7 other Ranks returned from Temp duty at 29th CCS	

1875 Wt. W593/826 1,000,000 4/15 J.B.C. & A. A.D.S.S./Forms/C. 2118.

WAR DIARY or INTELLIGENCE SUMMARY

Army Form C. 2118

Place	Date 1916	Hour	Summary of Events and Information	Remarks and references to Appendices
COUIN	July 14		DMS Reserve Army (Sgn. for MICHELL) called in afternoon & expressed his satisfaction with the Hospital accommodation. Walker Evans.	
	July 15		Stormy handed over Red Cross & Surplus Stores to the 129th Fd Amb & then finally returned both at 12.30 p.m. Hd Quarters & ADS by Motor until the Ambulance proceeded to WARLOY - Baillon - (The personnel being conveyed in Motor Lorries) to take over from the 90th Field Ambulance, which however had not yet had orders to move. Reported my arrival personally to DDMS 10"Corps at SENLIS & to ADMS 32nd Div at BOUZINCOURT. The 1/1st S.M.Fd. Amb. then stood up at Idolette place a 2 Sect. up in the evening to reinforce the bearers of that unit. 3 M.O.s & 3 bearer Subdivisions to reinforce the bearers of that unit. Weather fine.	info LENS.11 Howitzers
WARLOY- Baillon	July 16		Sent Burgoyne 1st Unit remained in Bivouacs at WARLOY. - A wet night & day. Four new officers.	
	July 17	10.30 AM	ADMS called & instructed me to relieve 75th Fd Amb at MILLENCOURT with 2 Sub-divisions of ~ to take over the Corps Hospital for Slightly wounded at VADENCOURT with 1 Sub-division (with whom would be 1 Sent Sub div of 1/1st S.M. Fd Amb). Also Stretcher bearers of 75th Fd Amb will 30 officers & a field Bearer Divn at their advanced Dressing Station at NORTH CHIMNEY ALBERT at BATAUME POST on the ALBERT-BAPAUME road were duly carried out. - Capt. Scott-Williams proceeding to VADENCOURT. Capt Hereford & 2 m.o.s going to the ADStation Sup. to MILLENCOURT & balance of the 1/2nd S.M. Fd Amb. relieved no 97th Officers Hospital at WARLOY. A wet day. Capt Morris Bennett proceeded for camp duty as M.O. 1/4 Royal Berks.	
MILLENCOURT	July 18		DDMS called in morning, afterwards visited the advanced Dressing Station & ADMS at BOUZINCOURT in afternoon visited Capt. Williamson at VADENCOURT. Received orders to further move tomorrow. A fine day.	

WAR DIARY or INTELLIGENCE SUMMARY

Army Form C. 2118

(Erase heading not required.)

Place	Date	Hour	Summary of Events and Information	Remarks and references to Appendices
MILLENCOURT	July 19		At 11.30 was relieved at MILLENCOURT by a party of the 125th Fd Amb. The Headqrs of the Ambulance proceeded to VADENCOURT with 1/2 Fd Ambulance and 1/2 Sect but division proceeded for duty at North CHIMNEY ALBERT. Weather fine.	
	July 20		Today I received report from ADS that 9 of my personnel (1 R.A.M.C & 1 A.S.C. M.T. attached) had been sent down suffering from gas poisoning & one other was also severely wounded (Comp Fracture of leg, bullet through arm). A very busy day. There have been heavy fighting also BRICKERS & known & POZIERES. VADENCOURT only been slightly wounded & sent to evacuation ACOs are chiefly by advising ammunition teams - weather fine.	
	July 21		These wounded of my unit have been sent down suffering from gas poisoning. They were all affected while collecting wounded from trenches N & S VILLERS. Another busy day as heavy fighting still continues - weather fine.	
	July 22		At Head Quarter all day. Transport all running Ambulance cars wounded to the 2nd Australian Field Amb. which has opened our near us. Weather dull but fine.	
	July 23		Another busy day, a fighting also got on several wounded fine.	
	July 24		A.M. visited BOUZINCOURT & thence with ADMS went to N. Chimney ALBERT & BAPAUME POST. DDMS 2nd Corps (8) which we are now a part - College. Weather fine.	
	25		A quick day a fighting on our front is not quite so severe. In afternoon transferred transport. ADMS called in Evening. Weather fine though.	
	26		Am visited ADMS at BOUZINCOURT. The division is heavy relieved & going out at weather. Fine but cold & dull	

1875 Wt. W593/826 1,000,000 4/15 J.B.C. & A. A.D.S.S./Forms/C. 2118.

Army Form C. 2118

WAR DIARY
or
INTELLIGENCE SUMMARY
(Erase heading not required.)

Instructions regarding War Diaries and Intelligence Summaries are contained in F.S. Regs., Part II. and the Staff Manual respectively. Title Pages will be prepared in manuscript.

Place	Date 1916	Hour	Summary of Events and Information	Remarks and references to Appendices
VADENCOURT	July 27		Informed by A.D.M.S. that we were being relieved by Australian Field Ambulance & as the Enemy 'Officer to part of the 7th Cand of that Corps arrived at VADENCOURT. One of my Motor Ambulances detained at LA BOISELLE was struck by Shell Splinter the Superstructure half damaged. The Wagon orderly was severely wounded. Weather fine, hot.	
"	July 28		The Australians had no orders to relieve the Australians but the D.D.M.S. 2nd Corps instructed the No. MS 12th Division to take over from us at those Stations & the lead of my Section arrived at that Quarter at 10.30 p.m. Received orders to proceed tomorrow to BEAUVAL. Weather fine	
"	July 29		in light marching order. The Field Ambulance Paraded at 7.30 am. Marched to BEAUVAL via RAINCHAVAL & BEAUQUESNE. Arrived at 1.30 pm. The weather was hot & Afternoon but the men completed the journey in good condition.	
BEAUVAL	July 30		The march was continued at 7 am to FRANQUEVILLE via CANAAS & BERNEUIL. The weather was again very hot. The transport particularly found the very hilly country near the End of the march very trying. The went has gone into Bivouac in the village as billets for Officers & men are very bad.	
FRANQUEVILLE	July 31		The day has been spent in making the men as much comfortable on moving down of the A.D.M.S. was one not genuine expect. But we have to collect the Rect from the Northern part of the Area. Again a hot afternoon day.	

J Agnew Major R.A.M.C.
O.C. 1/3rd South Midland Field Ambulance

WAR DIARY

OF

1/3RD SOUTH MIDLAND FIELD AMBULANCE

FOR THE MONTH

OF

AUGUST 1916

WAR DIARY
or
INTELLIGENCE SUMMARY

Army Form C. 2118.

Place	Date 1916	Hour	Summary of Events and Information	Remarks and references to Appendices
FRANVILLE	Aug 1		Received orders from ADMS to proceed today to LONGVILLERS. Horses billetted there. The Unit marched out at 6 am and reached LONGVILLERS at 7.45 pm. Capt DREZE (RAMCF) was permanently transferred to 4th Flanders as M.O. & Capt Wrigley RAMC (TF) reported for duty with this unit. Weather fine.	
LONGVILLERS	Aug 2		Routine duties. Section Cookery & Equipment. Weather fine.	
	Aug 3		ADMS called. Routine duties. Weather fine.	
	Aug 4		Opened hospital for the Old Chateau for sick of 144th & 145th Brigades & details. ADMS called. Weather fine.	
	Aug 5		Routine duties. Fine day. Capt KENION (RAMC, T.F.) left for duty as M.O. 1/6 Warwicks vice Lt. FAIRLEY (RAMC, T.F.) who rejoined the unit.	
	Aug 6		Church Parade 9 am by Chaplain Welshman & in evening by Chaplain MERK. Weather fine.	
	Aug 7		Routine duties.	
	Aug 8		ADMS called & informed us we marched to BEAUVAL tomorrow. Busy packing up & clearing hospital. Weather fine. The rest has been delightful but too short.	
	Aug 9		Paraded at 5.45 am & marched at 6 am. via 1/2 3 Co?. 8 Field Engineers. Reached BEAUVAL at 10 am when we bivouac'd in a field for the night. Weather hot but fine.	
BEAUVAL	Aug 10		Paraded at 5.30 am & marched to RAINCHEVAL which was reached at 9.30 am. Was showery most but fine after.	
RAINCHEVAL	Aug 11		Resting at RAINCHEVAL	

Army Form C. 2118.

WAR DIARY
or
INTELLIGENCE SUMMARY
(Erase heading not required.)

Instructions regarding War Diaries and Intelligence Summaries are contained in F. S. Regs., Part II. and the Staff Manual respectively. Title Pages will be prepared in manuscript.

Place	Date 1916	Hour	Summary of Events and Information	Remarks and references to Appendices
RAINCHEVAL	Aug 12		Reconnaissance & accordance with instructions from ADMS dispatched Capt Smythe & 1 bearer sub-division complete bereft to OC 4th S.W. 2nd and for duty at NORTH CHIMNEY ABBSOR(?) while the division is still in the line; also Lt SPIERT & 6 other ranks to Ofenborg hospital MARLOY	
	Aug 13		Paraded at 9:30 am and proceeded to LOUVENCOURT where in tour over the II Corps Officers Rest Hospital and the II Corps Rest Station from the 38th Field Ambulance. Showery weather	
LOUVENCOURT	Aug 14		Routine duties. Visited Capt Witman & took charge of Rest Station + Capt Hengbuck of Officers Hospital. ADMS called. Showery weather.	
	" 15		Routine duties. Weather cool & showery. Paid another interim acct. damaged to shell fire in BATOKE (?).	
	Aug 16		DADMS + Capt Robinson (?) Heavy Shower. Capt Knopfey left for temporary duty with the 1st South Ft at CHALKFAYE	
	17		DDMS + DADMS II Corps called Routine duties. Thunderstorm in afternoon	
	18		Routine duties. ADMS called. Fine day	
	19		Capt Simpson RAME (TC) reported for duty.	
	20		Church Parade 9 am. Sept Wolff of my unit who was killed in ORVILLERS last night was buried this evening at LOUVENCOURT	
	21		Routine duties - weather fine	
	22		AND D-S	
	23		Along with Capt Hengbuck & Capt Williamson (L/t 2nd Stafford) formed a Med Board to investigate 383 General men I saw to how conducted Butter	

2449 Wt. W14957/M90 750,000 1/16 J.B.C. & A. Forms/C.2118/12.

Army Form C. 2118

Instructions regarding War Diaries and Intelligence Summaries are contained in F.S. Regs., Part II. and the Staff Manual respectively. Title Pages will be prepared in manuscript.

WAR DIARY
or
INTELLIGENCE SUMMARY
(Erase heading not required.)

Place	Date 1916	Hour	Summary of Events and Information	Remarks and references to Appendices
LOUVENCOURT	Aug 24		Routine duties. Weather fine	
	25		ADMS called + said we were going the relieved in morning, went to BVS to report in morning but in afternoon received orders to interview ADMS 6th Div Ambulance accommodation there. Came over from there Ambulance at BERTRANCOURT. MAILLY-MAILLET + ACHONVILLERS with a view to taking over from their Ambulance	
	26		B/O section marched at 11 am to take over advanced posts of 16th + 17th Fd Ambulances at MAILLY + ACHONVILLERS. Capt Smythe then known returned from duty at ADMS Chaumy. ALBERT own service during the line. Wet day with Thunderstorm in afternoon	
BERTRANCOURT	27		Paraded at 11 am + after handing over Officers Hospital + Rest Camp 2nd Corps to the 17th F. and marched to BERTRANCOURT to relieve the 16th Fd. Here these moves are being carried out on the 1466th Bde Bgde have taken over as a portion of the line in front of ACHONVILLERS	
	28		Routine duties. Weather fine	
	29		" " Heavy Thunderstorm + persistent rain afterward	
	30		Visited ADS's at MAILLY - in morning - still raining	
	31		Routine duties. Weather fine	

J A Green Major RAMC
OC 13 South Midland
Field Ambulance

Vol 19

WAR DIARY
OF
1/3RD SOUTH MIDLAND FIELD AMBULANCE
FOR THE MONTH OF
SEPTEMBER 1916

COMMITTEE FOR THE
MEDICAL HISTORY OF THE WAR
Date 26 OCT 1916

Jasper
Major RAMC
Comdg 1/3rd S.M. Fd Ambulance

WAR DIARY or INTELLIGENCE SUMMARY

Army Form C. 2118

Place	Date 1916	Hour	Summary of Events and Information	Remarks and references to Appendices
BERTRANCOURT	Sept 1.		Fine day – Routine duties. Capt Scott Indermain left the unit to report to Base in Boulogne.	
"	2		Fine day. C.O. Col McGowan inspected the unit & congratulated it on its work on the SOMME front. Capt CARROL (R.A.M.C T.C.) reported for duty.	
"	3		Routine duties. Fine day.	
"	4		" " Wet day.	
"	5		Visited A.D.M.S. Sgt Dorman re evacuation of Men B. his Division thro' my unit. Weather favouring.	
"	6		Routine duties. A.D.M.S. & Capt Carrol & said I should proceed to BUS tomorrow on relief of BERTRANCOURT by 132nd Fd Amb. Who would also take over the A.D.S. at the Château MAILLY. In the evening an advance party of the 132nd Fd Amb proceeded to MAILLY. Weather fine.	1100–1 LENS
"	7		Capt HESFORTH & R.B. Dixon arrived at the D.H. at 11.30am on relief by 132nd F.A. at MAILLY. Capt KERR with A. Sebin with CO A.Sebin remained at RED HOUSE MAILLY. Left after a 2 hour hand over before AUCHONVILLERS. Remainder of the unit on relief by 132 Fd Amb marched at 2.15 pm to BUS where I relieved the 1/1st S. Md Fd Amb. O.D.M.S. & Capt entered at 3.30 pm. Weather fine to the Somme. REAUMETE.	Fd. Hosp. A.D.
BUS les Bertros	8		A.D.M.S. called. Routine duties – Fine day	
"	9		Routine duties. Fine day.	
"	10		9 am Church parade. An afternoon tour in cars from 1/1st Fd Amb as they are on move tomorrow. Fine day.	

WAR DIARY / INTELLIGENCE SUMMARY

Army Form C.2118

Instructions regarding War Diaries and Intelligence Summaries are contained in F.S. Regs., Part II. and the Staff Manual respectively. Title Pages will be prepared in manuscript.

(Erase heading not required.)

Place	Date 1916	Hour	Summary of Events and Information	Remarks and references to Appendices
BUS LES ARTOIS	6/11		Routine duties. Admitted patient from 1/2nd. S. Middx 3rd Amb. who are moving tomorrow to 145th Inf Bde. Weather fine	
"	12		Routine duties. Weather showery. Evacuating cases to C.C.S. & returning others to duty preparatory to moving tomorrow.	
"	13		Paraded at 9.30 am marched in rear of 144 Inf Bde to ORVILLE. arrived where the Bde is going into rest. B Section opened hospital for the sick of the Bde. Weather - wet. Been training in field.	
ORVILLE	14		Routine duties. Received orders that A/Dy H/Supt LAMBOURNE have been cancelled the holiday for [illegible] Conduct in front of POZIERES. on July last	
"	15		ADMS called & informed me that I would be ready to move at 2hrs notice if necessary. 9 a.m. parade & inspection. Sections are being instructed in stretcher waddles. Weather fine but very close at night.	
"	16		Routine duties. Quiet day. Weather fair.	
"	17		Church parade 9 am. ADMS called & said we were moving further back into rest — in afternoon went to see MON PLAISIR nr HEM 6 which we move tomorrow. fine day in rear of 144 Bde	
"	18		Paraded at 8.30 am & marched to MON PLAISIR from [illegible] Bde obtained the adjoining farm at Bivouac. A/c. Section, on account of heavy continuous rain it is impossible (or been to Bivouac. B Section opened up for sick of 144 Bde.	
MON PLAISIR	19		Quiet day — but weather still very wet.	

Ref Map LENS II 1-100,000

WAR DIARY or INTELLIGENCE SUMMARY

Army Form C. 2118

Instructions regarding War Diaries and Intelligence Summaries are contained in F.S. Regs., Part II. and the Staff Manual respectively. Title Pages will be prepared in manuscript.

(Erase heading not required.)

Place	Date 1916	Hour	Summary of Events and Information	Remarks and references to Appendices
MONTPLAISIR	May 20		Routine duties. Weather Excessive wet. Capt Curror left for duty as M.O. 1/5 Royal Fusiliers. Capt Wrigley rejoined from 17th Worcesters.	
"	21		Route marches in morning. St Eloi Hill wind in afternoon. Weather Showery & Close.	
"	22		Drill for duel in field Ambulance movements. Weather fine but close.	
"	23		Route march in morning. A.D.M.S. Called to Mc Sweeney. Left for duty with 25th Division.	
"	24		Church Parade 9am & Routine duties. Capt SOUTTAR R.T.M.C.T. Left for temp duty with 252nd Bde R.F.A. Weather fine	LENS. 11 1 – 15/5/1910
"	25		Field Ambulance moved in morning & routine duties. Capt Seymour R.T.M.C. left for temp duty with 16 /4th Gloster Batt". Weather fine	
"	26		Route march in morning & routine duties. Capt Theopold attended a preliminary Conference at 3pm at which the M.O.E. Explained the scheme for a field day tomorrow. Weather fine.	
"	27		Stretcher drill in morning & routine duties. Unit paraded at 9.30 am for a route march with 16 144th Inf Bde. followed by an attack on BERNAVILLE from FROZEN HERT. The Ambulance turned out 1st in its NEW FIELD for the collection & reception of wounded. Arrived at HEAD QUARTERS at 6 pm. Weather Showery	
"	28		Received instructions to Evacuate all cases not likely to be will in 3 days – in view of a probable move. Weather very wet	Rd. Hosp. Ed. ??

Army Form C. 2118.

WAR DIARY
or
INTELLIGENCE SUMMARY

(Erase heading not required.)

Place	Date	Hour	Summary of Events and Information	Remarks and references to Appendices
MON PLAISIR	Sept 30 1916		Received orders late last night - to follow the 144 Inf Bde billets for the night at IVERGNY. Parade at 9.15 am & after marched in accordance with instructions - A halt of 3/4 hour at 12.45 at MITTY to water & feed horses - & reached our billets at 4 pm. C Section moved up to assist 9/144 Inf Bde on our arrival - weather fine	Ref map LENS II. 1-100000

J Agnew Major RAMC
OC 1/3 South Midland Field Ambulance

140/168

48th Div

113 F.M. Field Ambulance

Oct 1916

COMMITTEE FOR THE
MEDICAL HISTORY OF THE WAR
Date -2 DEC. 1916

From O.C

[Stamp: 1/3rd SOUTH MIDLAND FD AMBULANCE, No 28/51, 1 NOV 1916, R.A.M.C.T.]

To:- ADMS - 48th Division

Herewith War Diary of 1/3rd South Midland Field Ambulance for the month of

OCTOBER 1916

1/11/16

[Signature]
LT. COLONEL
COMG. 1/3rd, STH. MID. FD. AMBULANCE.

WAR DIARY / INTELLIGENCE SUMMARY

Army Form C. 2118.

Vol 2

Place	Date 1916	Hour	Summary of Events and Information	Remarks and references to Appendices
IVERGNY	Oct 1		The Colonel was out back to old line at midnight. At 9 am received orders that Brigade was to move again. Temporary Hd qu Parly had at 11.30 am. Our destination was GRENAS where we billeted in a CHATEAU grounds. Very help comfort. RAMC called round as we were nearing to MONDICOURT & told me that BRS was tomorrow to meet us in afternoon troubs. Weather appeared - weather fine.	help LENS 1-two odd
GRENAS	" 2		C Section paraded at 8.30 am under Capt HERE marched to MONDICOURT & took over from an Adv of the 46th Div. Weather been wet & cold	
	3		Remainder of Unit paraded at 11 am & marched to MONDICOURT & completed taking over which was done by noon. There is a Small Officers hospital to "U" WB in a field dug but the driven weather one in huts which made a bit of a pair. Capt SOUTER returned from detached duty. Weather very wet	
MONDICOURT	4		ADMS called. Have commenced draining the Camp, which was very necessary. Weather very wet.	
	5		Having obtained a little material from RE began a new shower bath & standings for horse lines. Drainage of Camp continues - Weather still wet -	
	6		Routine duties. Weather cold but fine. The BRS is developing into a 1st Cys Rest Station	
	7		Attended Conference at ADMS office at 9.30 am in arrangement of works in event of action. Weather cold but fine	
	8		Church Parade 9 am - ADMS & routine duties - very wet day	
	9		Routine duties - weather fine	
	10		ADMS called & stated that we should evacuate patients more liberally in view of future French when we	

Army Form C. 2118.

WAR DIARY
or
INTELLIGENCE SUMMARY
(Erase heading not required.)

Place	Date 1916	Hour	Summary of Events and Information	Remarks and references to Appendices
MORLANCOURT	Feb 10 cont'd		Might have to take in Company wounded. KO's going in. Well with new bath house & sick Corp. Standing complete. New latrines re. track in more convenient place. Weather fine.	
	11		Graded 43 CES during morning. Army-Survey received notes that we should be prepared tomorrow by 52nd Div Arty. (17th Div.) that we were R.F. clear of MORLANCOURT by today (13th inst.) Weather fine after a wet morning.	
	12		Lieut Capt SMYTHE & MORLANCOURT returning, which has received orders to move. He found he belongs R.E. 3rd my move was postponed until Saturday (19th inst.) At 3 p.m. attended a demonstration on method of Artillery of hut to by Col GRAY Royal @ Capt O'MOORE reported for duty from sick leave. Weather fine.	
	13		Routine duties in morning. After Noon attended Divin'S officers which form in these two front line work. Sent a telephone party of 10 O.R. to prepare an O.P. dugout for Artillery H.Q. at Le HAIE Ferme. Weather fine.	
	14		Standard cart at MORLANCOURT at 11 a.m. I attended & 1 CHO dine. My usual duties carried on in between. Capt Mitchell marched with whole of B Section (Bearers) A section proceeded by 4 PONDILLIERS where they returned 11.5. and 2nd and 3rd in afternoon went with Nos 1 & 3 PONDILLIERS to investigate rides & proposed Elephant house for collecting post for battery ones (from HABITERNE. If necessary to BONNEGAY that such case shall all be evacuated by motor ambs. via PONDILLIERS. the Bearers if possible. Coming F S.B.R. function keep & weather fine but cold.	× Report 575
	15		Quiet parade 7.30 am. Rides to K. R. E. Si Morlancourt for Elephant traces re an which notches already been commenced. Afternoon attended a second rider by Col Gray Royal on two salient of no uses. Company of General agreed to his transfer to 3/r and 3rd Engineers. Commented on the proposed humps. Weather cold but fine.	

WAR DIARY or INTELLIGENCE SUMMARY

Army Form C. 2118.

Place	Date 1916	Hour	Summary of Events and Information	Remarks and references to Appendices
HENU	Feb 16		Visited ADMS at 9.45 am. Then went to FONQUEVILLERS with Capt Westfall, Major, & Smyth & an Engineer Officer. Walked along the present track (of Fonquevillers) making plans from HEBUTERNE. Also inspected a suggested site for a new underground dressing station in Calker village. On return K HENU reported enemy had K.A.M.S. who infiltrated HEBUTERNE. Also started improving huts we occupy at HENU – a stormy day.	HEBUTERNE 1:40,000
	" 17		Routine duties. Weather fine but cold.	
	" 18		Routine duties during morning. In afternoon rode over to the front Amb at D.26 Central where I had received orders to take over lorries from 51st Fd Amb – later on heard that this was only temp. Weather – fine day after a wet night.	
	19		Capt MOORE + 20 OR of A Section relieved 51st Fd Amb at ADS HEBUTERNE by 10 am in accordance with instructions from ADMS. At 1.30 pm Personnel of Unit at HENU paraded & marched to D.26 Central where we took over from 51st Fd Amb. During evening OC 1/1 E.12.F.A. called to say he was taking over from me tomorrow. Weather very wet.	
D.26 Central	20		Routine duties + handing over to an Advance party of 1/1 W.R.F.A. (49th Div) This is a big thing as there is an enormous amount of Stores re Capt Westfall returned 4 his 28- during morning on relief at FONQUEVILLERS. Later Capt MOORE + his party also returned on relief at HEBUTERNE. DDMS via Corps called. Weather fine but cold.	
	21		Paraded at 10.30 am + unit marched to COURCELLES where we took over an Empty Hospital from 1/3 W.R.F.A. Weather fine but cold.	

WAR DIARY or INTELLIGENCE SUMMARY

Army Form C. 2118

Place	Date 1916	Hour	Summary of Events and Information	Remarks and references to Appendices
COUTERELLE	Oct 22		Church parade at 9.30 am. ADMS 48th Div called round by Corp Order. Saw clerk & leave the place at 11.30 am. Horses reviewed as orders hither effect. I first went to 144 Bde Hd Quarters about it & after K DHQ (Noullens) where I found that a line had been dispatched ordering me to move to HALLOY after I saw ADMS who returned to 144 Bde Hd Qrs (Authieville) I am (very) & (ailerthed) to get instructions as impending move South. A very cold frosty day.	
HALLOY	23		Routine duties — washed billets	
	24		Lord Haig reviewed troops to move. The transports go by road tomorrow. Remainder of Unit will proceed by motor buses. The H. transports paraded at 9.45 am under Capts & bus home. 2 Lieutts & proceeded with rest of 144 Bde transport to TALMAS. I went the way to BRESLE & AMIENS. Weather wet — but warm.	1-100000 AMIENS
	25		Remainder of unit paraded at 10 am marched to MONDICOURT where they Embussed for BRESLE where Ambulance went in advance with billetting party. Arrived at BRESLE 4.40 pm & felt somewhat billets frozen. Billets for officers. Disposed but not across. Under a 30 pm after a very hard 2 days march. Failed at night received orders hence to temporarily take over 51 Corps Rest Station at BECOURT.	
BRESLE	26		Went to 51 Corps Rest Station Capt Hereford & B & Lt Subbleman also proceeded there to take over the 29th FA which is at present moving. The place is of recent growth & unsuitable, the trouble laying out of the Camp (all marquees) & the wind of recent frost having frozen the materials worse. the bad weather has prevented burials around to make matters worse the bad weather has turned everything into a sea of mud. There are about 1000 patients in all. After I visited ADMS 4 & Enemy at B. Seelen had precedent.	1-100000 BRESLE AMIENS

WAR DIARY or INTELLIGENCE SUMMARY

Army Form C. 2118

Place	Date	Hour	Summary of Events and Information	Remarks and references to Appendices
BECOURT	Oct 27 1916		Completed handing over as far as possible during morning. A more detailed survey of the Camp only increases the difficulties that have to be overcome. Through preparation is necessary but everything is hampered by the mud. Rations promised by the 9th Divn did not arrive & I was obliged to draw on my reserve. Dlls depot halts supply and feeding accommodation needs extending. Have closed the packstore until it can be renovated – weather very wet. DDMS called – He is very anxious to attempt get things straightened up.	
	Oct 28		Another day of hard continuous work. Difficulty with daily state (Return of Sick & wounded) since we erected pt right. Rations difficulties improved but not yet adequate to. Have arranged to have details A+D Bn 7th parade during to & have got 2 SRs from Back of the 2 other divisions in the Corps who keep their own A+D book. Two officers came I lent Ambulances of the 1st Northumbrian FA are sent for assistance here. Several Carrying Store & other Equipment arrived today. That has helped the feeding arrangements. The difficulties of running a Corps Rest Station with continually changing of these medical units are very great to my mind success can only be attained by a permanent personnel with lines of a CCS – want of continuity of records will be partly met. Another very wet day.	
	Oct 29		Today the weather is again appalling. I have decided to divide the Camp into sections. One for Each Division of the Corps & another for Corps & other Divisional troops. The officers hospital quarters are not yet complete remainder to be keep Officers in. I have found it necessary to organize Day & night orderly med Officers & cross pour in at all hours. There is also an out patient Casual sick Dept. – Pm this there are the RAP 100 behind the scene. The miller a great drain on the line of my med Officers (& a Chaplain) with RDLJS Sel-aroni rest. I have formed Salvage &rubbish Gree	

WAR DIARY or INTELLIGENCE SUMMARY

Army Form C. 2118

Place	Date 1916	Hour	Summary of Events and Information	Remarks and references to Appendices
BECOURT	Oct 29 (Cont)		Salving the practise. Another clearing up report from the Camp & its surroundings. the french re. Another party is filling up old trenches at the entrance to the Camp with a new burying proper road of Ruhineaux End. Still another party scraper mud all day but find it difficult to cope with the wet damp supplies of clothing & equipment. having shown the stores away somewhere under the snow section is alright now. DDMS III Corps again called. also DADMS 4th Divn	
	Oct 30		Completed the drainage of latrine in their own section today the home duties of yesterday. the day before Continues. in addition to on another fatigue clearing out & Covering in shell hole trenches which are full of refuse re DDMS III Corps & ADMS 4th Div called during morning. Old practise trench cleared. Am installing a parachute for Each bysan Section T Camps. No mainstud is not by troops to know all forces an oblong deep trench pit with the parapet slab behind accumulates must be increased. Considering further. are needed at all these fatigues are being utilized freely from Communicating trench are needed at all these fatigues are being utilized freely from another day auxillary rain though worrisome at night well a bomb & ammunition store in part of the of the old trench the every necessary. Weather ditto not during day another day auxillary rain though worrisome at night An officer of the III Corps Engineers called & passed into Camp which is the most pressing need	
	Oct 31		The rain turned during tonight was nasty was a regular 8 morning were blown over to had the re sections. Some fatigues are going on - better today but weather worse the burying	

J A Green. Lieutenant Colonel. RAMC.
O/C 1/3 South Midland Field Ambulance.

COMMITTEE FOR THE
MEDICAL HISTORY OF THE WAR

Date −3 JAN. 1917

War Diary

of

1/3rd South Midland Field Ambulance

For The Month of

November 1916

WAR DIARY or INTELLIGENCE SUMMARY

(Erase heading not required.)

Army Form C.2

Place	Date 1916	Hour	Summary of Events and Information	Remarks and references to Appendices
BECOURT WILL Th (Corps Post Station)	May 1		ADMS 48th Div called at 10 am Visited first the Camps with me - making suggestions as to temporary huts. The DDMS called subsequently in afternoon (Col MacDonald) being very so taken with hurricane & began trying to clear things up. The large party clearing went away. Another damp road (?) close of dumps re - others digging sites (?) trench latrines to improve the accommodation The officers engaged in improving the latrines. Commenced today a log road into the Entrance of the Camp. This ought to be a great help when finished. Went to see some of the most difficult hutter ambulances to get off the road which has been impassable. In the last few wet days. At 9 am took a movement road & patients in the Road station with a view to checking the trying leather time in morning but not urgent.	
	May 2		A pouring wet day + mud and slush work had the ambulances to contend with. Patients had been coming in large number had our accommodation in several places been overcome. But thankfully proper portion were pressed into putting across into patients marquees.	
	May 3		DDMS Corps called twice enquiring over the Camps - making numerous suggestions for carrying on. Had a party of Conscendeers (?) patients following on the Camp which were well ranked. Visited him afterwards. Continued digging deep latrines where our unit remark.	
	May 4		Routine duties all day. beginning to improvement - The advance road in progress up(?) repair line to breed (?) with afternoon the teams called + gave me invitations to gradually relieve my patients to 500 - arrangements having been made for others to (?) Etaples. The Sanitary Officer of the 50th Div called at my quarters. ADMS 1st Div took me the faun of further Sanitary arrangement of the Camp + provision meas for the purpose within five subjectional cross drainage (?)	

WAR DIARY or INTELLIGENCE SUMMARY

Army Form C. 2118

Place	Date 1916	Hour	Summary of Events and Information	Remarks and references to Appendices
BECOURT HILL III Corps Rest Stn	Nov 5		8th Sanitary Sqd (20 men) of 50th Division arrived & commenced Sanitation throughout dists. Routine duties — including all usual fatigues — Found it is going to the different latrines, number of patients to various conditions are very bad & admissions very high weather — fine during day but wet at night.	
	Nov 6		WMR as usual — latrine work is progressing. Stores still being fitted in marquees but Cond has been rather difficult to obtain. Road is not being substitutes as all for the Corps Rest Station has to the 4th who are chairman. Have cleaned the bell pickets which has lately been opened as an Admission Centre. Three separate pockets are being opened — The first and dinner in the line of the 8th for Corps & Other Ranks Camps arrangements kept all facilities in Shucabous weather fine after a very wet night. Capt NICHOLS left for battalion duty.	
	Nov 7		A dreadfully wet day. Am managing to get the number of patients in the Station reduced. An arrangement to have only 12 in each marquee. This should enable an improvement. C.E. III Corps called & expressed himself Capt MORRIS RAMMET dreadfully wet. Reported for duty.	
	Nov 8		Routine duties. Weather fine after a very wet night.	
	Nov 9		A fine morning. HRH S.M.S. trained round the camp. At 1.30 pm the Corps Commander called with his staff. Weather fine.	
	Nov 10		Routine duties — things are running better. The Latrine road is forming & Sanitary arrangements are now different. A new moveable pan has been tried. Weather after fine but cold.	

WAR DIARY or INTELLIGENCE SUMMARY

Army Form C. 2118

(Erase heading not required.)

Place	Date 1916	Hour	Summary of Events and Information	Remarks and references to Appendices
BECOURT HILL Nr Corps Rest Station	Nov 11		ADMS 48th Dn. + DDMS III Corps both called during the morning. The latter said I/c had been directed to remove the Corps Rest Station to MILLENCOURT where it will be replaced by the 2nd Fd. Ambulance. (19 Divison). The chief difficulty here is the lack of water. Meantime we carry on here. Erected a large store tent near entrance to camp for use as a CCS dressing tent. Turned old dressing tent into a drying room. Weather fine but dull. In evening the road outside camp was shelled but no damage done.	
	,, 12		Routine duties. DC RSn of 2nd Fd Amb called re removal of Equipment to MILLENCOURT. Weather - dull but fine.	
	,, 13		Routine duties. - Sickness all troops. DDMS called. Weather fine but dull.	
	,, 14		Routine duties. DDMS called. also OC 2nd Fd Amb. re transfer of Equipment. Weather fine but dull.	
	,, 15		Routine duties. 6 motor lorry loads of Equipment sent to MILLENCOURT. Capt SMYTHE RAMC arrived. Leave from 4/1 SM CCS - Scots Very cold day. - ADMS 50th Div. called re brendan tces of Capes of this division.	
	16		A cold frosty day. 3 lorry loads of Equipment despatched to MILLENCOURT. ADMS called. - Routine duties.	
	17		Frost very keen. Enemy night a German Aeroplane overhead – found rocket hopper opposite in damage. Found the following names in recent list of awards Military Medal - Cl Caller RSM. Sgt Stewart & Cpl Beacon - all of this unit. Detailed 2 NCOs + 25 men for duty as Stretcher bearers on the front here a Stretcher number of . . .	

WAR DIARY
INTELLIGENCE SUMMARY

(Erase heading not required.)

Army Form C. 2118

Place	Date 1916	Hour	Summary of Events and Information	Remarks and references to Appendices
BECOURT HILL Th Cop Red Station	Nov 18		Routine duties. Detailed a second party of 2 NCO+men for duty on front line fireplaces. A similar number coming down for a week rest. Weather. Snow in night but fine + healthy warmth in afternoon.	
	Nov 19		D.D.M.S. called. Said that I would have all funked here being as comfortable as possible. Supplement. I could send any fracture questions to No 1 hunstonian Station BECOURT Chateau. She will help on every thing for B. 10 Solemn magpie (with wooden floor) I have had good accommodation for 120 patients. In afternoon visited No.1 hunstonian Station. I made arrangements for this with OCR 97th d Station. Capt SOUTER left for temporary duty with 1/8 Arcadi Outt. Weather — dull but warm.	
	20		Capt Shiell + Mr McReuchlin F.d. Amb on temp duty here. Went on leave. Routine duties. Capt MORRIS left for duty at 48th Div. School of Instruction. Weather. Dull but warm.	
	21		Routine duties during morning. P.M. visited DDMS at Corp. HA. Duerlois — Cold + foggy day. SD4 + Cav have opened a Dr S at LAVIEVILLE (Which we are Depopulating). Hospitals away. DDMS called — morning but fine otherwise. Capt Scott RAMC No2 15 DAC reported for duty. He will come in each day between 9 + 12 noon.	
	22		Routine duties — fine but dull day.	
	23			
	24		Usual work about camp. DDMS called. Equipment still going to MILLENCOURT. Rain in night.	
	25		A very wet day + all out door work suspended	
	26		Afti a wet night weather cleared + outside work continued. Engineers have commenced wage on Entrance road (which had been suspended for some days) Special Plymout gang checking Recket, from A+D Boots of my Pickmann which have returned to me. Frosty at night	

2449 Wt. W14957/M90 750,000 1/16 J.B.C. & A. Forms/C.2118/12.

Army Form C. 2118

WAR DIARY
or
INTELLIGENCE SUMMARY

(Erase heading not required.)

Instructions regarding War Diaries and Intelligence Summaries are contained in F. S. Regs., Part II. and the Staff Manual respectively. Title Pages will be prepared in manuscript.

Place	Date 1916	Hour	Summary of Events and Information	Remarks and references to Appendices
BECOURT HILL	Nov 27		Major GOVER & the tent Sub division of the 11th Northumbrian Fd Ambulance who have been on temp. duty here left to rejoin their unit. Lt FANSTONE of 1st Fd Amb. reported for duty. ADMS called. Weather fine but dull.	
III Corps Rest Station	28		Routine duties all day - weather fine but fog & frost at night.	
	29		ADMS called. Routine duties - Continued checking of kit from A-N-ZOTF & 28th Fd Amb. depôts. Weather thick but fine.	
	30		DDMS called. Routine duties. Capt REID of 2nd Fd amb. reported for temporary duty vice Lt FANSTONE who rejoined his unit.	

J A Green Lt Col. RAMC

OC 1/3 South Midland Field Ambulance

B.E.F

Vol 22

140/900.

4th Div.

Rec'd

WAR DIARY

OF

1/3RD SOUTH MIDLAND FIELD AMBULANCE

FOR THE MONTH

OF

DECEMBER

1916

11 JAN 1917
3rd South Midland Fd Amb
R.A.M.C.

COMMITTEE FOR THE
MEDICAL HISTORY OF THE WAR

Date   31 JAN. 1917

J. Green
LT. COLONEL
1/3rd. Sth. Mid. Fd. Ambulance

WAR DIARY or INTELLIGENCE SUMMARY

Army Form C. 2118

(Erase heading not required.)

Instructions regarding War Diaries and Intelligence Summaries are contained in F.S. Regs., Part II. and the Staff Manual respectively. Title Pages will be prepared in manuscript.

Place	Date 6/16	Hour	Summary of Events and Information	Remarks and references to Appendices
BECOURT H14 (III Corps Rd) S4h	Dec. 1		Routine duties. Weather fine	
	" 2		Routine duties. Capt KERR proceeded on leave. Rev E C Young C.F. (W.O.) joined us vice Rev H.A. MEEK (A.I.F.) Weather fine	
	" 3		Routine duties. DDMS called. Weather – ground thaw & everything muddy – no rain	
	" 4		ADMS HQ afterwards proceeded to CONTALMAISON to arrange about relief of bearers in front line. DDMS called. Capt SCOUTER rejoined from detached duty. Weather fine	
	" 5		Routine duties. At 7pm sent 6 motor ambulance to No.1 bearer rear Stabn, & repaired in bus and if patients. So it had been advised at 6.30 pm. (53 casualties including skilled & sick duty adm!) So Sdns left for Terif, but only 1/5 wanted. Weather fine	(intact 30-40 from)
	" 6		Routine duties – strong sunday Equipment enemy. Closed. The rest station for admission of patients at midnight. Weather fine	
	" 7		Routine duties – weather fine but dull	
	" 8		Routine duties – patient pulmonary diminishing – weather dull but fine	
	" 9		A dull wet day. At R.M.C. (III Corps) called re knapsack reserve park & Stop Enhance to CRS	
	" 10		Handing over Stores to. Sent out div J. F. S in 9d. and where has been on duty, new relieved to their unit. A.C. went in leave. Weather wet.	
	" 11		Weather fine. Sent tent & other equipment to 141 Fd Amb. DDMS called – wet weather	
	" 12		Sent 1 H.trap & arms 15" Bn. - Weather hen.	
	" 13		DDMS called – various other Equipment sent J.B.	
	" 14		Lt Edwards & Caddy reported for duty. Received orders to send 1 Section complete. (Sec.Motor.Amb) for duty at 3rd Corps Rest Stabn at H14c. 5 temporary funeral	

WAR DIARY
or
INTELLIGENCE SUMMARY

(Erase heading not required.)

Army Form C.2118

Place	Date	Hour	Summary of Events and Information	Remarks and references to Appendices
BECOURT HILL	1914 Dec 15		C Section paraded & left for duty at II Corps Rest Stn. Capt SOUTTER in charge with him Lt Edwards Party — one lorry load of Equipment from MILLENCOURT daily.	
	16		AMMS called. Lt Edwards left for leave three sluices off the strength of the unit. At Parks joined for duty. Lt Oakley transferred to "B" Sn 2/e Amb. 2 sluices off strength. Transport J.C. Section reported having been sent here by DDMS No 2 7/e Amb from MILLENCOURT.	
	17		Routine duties —	
	18		Visited A.D.M.S. who arranged for broken things. Arranged when trying to collect new horse tried to carry in the right door way and blocked their rest. Vlait — Cannot get anything done & we are losing so many horses At ALBERT (illegible) Capt KERR returned from leave	
	19		Capt MOORE & A Section hatched to ALBERT to take over where there had have not General forcast. Meantime they are preparing new horse standings outside ALBERT. All patients within Capt Rest Station cleared out today & all new arrivals sent to New Corps Rest Station today. Capt KERR joined the section at MILLENCOURT. Capt SOUTTER admitted sick to III Corps Rest Station DTOMAS II Corps called.	
	20		were k Officer hopful Markup	
	21		A MAUDSLEY recommended for a commission & endorsed by 9.P.O. Sailor for recommend under date Dec 26 for England was received. Transp Equipment (except two guns) has now been sent to NEAR MILLENCOURT. According Instructions Stamp hole & latrine pits are being filled in. Amb with horse Standing at ALBERT.	

2449 Wt. W14957/Mg0 750,000 1/16 J.B.C. & A. Forms/C.2118/12.

WAR DIARY
or
INTELLIGENCE SUMMARY

Army Form C.

(Erase heading not required.)

Place	Date 1916	Hour	Summary of Events and Information	Remarks and references to Appendices
BECOURT HILL	Dec 22		Wet weather interfered with chicken marquees. Had other work carried on. DROMS cellar	
	23		Fine day, but high wind which blew down 2 store huts & marquee. Horse standings at ALBERT very finished.	
	24		Transport transferred to ALBERT. DROMS III Corps cellar	
	25		Xmas day. Church Service. Sam. Divided between ALBERT & BECORT	
	26		Transport of C Section returned to MILLENCOURT on orders of A.D.M.S. Wet day.	
	27		Weather fine. Received instruction to send remainder of Equipment (see MIRRVEES) to BRAY. Stores at BECOURT which has been taken over by 1/1 S. M. Z.A. DROMS cellar. Routine duties	
	28		" " DROMS 48th Div cellar	
	29		" " Capt SOUTTER returned from 3rd CCS for duty. Weather wet.	
	30			
	31		A.D.M.S. called. Reported that A.D.V.S. does not like new horse standings. Weather wet. O.C. returned from leave.	

J. Agnew Lt Col.
OC 1/3 South A.D. Amb

WAR DIARY

OF

1/3RD SOUTH MIDLAND FIELD AMBULANCE

FOR

THE MONTH OF JANUARY - 1917

COMMITTEE FOR THE
MEDICAL HISTORY OF THE WAR
Date 13 MAR. 1917

WAR DIARY or INTELLIGENCE SUMMARY

Army Form C. 2118

Place	Date	Hour	Summary of Events and Information	Remarks and references to Appendices
BECOURT HILL	1917 Jan 1		Remainder of Ambulance (bar details) moved & joined A Section at ALBERT where we remain to rest. Lt EDIS left for duty c 1/1st South Midland Field Ambulance. Weather fine	
	2		Routine duties - Walked home at TOURSIEUX. Weather fine	
	3		Routine duties - Walked BECOURT HILL where party is still clearing up things	
	4		Routine duties - weather wet	
	5		Walked BECOURT HILL	
	6		A.D.M.S. called - Routine duties. Walked C Section at MILLENCOURT in afternoon	
	7		Transport of A + B Sections left ALBERT with that of 144th Fd Bde. En route for back area South of ABBEVILLE. Handed over "Charge B" Equipment to A.D. at BECOURT HILL to OC 1/1 S.M. Fd Amb. Weather fine.	

WAR DIARY or INTELLIGENCE SUMMARY

Army Form C. 2118

(Erase heading not required.)

Instructions regarding War Diaries and Intelligence Summaries are contained in F. S. Regs., Part II. and the Staff Manual respectively. Title Pages will be prepared in manuscript.

Place	Date 1917	Hour	Summary of Events and Information	Remarks and references to Appendices
ALBERT	Jan 8		A+B Sections paraded at 3 am & marched to HEILLY where they entrained & proceeded to PONT REMY with 144th Bde. Thence they marched to HUPPY (south of ABBEVILLE) where the Divisn (non artillery +RE) is going into rest. I proceeded in motor ambulance to AIRENNES where A Section opened for the Sick of the 143 Inf Bde. afterwards visited A+B+VS at HALLENCOURT & then proceeded to HUPPY to meet the Sec Lieut in Seclines - Very wet in morning - Snow & sleet at night. Weather officering.	
AIRENNES	9		A Section marched from HUPPY to AIRENNES. Busy arranging hospital accomodation with for personnel in Evening. Went to 143 Inf Bde. HH Duartes re Sick records &c. Weather - Cold frost	
	10		Opened Hospital for Sick & Commenced Outpatients. Visited HUPPY in afternoon. Weather Cold frost	
	11		Routine duties from 4 AM to 8 PM - Weather - bad - Snow & rain	
	12		ADMS, AA+QMG; A+VS; Called. Received orders to move horses from AIRENNES as horse vaud on a french bil? Hospital for Glanders, Mange &c. Found accomodation for them at BETTENCOURT - Smith River - Weather bad - Snow & rain	
	13		Routine duties during morning. DMV visited RA+Own Depot at HEM & fat material for troughed Moved all horses from AIRENNES to BETTENCOURT. Rev A.H.MEEK Chaplain of Forces. rejoined the unit from Sick leave - Weather cold frost	

Army Form C. 2118

WAR DIARY
or
INTELLIGENCE SUMMARY
(Erase heading not required.)

Instructions regarding War Diaries and Intelligence Summaries are contained in F.S. Regs., Part II. and the Staff Manual respectively. Title Pages will be prepared in manuscript.

Place	Date 1918	Hour	Summary of Events and Information	Remarks and references to Appendices
AIRENNES	Jan 14		Routine duties. Attended a Church parade in afternoon, went to Bde Hd Qtrs to arrange about billetting the Bde after 6th R. Warwicks (whom 6th R. Warwicks are relieving) to disembark tomorrow. Gallops & Regimental M.O. Weather fine but cold.	
	15		Routine duties during morning. In afternoon travelled 5th F.E.& (5th Warwicks) in Sandbells to Other trams. Weather cold but fine.	
	16		Routine duties. Weather cold & frosty.	
	17		Went to III Corps rest station MILLENCOURT to see C Section on detached duty there. Weather very cold - heavy snow.	
	18		Routine duties. Weather cold & fine. Shower baths in working order.	
	19		Routine duties. Tested transport during afternoon. Weather cold but fine.	
	20		" " Weather very cold & fine.	
	21		Church parade 10 am. Routine duties. Weather MMS wet afternoon. Weather very cold - hard frost.	
	22		Routine duties - very cold & frosty.	
	23		Routine duties - Route march for men - weather cold, dry & frosty.	
	24		Routine duties. During evening received orders that transport & A Section march tomorrow to transport of 143 Bde en route for new area south of the Somme.	

WAR DIARY or INTELLIGENCE SUMMARY

Army Form C. 2118

Place	Date 1917	Hour	Summary of Events and Information	Remarks and references to Appendices
AIRAINES	24 (cont)		When the Division is taking over from the French.	
	25		Routine duties during morning. In afternoon visited HOPPY there B Section where transport when known. C Transport to 144 Bde Transport of A Section left at 10.30 am. Weather very good. Tried	
	26		Routine duties. In afternoon preparation for moving tomorrow. An advanced party proceeded to MERICOURT on SOMME to arrange accommodation there. Weather very good indeed.	
	27		A Section proceeded by train to MERICOURT on SOMME. Transport formed their Convoy. Afternoon — opened Hospital in the MAIRIE there	
	28		Church Parade 10.30 am In afternoon visited CERISY & found that B Section had arrived with 144 Inf. Bde. Weather very good	
MERICOURT sur SOMME	29		Have received orders to take over front line posts when the Division goes in. Proceeded to French Amb. at ECLUSIER which will be my Head Quarters when B and C Section reported the Rte at MERICOURT weather very good	
	30		Routine duties all day Weather still frosty	
	31		At 9.15 am. left with Offenpark on a tour of posts we are taking over extended that HQS. moved to at FRHUCOURT. After to arranged for more tomorrow. Still hard frost	

J A Green, Lt Col RAMC
OC 1/3 South Midland Field Ambulance

WAR DIARY

OF

1/3RD SOUTH MIDLAND FIELD AMBULANCE - R.A.M.C. - T.F.

FOR
THE
MONTH
OF
FEBRUARY
1917

COMMITTEE FOR THE
MEDICAL HISTORY OF THE WAR
Date 4 — APR. 1917

WAR DIARY or INTELLIGENCE SUMMARY

Army Form C. 2118.

Place	Date 1917	Hour	Summary of Events and Information	Remarks and references to Appendices
ECLUSIER (hut) 61.5 c.5.0	Feb 1.		At 11 am the Unit marched from MERICOURT-SUR-SOMME & took over from 10 French Field Amb at 6.15 C.5.0. An advanced party of heavy proceeded to FLAUCOURT for instructions in front line work by the divisional stretcher bearers of the 152 - French Infantry Division — weather fine but very cold	MAP REF FRANCE 62d 1:40,000
	Feb 2		A.D.M.S. called at H.Q. Quarters. B Section (Lt Capt HEDRAPATH & Capt BALL) took over collection of wounded from whole divisional front & relieved the French tourangine stretcher bearers there. The A.D.S. has been established at FLAUCOURT. — weather - very cold	
	Feb 3		Party at HQ Quarters all day - preparing for wounded accommodation - all trench wagons having been removed. The Lower Ambulance on the trench of the Canal will have to be taken into use. C Section returned from duty at III Corps rest Station (MILLENCOURT). Commenced making Camphor bags. Camphor + sac powder + issuing it to each. French motorpouche treatment of frostbit. Church parade 10 am. The Germans made a big raid on our trenches opposite BIACHES & wounded began to come in at 4.30 from Advanced Exchange Cars from 1/1 + 1/2 S.M.F.A. (who are not yet New) for evacuation of wounded. — weather keen frost	
	Feb 4		The wounded were coming in all night + Capt Moore + Capt R + Sergt Lumpe were working all night. The A.D.S. was Brandeley, Kopting both Ambulances were kept continuously spreading to CCS & about 130 wounded were dealt with in 24 hours. There was an unusually large proportion of dangerously & seriously wounded amongst the cases. Walking cases - large numbers of sick from the whole division were also dealt with during the day -	
	Feb 6		Received orders that I have to open an "Divisional Main Dressing Station - Much trouble with cases - weather cold -	

WAR DIARY or INTELLIGENCE SUMMARY

Army Form C. 2118.

Place	Date 1917	Hour	Summary of Events and Information	Remarks and references to Appendices
G.15.c.5.0	7		ADMS called – Routine duties – weather Cool – Lower Camp Sunnel completed Block	
	8		Routine duties – Lt ASHBY RAMC (T.C.) left for duty with 1/6 Glosters – Capt SOUTTER returned. Weather – very Cold – Keen frost –	
	9		ADMS called. 1 Bearer Subdivision of 1/1st S.M. Fd Amb. joined for duty at Advanced Dressing Station – where Advanced Aid Posts are being established. Weather – very Cold	
	10		Routine duties – Weather temperate –	
	11		Church services during morning. The Extension of the line to the Right has entailed a further Extension of Advanced Aid Posts & we have acquired more hut accommodation from the 1st Divn. for our ADS at FLAUCOURT. – Weather still very Cold.	
	12		Routine duties ADMS called – Put a small party of SUSSEX Pioneers to help with Building extensions. Cold & fine	
	13		Routine duties. In the afternoon ADMS & 2 Capts + ADMS College I NCO & 36 men of 1/1st S.W. Fd Amb. joined for duty at A.D.S. Slight thaw during day –	
	14		Routine duties. ADMS called – The "New Aluminium Hut" has now been completed. Weather fine	
	15		Visited ADS at FLAUCOURT along with ADMS during morning – Slight thaw –	

WAR DIARY or INTELLIGENCE SUMMARY

Army Form C. 2118.

Place	Date 1917	Hour	Summary of Events and Information	Remarks and references to Appendices
G.15.c.S.o. Feb 16			Started AMIENS to buy Acetylene Lamps for ADSK. Capt MORRIS returned for duty from Div School. Thaw + Snow again. A Soup Kitchen opened at HERBECOURT under my supervision.	
	17		ADMS called. He informed me that I must greatly increase my accommodation – Looked forward with Ikestead – Treves – the large ANEIAN HUT has now been completed as a dope department. Heavy rain during night.	
	18		Halted Red Cross Stores ad HQM to get things for Hospital – very cold two days – Roads may be English.	
	19		Routine duties. ADMS called. Weather very wet + foggy.	
	20		ADMS called. Routine duties. Weather – wet + foggy.	
	21		Lt + Qu S.to HILL returned for duty after protracted Sick leave. ADMS called. Men of SUSSEX Pioneer taken away – the will reduce our building rate – wet day.	
	22		Traveled ADMS at AHQ. Then went to HERBECOURT to see Soup Kitchen. Another Soup Kitchen general today at BOIS de MENEAUCOURT (A20 c.1.1).	
	23		A sudden rush of trench feet cases from 143rd + 144th Bde. who have had a very difficult + very protected relief. The 4.16th Brohis have suffered most. ADMS called – very hot day.	
	24		ADMS ☐ Capt + ADMS called here. Trench feet cases – all partures are being hindered by trench method. Weather fine but mud everywhere.	

WAR DIARY or INTELLIGENCE SUMMARY

Army Form C. 2118.

Place	Date 1917	Hour	Summary of Events and Information	Remarks and references to Appendices
G.15.C.5.0.	Feb 25		Routine duties - Rendered special report on trench treatment of wounds sent to ADMS. Weather fine + warm - Snow toward evening. Kitchen furnace.	
	26		Routine duties ADMS called. Got so many convoy trench feet to-day. A Motor Amb. of 1st Divn. attached time to prepare for conveying any cases of the Division to their own trench ambulance direct. Weather fine.	
	27		ADMS called in morning + informed me that we should by reference at ADS/5 on the 1st Army. by 1/1 S.M. I had talk in the day received instructions written. Reference the necessary hours - The Bearer Subdivision of the 1/1st S.M. Amb. on duty at ADS/5 returned to its unit - bearer sub. Received information that Capt R. Henry Army went have been attached to military for general conduct while temporarily attached to the 1/6 Roy.l Warwicks.	
	28		Routine duties ADMS called during day. Weather fine	

J Aylmer Lt Col.
OC 1/3 South Midland Field Amb.

SECRET Vol 25

140/204"

COMMITTEE FOR THE
MEDICAL HISTORY OF THE WAR
Date 11 MAY 1917

WAR DIARY

OF

1/3RD SOUTH MIDLAND FIELD AMBULANCE

FOR
THE
MONTH
OF

MARCH 1917

Army Form C. 2118

WAR DIARY
or
INTELLIGENCE SUMMARY
(Erase heading not required.)

Instructions regarding War Diaries and Intelligence Summaries are contained in F. S. Regs., Part II. and the Staff Manual respectively. Title Pages will be prepared in manuscript.

Place	Date 1917	Hour	Summary of Events and Information	Remarks and references to Appendices
ECLUSIER G. 21. c. 5.0	March 1		Advanced dressing Station at FRISECOURT handed over to 1/2nd S.M. Fd. Amb. "B" Section returned to 41st Divn.	MAP FRANCE 62c
Divisional main dressing station			Recce. Bid. Durrie C Section left for duty at A.D.S. 1st C.O. & 23 men of "A" Section left for duty at New CR Stn. at CERISY. Wind N during night. Fine day.	
	2		Routine duties. A+M S called. Weather fine	
	3		" " " " "	
	4		" " 5 horse huts arrived, forwards. Weather fine	
	5		" " A+M S called. Heavy snow in night.	
	6		" " A+M S called	
	7		" " Weather very keen	
	8		" " A+M S called " "	
	9		A busy night freeing a successful raid by the barriers. A+M S called.	
	10		Routine duties. 6 case typhoid for hospital admitted. Weather fine & warm.	
	11		Slight — Two more cases of poisoning admitted A+M S III Corps + A+M S called – Opened & fixed up special pier war. Weather fine.	
	12		Routine duties – Weather dull.	
	13		" " Divisional band played at MAIN DRESSING Station. Weather fine.	
	14		A+M S called. Hon Lt. & Qr. Wk. 14th Hill. Left for England Undergo Course of Induction at Extras R.E. Having ceased NEWARK from Sheet off his Strength.	

1875 Wt. W593/826 1,000,000 4/15 J.B.C. & A. A.D.S.S./Forms/C. 2118.

WAR DIARY or INTELLIGENCE SUMMARY

Army Form C. 2118

(Erase heading not required.)

Place	Date 1917	Hour	Summary of Events and Information	Remarks and references to Appendices
ECLUSIER	March 16th		ADMS Corps. Routine duties. Weather fine.	
NW Haven PERONNY 5.7.	March 16th		Routine duties. Weather fine. There are signs of a German retreat on their front - numerous fires are reported in front of PERONNE.	
	17		Routine duties. Weather fine.	
	18		In the morning a patrol of K.R. Warwicks crossed the SOMME & entered PERONNE which they found empty. Weather fine.	
	19		A quiet day. No wounded admitted for 24 hours. Our troops across the SOMME are not yet meeting any serious opposition as they push forward. Very wet and day at 11:15 p.m. B Section marched to HERBECOURT for duty across the SOMME. Everything good at M. Sir. Weather cold & dull some snow.	
	20			
	21		B Section ordered to report to Lt Col WARD CRA who is commanding a Mobile Column. Rode into PERONNE & saw Col WARD. Cold fine day. 1 NCO & 23 men who have been a working party at New CAS & CERISY returned to the quarters.	
	22		B Section attached at DOINGT East of PERONNE. Routine duties. Weather very cold. — Snow showers.	
	23		Routine duties. Weather fine.	
	24		" " " Everything quiet.	
	25		DDMS III Corps & ADMS IV Army called round in tour from 5 p.m. In afternoon went round area West of SOMME which has been put under my control. Weather fine.	

WAR DIARY
or
INTELLIGENCE SUMMARY

Army Form C. 2118

Place	Date	Hour	Summary of Events and Information	Remarks and references to Appendices
ECLUSIER	March 26 [1917]		Received orders to move to PERONNE area tomorrow. B Section moved to BUSSU (NUDOIR?) in succession of MRAC's mobile Column. Weather Cold & dull.	
	27.		The Unit (less B Section) marched to DOINGT (I.36.a.5.6. - map 62a). Marched TINCOURT. Whole Joined an MSB tonight. Cold weather.	
	28.		Received orders that B Section had taken over ADS at TEMPLEUX la FOSSE & Albert. At site for Soup Kitchen on the road that bridges. Visited TEMPLEUX with OC B Section & arrived at Site for ADS. Took note to TINCOURT & found ADS working there. Later visited ADMS at PERONNE & reported on both ADS's. Weather frosty but clear. ADMS ordered to visit him tomorrow ADS TINCOURT in afternoon. Visited Soup Kitchen also opened at BUIRE and arranged for R. Collection in back area. weather Cold Frost.	
	29.		Visited ADMS in morning. In afternoon visited OC MBSN's Force at CARTIGNY to arrange for Collection of his sick & wounded. As 7 p.m. learnt that he shortly had a Adv.(?) Dressing(?) in taking (think village?) LE MILLE (and Q. VILLERS punam). So proceeded with Capt Hume to ADS TINCOURT then I returned at 11.15 am we had evacuated 55 wounded. Slipper to MBS PERONNE. Weather fine but Cold.	
	30.		ADMS called & informed he had arrangement for attack on EPEHY which is being continued. I left 8th app't route to TEMPLEUX to see OC ADS there. On advanced post was Established with our MO at LONGAVESNES & ADS reinforced with 1 MO & Extra bate ambulances. To Shilda Cannon marched equipment & transport. In Evening visited TINCOURT ADS which I have also reinforced with 1 MO & 6 Bearers. Weather fine	

J.A. Green
LT. COLONEL
Comm'g. 5TH. MID. FD. AMBULANCE

SECRET
Vol 26

140/2086

48 Rm

WAR DIARY
OF
3RD SOUTH MIDLAND FIELD AMBULANCE

FOR THE MONTH OF

APRIL 1917

COMMITTEE FOR THE
MEDICAL HISTORY OF THE WAR
Date -6 JUN. 1917

LT. COLONEL
COMDG. 1/3rd STH MID FD AMBULANCE

WAR DIARY or INTELLIGENCE SUMMARY

Army Form C. 2118

(Erase heading not required.)

Instructions regarding War Diaries and Intelligence Summaries are contained in F.S. Regs., Part II. and the Staff Manual respectively. Title Pages will be prepared in manuscript.

Place	Date 1917	Hour	Summary of Events and Information	Remarks and references to Appendices
DOINGT	April 1		The village of EPEHY (Map 62.C 1-40,000. F.1.) was attacked this morning at 5am – all dispositions for Evacuation of wounded had been made in advance and 88 wounded (including 7 prisoners of war) were evacuated thro' my ADS at TEMPLEUX la Fosse. Weather very bad – heavy sleet storms. At night Capt KENMONT-SMITH ADMS, proceeded to VILLERS FAUCON (E.22,23,28) & took possession of Billet 215 with a view to opening an ADS there.	Map 62.C 1-40,000
	2		ADMS called during morning. In afternoon started prepared Site of Baths & Soup Kitchen at TINCOURT. Weather – Heavy rain.	
	3		The Bearer Sub division of ½ Shire Fd Amb. took over ADS TINCOURT & my personnel were promoted to VILLERS FAUCON to open up new ADS in that village – Capt Moore i/c – Commenced erecting VILLERS FAUCON — LONGAVESNES & TEMPLEUX la Fosse bearer posts	
	4		An orderly was today being Erected at TINCOURT + Soup Kitchen which open there today. In afternoon ADMS informed me of attack impending attack on RONSOY Base BOULOGNE & LEMPIRE arrangements made accordingly. Capt PRATT & 2 Bearer Sub Division ½ B Section from TEMPLEUX la Fosse reinforced ADS VILLERS FAUCON. Heavy snow at night	
	5		The attack on the 3 villages took place at 5am in fine weather. Collection of wounded worked smoothly & 136 casualties (including 20 prisoners of war) passed thro' ADS VILLERS. An attack in a ridge S.E. of RONSOY was later piece successfully & 38 wounded (including prisoners of war) were passed thro' the ADS TINCOURT.	
	6		Visited ADMS & ADSs at TINCOURT & TEMPLEUX la Fosse. Weather fine all ADSs in trouble all ADSs in today.	
	7		Everything Quiet ADMS called weather – wet. Weather – Generally fine but some rain	

Army Form C. 2118

WAR DIARY
or
INTELLIGENCE SUMMARY
(Erase heading not required.)

Instructions regarding War Diaries and Intelligence Summaries are contained in F. S. Regs., Part II. and the Staff Manual respectively. Title Pages will be prepared in manuscript.

Place	Date 1916	Hour	Summary of Events and Information	Remarks and references to Appendices
BOUZINCOURT	Apr 8		Routine duties during morning. In afternoon visited all ADSpns & found things satisfactory. Conf. Kitchen at VILLERS proved specially useful. Fine day	
	9		Routine duties at Hd Quarters - weather fine	
	10		" " " " " "	
	11		Visited ADMS at AVELUY & TINCOURT & TEMPLEUX le Fosse. Weather Cold - Snow storm	
	12		Visited ADSpns & made arrangements for collecting wounded from a Div Brigade attack intended East of LEMPIRE & RONSOY. Weather very bad - Snow storm in afternoon & night	
	13		The attack came off as arranged — was successful. the 1 Brigade attacked at 4 p.m. last night & the R.B. Bde at 4.30 a.m. In spite of appalling weather conditions the Evacuation of wounded proceeded steadily & successfully & all was got away in good time. There were 40 wounded. Much of the Stretcher bearing was done under heavy shell fire. Visited all ADSpns	
	14		Quiet day at Head Quarters - Weather finer - Nothing of importance on the front.	
	15		Visited ADS TEMPLEUX le Fosse. Weather wet	
	16		to ride on a big attack on a 2 brigade front. tomorrow. Strengthened personnel of ADS VILLERS FAUCON & made necessary arrangements. 40 extra bearers were sent forward to Relieve Corps. Weather finer	
	17		A wet morning. At 7.30 am rode round all ADSpns & found work well in hand but a large number of casualties. The attack on 3 farms had only been fairly successful. Visited ADMS. Weather wet. 137 wounded (including 1 prisoner & 1 man) admissions passed through the ADSpns	

1875 Wt. W593/826 1,000,000 4/15 J.B.C. & A. A.D.S.S./Forms/C. 2118.

WAR DIARY or INTELLIGENCE SUMMARY

Army Form C. 2118

Place	Date (1917)	Hour	Summary of Events and Information	Remarks and references to Appendices
DOINGT	Apr 19th		During the day Colonel Exploring ADMS gave his instructions to evacuate Greek 21st at VILLERS FAUCON. The ADS was transferred but up to Marques think at ST EMILIE who arrived at 9 pm on Reims. Relief of Wng unit was wounded — weather fine. Arrangements made for attack on Settlement farm. ADS called during morning. In afternoon visited all ADSs and off's sent in report to him on arrangement of Front line Stations accompanied by record advance thro' undressed theoSuction of ADS at VILLERS FAUCON who took thanks on a new site and the Refotohooking	Map. 62 C 1—40,000
	20		of 2 advanced Collecting posts each with 1 m.o. — One at EPEHY 7 one at F 20-a, 7-4 South-West of RONSOY road — weather fine but dull — attack on Gillemont Farm arranged for tea night post pond made brighter.	
			The attack on GILLEMONT Farm little place level my. Md that did not succeed. There were 45 Casualties evacuated through ADS. This was rather slow & hard work to all darkness people who very dim from the front line.	
	21		The new ADS at VILLERS FAUCON was opened today with an increased personnel. Cap't Killanin being in charge. Cap't Moore continued to Superintend the Evacuations from the R.A. Posts. ADMS called — weather fine.	
	22		Moved 7 wounded J Ambulance from DOINGT to TEMPLEUX La fosse. where we encamped in orchard behind the ADS. The Building has now been Evacuated as far as billets are concerned of the mined cellars to be used during day as little as possible - weather fine.	
TEMPLEUX La fosse	23		Another allied being arranged on Gillemont farm — visited ADS in VILLERS + Saw all arrangements made for dealing with the wounded. One Section of the Mt J Lowe J.C. Amb (42nd Div) reported for duty attached to the Brigade to ensure firmer... weather fine.	

WAR DIARY or INTELLIGENCE SUMMARY

Army Form C. 2118

(Erase heading not required.)

Instructions regarding War Diaries and Intelligence Summaries are contained in F. S. Regs., Part II. and the Staff Manual respectively. Title Pages will be prepared in manuscript.

Place	Date 1917	Hour	Summary of Events and Information	Remarks and references to Appendices
TEMPLEUX la FOSSE	Apr 24		The front attack on Guillemont Farm took place at 3.30 am without success. The evacuation proceeded smoothly. All Sitting Cases were taken to A.D.S. VILLERS FAUCON. All Lying cases direct from ST EMILIE to TEMPLEUX la FOSSE. 11 Motor Amb. & 4 Horse Ambulances were between Advanced Collecting Posts + Main Dressing Station at PERONNE. In all 128 wounded passed thro the Unit A.D. Station. Msn. During the day the Section of the M.T.E. Lane Fd Amb. proceeded to VILLERS FAUCON prepared for the left Sector of the Line behind their own Brigade — weather fine. Whilst VILLERS & ST EMILIE were Capt MORRIS R.A.M.C. left for duty at III Corps. School of Instruction.	
	Apr 25		The attack on Guillemont Fm. was renewed at 11pm last night & this time proved successful. The Casualties were heavy but all were dealt with quickly & successfully — 195 wounded passed thro. the two Advanced Dressing Stations. Three Motor Large Ambulances of the 4th Siberian Fd Amb. conveyed most of the Sitting cases from TEMPLEUX & FOSSE to M.D.S. PERONNE. A feature of the Casualties of the last 2 days has been the large number of German Bones 50% of the total being Shoulder cases. The Left Sector of the line was handed over to the M.T.E. Lanc Fd Amb. & my own personal withdrawn from it. Fine but cold day	
	Apr 26		Quiet day — Capt Scott Williams R.a.m.C.T.F. left the unit on being appointed to command the 2/3rd South Midland Field Ambulance. (61st Division) — Weather fine but cold.	
	" 27		Quiet day — Routine duties. Visited A.D.S. VILLERS FAUCON in morning. A.D.M.S. called — weather fine	
	" 28		Visited VILLERS FAUCON in morning — Capt Park R.a.m.C. T.C. left the unit & proceeded to England on completion of his Contract — Weather fine —	

Army Form C. 2118

WAR DIARY
or
INTELLIGENCE SUMMARY
(Erase heading not required.)

Instructions regarding War Diaries and Intelligence Summaries are contained in F. S. Regs., Part II. and the Staff Manual respectively. Title Pages will be prepared in manuscript.

Place	Date	Hour	Summary of Events and Information	Remarks and references to Appendices
TEMPLEUX la Fosse	Apr 29 1917		ADMS called round the Division would be relieved in a few days by the 42nd Division. In afternoon ADMS 42nd Div. called & I went round A+B Stretcher & at MILLERS Farm & Advanced Collecting posts at LEMPIRE & EPEHY. Weather fine	
	" 30		At Head Quarters all day busy with reports re weather fine. During the whole month my unit has been engaged in Advanced Dressing Station work.	

I agree to Col RAWCTF;
OC 1/3rd South Midland Field Ambulance

SECRET

This detailed Report of the work of my unit from March 21st to April 25th 1917 is now forwarded as an appendix to my War Diary for April 1917

J Agnew Lt Col RAMC T.F.
OC 1/3 South Midland Field Ambulance

COLLECTION OF WOUNDED

FROM AN ADVANCING ARMY

IN OPEN FIGHTING.

REPORT ON THE WORK OF 1/3RD SOUTH MIDLAND FIELD AMBULANCE FROM MARCH 21ST TO APRIL 25TH 1917.

MAPS:- SHEETS 62C AND 62B, FRANCE, 1/40,000.

I.

On March 21st 1917, B Section of my Unit, under the Command of Capt. Herapath was attached for duty to WARD'S COLUMN, and on the 22nd took up its quarters in DOINGT where it remained until March 26th when that force was disbanded. The same day the Section moved to BUSSU.

On the 27th the remainder of the Unit left ECLUSIER and marched to DOINGT where its Headquarters were established. The same evening Capt. KENNON and 12 other ranks (afterwards increased in number) proceeded to TINCOURT for the purpose of opening an A.D.S. in that village. They slept in the Church, but next morning selected an excellent undamaged house which had just been evacuated by Refugees.

B Section, on the same day (28·3·17), was ordered to proceed to TEMPLEUX-LA-FOSSE for the purpose of opening another A.D.S. in that place. The possibilities here did not appear to be very good at first, but we managed to secure part of a large ~~ruined~~ house, with three gardens and an orchard and a large yard behind it. The whole place was littered with felled trees and debris of the usual kind. The whole house with three cellars was ultimately acquired.

The Scheme was that the A.D.S. TINCOURT should receive sick and wounded from the Right Sector, and the A.D.S. TEMPLEUX-LA-FOSSE from the Left Sector of the advancing line.

As will be seen later, owing to the front of the Division side slipping somewhat to the left, and the general line of advance being in a N.E. direction, the TINCOURT A.D.S. gradually decreased in importance.

Until this time the fighting on our front East of

the SOMME had been chiefly carried on by cavalry who had one of their own Field Ambulances working behind them, but now they were withdrawn and infantry alone participated in the further advances.

On March 30th, late in the afternoon, the O.C., A.D.S. TINCOURT and later the A.D.M.S. were informed that the 1/4th Glosters would attack the village of ST. EMILIE that evening and preparations had to be made hurriedly to deal with an unknown number of casualties. The R.A.P. was located at VILLERS-FAUCON. It was decided to evacuate the cases along the road through E.28. K3.8.14 to MARQUAIX, HAMEL and TINCOURT. Fortunately Capt. Moore of my Unit had reconnoitred this road during the afternoon and reported that cars and horse ambulances could get as far as the cross-roads at K3.b.7.0. where they could turn. Three squads of bearers were sent to the R.A.P. with 2 wheeled stretcher carriers. Meantime the A.D.M.S. provided further motor ambulances; and extra dressings. Medical comforts were sent up. Capt Moore and myself went to the A.D.S. TINCOURT.

Capt. Moore volunteered to direct the evacuations from the Wagon Rendezvous, which later in the night was, on information supplied by the G.O.C., advanced to the crater outside VILLERS-FAUCON. In this way the carry from the R.A.P. was reduced by 3/4 of a mile, — a great help to the hard worked bearers. The advantage of having an officer superintending the evacuations proved of great value, for horse ambulance wagons were being used, the road was long, unknown and shelled at intervals; the night was very dark, and new as well as old shell holes had to be

avoided. The work however ran smoothly.
The first cases arrived at TINCOURT about 7 p.m. and by 4 a.m. 55 cases had passed through the A.D.S. and the bulk of the work was done.

On March 31st I received information that EPEHY would be attacked next morning (Apr. 1st). It was decided that casualties should be evacuated via LONGAVESNES through A.D.S. TEMPLEUX-LA-FOSSE. The M.O. i/c that Station got into touch with the 143rd Bde., and having heard afterwards that the 144th Bde. were also taking part in the attack, he saw the R.M.Os. concerned and arranged to send 2 bearer squads and 1 wheeled stretcher carrier to each R.A.P. A Collecting Post was established at LONGAVESNES at which one M.O., 3 Tent Sub Division Orderlies, and 1 Bearer Sub Division were held in reserve. The R.M.O's. promised to send guides to LONGAVESNES to conduct the squads allotted to them to their R.A.P's.
Motor ambulances were sent to E9.d.3.10 (SAULCOURT) to transport wounded of 1/6th Warwicks, and to E16.d.1.3. for those of 1/6th Glosters and 1/7 Worcesters.
The R.A.M.C. bearers attached to the R.A.P's. received instructions to go forward with the Regimental Stretcher Bearers to assist in the collection of wounded if necessary, and this was done in several cases.

The attack commenced about 5 a.m. on Apr. 1st, and the first cases reached TEMPLEUX-LA-FOSSE at 9 a.m. They continued to arrive throughout the day. In all 88 wounded were evacuated, including 7 Prisoners of War.

The scheme of evacuation did not turn out as successful in practice as was hoped in advance, for

the following reasons:-
   (a) The weather was very bad.
   (b) The nature of the ground and the bad roads over which the cases had to be carried for long distances necessarily made the process of evacuation slow.
   (c) The collecting post at LONGAVESNES proved to be too far back to be of much use and the personnel stationed there became of little value.

The wounded of 1 Company of the 1/7th Worcesters who were stationed on the right of the attack were attended to by the M.O. of the 1/8th Worcesters then stationed at VILLERS-FAUCON and were evacuated through the A.D.S. TINCOURT. 15 cases were treated at this place.

     My experience of these two attacks led me to the conclusion that with the advance of the line, both TINCOURT and TEMPLEUX-LA-FOSSE were no longer suitable sites for a principal A.D.S., and after consultation with the A.D.M.S. the latter instructed me to take over Billet 215 in VILLERS-FAUCON and form an A.D.S. there. Accordingly on April 1st Capt. KENNON and a small party proceeded there for that purpose.

     On the 3rd inst 1 Bearer Sub Division of the 1/2nd S.M. Fld. Amb. took over the A.D.S. TINCOURT and the remainder of my personnel at that Station proceeded to VILLERS FAUCON, where I also sent another Bearer Sub Division from DOINGT.

     The A.D.S., VILLERS-FAUCON was put under the command of Capt Moore, who had with him

Capt KENNON, A Section (less details) and the Bearer Sub Division of C Section. Later in the day, as a result of information received from Brigade H.Q., Capt PARK and B Section Bearer Sub Division was also sent to VILLERS-FAUCON from TEMPLEUX-LA-FOSSE.

On April 4th the A.D.M.S. informed me that there would be an attack next morning on an extended front with a view to the capture of three villages - RONSSOY, BASSE BOULOGNE and LEMPIRE, and in addition to the villages, a ridge situated in E 28 would also be occupied.

145th Bde. who were making the attack on the villages also notified O.C., A.D.S. early and supplied him with a copy of the scheme. On this occasion ample time was given to make suitable dispositions for the evacuation of the wounded, and the ground behind the 145th Bde was carefully reconnoitred by Capt. MOORE. The scheme of evacuation was that already arranged by the A.D.M.S. with slight modifications rendered necessary by local circumstances.

R.A.P's. were located as follows:-

Rt. Battn.	F 20 c central	4 R.A.M.C. bearers and 2 wheeled stretcher carriers.
	F 19 a.1.5.	Relay post, 1 N.C.O, 6 bearers and 1 wheeled stretcher carrier.
Centre Battn.	F. 8.c. 1.8.	4 R.A.M.C. bearers and 1 wheeled stretcher carriers.
	E 24.a.9.5.	Relay post, 1 N.C.O., 6 bearers and 1 wheeled stretcher carrier.
Left Battn.	F 1. c. 9. 6.	1 N.C.O, 4 bearers and 2 carriers

4 motor ambulances worked from the front to TEMPLEUX-LA-FOSSE
5   "   "   "   "   "   " TEMPLEUX to PERONNE.
Horse Ambulances were also used.

To deal with the attack in F28, two Bearer Sub Divisions were sent forward from TINCOURT and a Collecting Post was established at TEMPLEUX-LE-GUERARD. Motor and horse ambulances collected through this front. A Tent Sub Division from DOINGT temporarily took over the A.D.S. TINCOURT.

The attack on the villages commenced at 5 a.m. on the 5th inst. in fine weather. The whole of the arrangements for evacuating the wounded worked smoothly. The first casualties arrived at the A.D.S. VILLERS-FAUCON at 7 a.m. and at 11 a.m. the R.M.O's. reported all clear. It was 2 or 3 hours before the A.D.S. TINCOURT was cleared, but this was owing to the serious nature of many of the wounds which required careful dressing. During the time of waiting the wounded were made comfortable and supplied with hot drinks, food etc.

136 casualties (including 20 Prisoners of War) passed through this A.D.S.

On the right the objective in F28 was quickly reached and 38 cases (including 1 Prisoner of War) were quickly passed through the A.D.S. TINCOURT which was cleared by 10 a.m.

On the night of the 12th and early morning of the 13th an attack was made on a two Brigade front East of LEMPIRE and RONSSOY. Ample notification had been given to O.C, A.D.S. and necessary dispositions were made. The Left Bde (125th) attacked at 9 p.m. on the 12th inst. There were only five slight casualties and these were easily evacuated through an advanced post which had been established at the south end of EPEHY (F.I.c.6.5.) by wheeled stretcher carriers to ST EMILIE and thence by car to A.D.S. VILLERS-FAUCON, where they arrived at 1 a.m.

The Right Bde. (144th) attacked at 4 a.m. on the 13th. The Rt. Battn. R.A.P. had been located at F.21.c.1.3. It moved forward afterwards to F.21.d.4.3.

The Lt. Battn. R.A.P. was established at F.20.b.0.5. where it remained.

At 3.30 a.m. an Advanced Collecting Post, - previously notified to R.M.O's. - was established at F.20.a.7.4. in tents, with a reserve of 12 stretcher bearers and 30 blankets. Motor ambulances were able to reach this post and turn round.

4 Bearers and two wheeled stretcher carriers were attached to each R.A.P. and later on 2 extra squads were attached to advanced R.A.P. of the Rt. Battn.

A relay post was also established later on at the cross-roads S. of RONSSOY.

In spite of terrible weather conditions the evacuation of casualties from the Bde. front worked smoothly. The first cases reached the A.D.S. at 5.30 a.m. and at 9 a.m. the R.A.P's. reported all clear. In all 35 cases were evacuated during this time, 15 being stretcher cases. From 7 a.m. onwards the village of RONSSOY was heavily shelled and a good deal of stretcher bearing was carried on under this shelling. Sitting cases, - non urgent - were taken to TEMPLEUX-LA-FOSSE by horse ambulance. All lying cases were dressed at VILLERS-FAUCON.

VIII

On the night of Apr. 16th an attack was made by 2 Bdes on an extended front of 2 miles, the objective including the 3 Farms of LE PETIT PRIEL, TOMBOIS and GILLEMONT. Dispositions for the evacuation of wounded were made as follows:-

Rt. Sector (145th Bde)
 Advanced Collecting Posts (2 Tents) F.20.a.7.4. - 1 N.C.O., 8 bearers, 12 stretchers, 20 blankets, 1 wheeled carrier.
Rt. Battn. Aid Post (1/4th Berks) F.21.c.1.3.
Lt.   "   "   "   (Bucks) F.15.b.2.1.
 4 R.A.M.C. Bearers, 3 extra stretchers and extra blankets to each of these R.A.Ps.
Route of evacuation from Lt. Battn. Aid Post - across country behind RONSSOY WOOD to Collecting Post at F.20.a.7.4.

Left Sector (143rd Bde.)
 Collecting Post F.1.c.6.5.   1 N.C.O., 4 Bearers, 12 stretchers 20 Blankets, 1 motor ambulance.
 Rt. Battn. Aid Post. F.8.a.10.8. (MALASSISE FARM) - 2 Bearer Squads, 6 stretchers, 12 blankets, 2 wheeled stretcher carriers.
 Lt. Battn. Aid Post. F.1.b.8.10. - 2 Bearer squads, 6 stretchers, 12 blankets, 2 wheeled carriers.
 Relay Post. F.1.b.5.5. - 2 Bearers in temporary shelter.

The road having been repaired a motor ambulance was able to proceed to Collecting Post at F.1.c.6.5.

A horse ambulance was stationed at F.8.a.6.3. (S.W. of MALASSISE FARM)

Reserve Bearers at ST. EMILIE and A.D.S. VILLERS-FAUCON, and 1 motor ambulance at ST. EMILIE.

The night was excessively dark and the weather conditions appalling.

In the Rt. Sector, the Rt. Battn. casualties were easily cleared, but the Lt. Battn. (Bucks) had a large number of casualties, and as these had to be carried across country for a mile, their evacuation was necessarily slower. 16 extra Bearers were got forward in returning empty ambulances however, and most of the cases were got away by 6.30 a.m.

On the Left Sector, the cases from the Lt. Battn. (1/6th R. Warwicks) arrived smoothly at the Collecting Post, but for a while there was some difficulty with those of the Rt. Battn. (1/5 Warwick)

Notice of the attack had been rather short and time for complete reconnoitring was not quite sufficient. As a result some delay was at first caused in establishing touch between the R.A.P. and the horse ambulance stationed at the cross roads, S.W. of MALASSISE FARM). The roads were also badly pitted with shell holes and the darkness was intense. Sgt. Cann however, who superintended the evacuations, managed to locate the route by means of a flash light about midnight. Three extra squads of Bearers were sent forward to this R.A.P.; thenceforth everything worked smoothly, and at 7 a.m. all cases were cleared. At 8 a.m. all was clear at the Collecting Post at EPEHY.

A steady stream of wounded continued to arrive at A.D.S. VILLERS-FAUCON, where the medical staff had been strengthened, and by 11 a.m. that Station was all clear.

About 140 cases (including 1 Prisoner of War) were dealt with.

Owing to various explosions taking place in our area, the A.D.S. at VILLERS-FAUCON (Billet 215) was vacated on the 18th. and was temporarily transferred to ST EMILIE where marquees and tents were erected.

While visiting the Aid Posts this day, O.C., A.D.S. was informed of a probable attack on GILLEMONT FARM that night, and made his dispositions accordingly.

Rt. Battn. R.A.P. F.23.c.2.8.   4 Bearers, 4 stretchers and 2 wheeled stretcher carriers.

Lt. Battn. R.A.P. F.15.b.2.0. (acting also as a Relay Post)
    8 Bearers, 5 stretchers.

Relay Post N.W. of RONSSOY WOOD   4 Bearers, 2 stretchers

Collecting Post. F.20.a.7.4.   1 N.C.O., 4 Bearers, 12 stretchers and 1 motor ambulance.

In reserve at ST. EMILIE   4 Bearer squads.

The attack was postponed.

At 9 p.m. while cases were being dressed at the A.D.S. ST EMILIE, the village was heavily shelled and one R.A.M.C. orderly was wounded.

On the 19th at 9 p.m. the postponed attack on GILLEMONT FARM was made by 1 Company of the 1/4th Ox. & Bucks. After the attack there was considerable congestion of cases at the R.A.P and some delay in getting them evacuated. The chief reasons of this were

(a) During the day the R.A.P. was removed from F.23.c.2.3. (where it was stationed when the dispositions were made on the 18th) to F.16.c.5.2. without the knowledge of the M.O. i/c evacuations, and the new situation was only discovered by the R.A.M.C. Bearers after the attack had commenced. This caused re-arrangement of the line of evacuation.

(b) The wounded were collected "en masse" from

the front line — an unusual method.
(c) The long distance (3000 yards) which the stretcher
    cases had to be carried over difficult ground
    in utter darkness to the Collecting Post.
Reserve Bearers and stretchers were got forward
as soon as possible.
In spite of these difficulties the first walking
cases reached the Collecting Post at 10 p.m. and
the first stretcher case at 11.30 p.m. The last
stretcher case reached the Collecting Post at 5 a.m.
In all 46 cases were evacuated from this Battn.

On the 21st the A.D.S. was moved from St EMILIE
to a new site at VILLERS-FAUCON where it was established
in marquees and improvised huts on a plot of ground
opposite the cemetery (E22 d. 5.7.)

On the 23rd arrangements were made for a
further attack on an extended front, including
GILLEMONT FARM, by the 144th Bde. and 126th Bde. and
                          Dispositions were made as follows :—
144th Bde.
Rt. Battn A.P.   F22 c. 0.9.   4 Bearers, 1 wheeled stretcher carrier
Lt   "   "   F16. c. 0.9.   4   "   1   "   "
    Extra stretchers and blankets at each.
    Two wheeled carriers were also lent to Rt. Battn.
    R.M.O. for conveying cases from the front line,
    and 1 wheeled carrier to R.M.O. of Lt. Battn for the
    same purpose.
A new Collecting Post was opened at LEMPIRE at
F15 central, opposite the Soup Kitchen (from which hot
drinks were served.)
2 M.O's, 4 Bearer squads, extra stretchers and blankets

and 2 horse ambulances were stationed here. Motor ambulances plied between the Collecting Post behind RONSSOY WOOD at F.20.a.7.4. (where 2 squads of Bearers were stationed) and the A.D.S. at VILLERS-FAUCON E.22.d.5.7.

126th Bde:-
   Rt. Battn. Aid Post, F.8.b.0.9. (MALASSISE FARM) 2 Bearer squads.
           Relay Post at F.7.b.8.10. 1 Bearer squad and 2 wheeled carriers.
   Lt. Battn. A.P. F.3.b.9.9. 2 Bearer squads and 2 wheeled carriers.
   Collecting Post. F.1.c.6.6. 1 M.O. and 1 squad.
   Motor ambulances at this post for lying cases.

It was arranged that all stretcher cases should be dressed at VILLERS FAUCON and dispatched direct to M.D.S. PERONNE, and that all walking cases were to be collected at ST EMILIE - where 8 squads were in reserve - whence they would be transported by horse ambulances to TEMPLEUX-LA-FOSSE, at which station they would be dressed before evacuation to M.D.S. PERONNE.

4 extra motor ambulances were obtained from the 42nd Division. In all 11 motor ambulances and 4 horse ambulances were used (during the first phase of the fighting) between Advanced Collecting Posts and the M.D.S. PERONNE. They were distributed as follows:-
1 Horse amb. between ST EMILIE and EPEHY;
1 " " "   "   and LEMPIRE;
3 Motor ambs. " VILLERS FAUCON and the front line;
5 "   "   "   "   " M.D.S. PERONNE;
3 "   "   "   TEMPLEUX-LA-FOSSE "   "   ";
2 horse ambs and G.S. Wagons between ST EMILIE and TEMPLEUX-LA-F.

The ~~first~~ attack took place at 3.30 a.m. on the 24th inst. and the whole scheme worked smoothly and well although the number of casualties was fairly large. 56 stretcher cases and 10 sitting cases had been evacuated from A.D.S. VILLERS-FAUCON by 3.30 p.m. and 62 sitting cases from A.D.S. TEMPLEUX-LA-FOSSE by 6.30 p.m. The latter cases were advisedly retained for some time after being dressed, in order to facilitate the early evacuation of the stretcher cases.

During the day 1 Section of 1/1st E. Lancs. Fld. Amb. arrived and proceeded to EPEHY where it worked with my bearers with a view to its taking over that sector of the line next day.

In view of a renewal of the attack that night I asked O.C. 1/1st Sth. Mid. Fld. Amb (on instructions from A.D.M.S.) to lend me his 3 horse ambulances, and these were supplied.

The dispositions of the various posts remained the same.

The attack was renewed at 11 p.m., and again the wounded were dealt with successfully. About 95 stretcher cases were passed through the A.D.S. VILLERS-FAUCON and about 100 sitting cases through the A.D.S. TEMPLEUX. The latter were nearly all evacuated to M.D.S. PERONNE by the 3 horse ambulances of the 1/1st S.M.F. Amb. and this enabled me to use 2 more motor ambulances for the evacuation of stretcher cases from VILLERS-FAUCON to M.D.S. PERONNE.

After the capture of GILLEMONT FARM the dispositions of R.A.M.C. Posts and Bearers remains as under:-

Rt. Bde Collecting Post at LEMPIRE F.15.b.2.1. – 1 M.O., 4 Bearer Squads, 2 Tent Section Orderlies and 1 Cook; reserve stretchers and blankets and 1 motor amb.

Each R.A.P — 1 squad of Bearers, 3 wheeled carriers, 6 stretchers & 10 blankets — supplied by 1/3rd S.M. Fd. Amb.

Left Bde.:-
Collecting Post at EPEHY (F.1.c.6.6)   1 M.O., 4 squads of bearers, 2 wheeled carriers, 1 motor amb, reserve stretchers & blankets.
At R.A.P's. — 1 squad, 6 stretchers, 10 blankets.
Relay Post at MALASSISE FARM (F8 b. 0.9) - 1 squad of Bearers, 2 stretchers, 1 wheeled carrier.
Personnel supplied by 1/1st E. Lancs Fd. Amb.

A.D.S. VILLERS-FAUCON
  3 Officers, 2 Tent Sub Divisions, 1 bearer Sub Division & Reserve Bearers.
  Cars — 3 motor ambs. and 1 Ford.
  Transport — A & C Section 1/3rd S. M. Fd. Amb.
              C   "   1/1st E. Lancs. Fd. Amb.
Railway Embankment near ST EMILIE —
  Reserve Bearers E. Lancs. 4 squads.

During the whole of the preceeding operations, all wounds have been carefully cleaned, dressed and splinted, and obvious fragments of foreign bodies removed at the A.D.S. Even when casualties were fairly numerous it has been found possible to do this.

Arrangements were also made for the supply of hot drinks & bread and jam at Collecting Posts and A.D.S.

The chief lessons learnt from the preceeding events are:-
1. Necessity for early and full information from Brigades re impending operations.
2. Importance of Reconnoitring.
3. " " conferences between M.O., Fld. Ambs. and R.M.O's.
4. Necessity for early and mutual notification of change of dispositions between M.O's Fd. Amb. and R.M.O's.
5. The most direct route for motor ambulances, compatible with operation arrangements should be conceded, irrespective of official traffic routes.
6. Need for increased number of flash lights for bearers working on dark nights.

30/4/17

J Agnew
LT. COLONEL
COMDG/ 3rd. STH. MID. FD. AMBULANCE

SECRET

WAR DIARY

of

1/3rd South Midland Field Ambulance

for the month of MAY 1917.

COMMITTEE FOR THE
MEDICAL HISTORY OF THE WAR
Date 10 JUL. 1917

WAR DIARY or INTELLIGENCE SUMMARY

Army Form C. 2118

MATS France
62ᵈ & 57ᵗʰ
1-40,000

Place	Date	Hour	Summary of Events and Information	Remarks and references to Appendices
TEMPLEUX la FOSSE MAP 62ᶜ 1-40,000 D.28.d	May 1		The Details of the 1/1ˢᵗ S Lanc Fd Amb. (42ⁿᵈ Div) arrived preparatory to taking over the Front Line Section duties – weather fine	
	2		Handed over AMTS VILLERS FAUCON (E 29.a) + front line posts to 1/1ˢᵗ S Lanc Fd Amb. Tent Sub Section of 1/1ˢᵗ S Fd Amb. arrived at TEMPLEUX la Fosse. Received instructions that tomorrow we were to proceed to HALLE (I 19.6) to go into rest. No rel relief tomorrow the units proceeds on free marching order at 10 a.m. Having handed over to 1/1ˢᵗ S.C. Fd Amb at TEMPLEUX the units proceeded in free marching order at 10 a.m. Marched to HALLE – weather very hot.	
	3			
	4		ADMS called + proceeded to go + inspect a site to proposed DRS¹⁰ Belateel? Officer to go over to fatigue duty at the CHAPELETTE Station – unloading train for new C.R.S¹⁰ weather fine + hot –	
	5		Routine duties – weather very hot	
	6		Received instructions to direct DRs on selected site at HALLE. weather fine but cold after heavy rain during the night	
	7		Routine duties – commenced new DRS – weather fine	
	8		" " " " "	
	9		Working on new DRS	
	10		Quantity of building material arrived from SCLOSIER – (on forms M.R.S.17)	
	11		Thunderstorm at night. 80 men to LA CHAPELETTE for unloading trains. P.M. Received sudden orders that we were proceeding North tomorrow to relieve the 1ˢᵗ Division in front of BAPAUME. Capt SOOTTER went on leave Y Capt Kerr M.C. left for temp? duty with 1/5 K.R.R.C. barricale. Weather very hot.	

Army Form C. 2118

WAR DIARY
or
INTELLIGENCE SUMMARY

MAP 57c
1 - 40000

(Erase heading not required.)

Instructions regarding War Diaries and Intelligence Summaries are contained in F.S. Regs., Part II. and the Staff Manual respectively. Title Pages will be prepared in manuscript.

Place	Date 1917	Hour	Summary of Events and Information	Remarks and references to Appendices
HALLE	May 12		Paraded at 8.20 am in full marching order & marched in May 12 145 Inf Bde to COMBLES (T.23) via CLERY & MAUREPAS. The infantry were in full marching order traversing Sharpnel helmets + Small for the function in the alert position. The day was temporarily hot. A large number fell out on the march we brought in 96 in Ambulance wagons. After saw the Brigade Commander + suffered the almost all marching mid day with S.B. Perkinson kieu + new wagons. The Capt Batts in afternoon visited ADMS 115 Div at N.11. Cantral, as represetative of our own ADMS and subsequently moved nearer to DG (r.) 3d Aust. 4/5' Div) to take over the ADMS's brigades at LEBUCQUIERE + front posh of the Bde Sector of our new line. Sent full refort of arrangements to ADMS at TERONNE	
COMBLES	13		Marched at 9 am to N.11.C near BEAULENCOURT where we took over a convoy from the 2nd Australian Field Amb. Met the ADMS who travelled with him to BAPAUME where we took over a few tenements. Weather very hot wrk. Thunderstorm at night	
N.11.C	14		Opened at N.11.C as a field Amb. for the front of the 46th Division. Finally received recomm stations will be opened. The other White Camp tenements as no BC have been returned his firing. Capt Marr + 20 other ranks proceeded to BAPAUME & relieving the 35th Fd. Amb. there. There is still a station for seeing to cut tent. B Section FSC own bringdale. Routine duties - Weather fine -	
	15		" Div HQ Regulars arrived at N.M. Central . Weather fine -	
	16		" " visited Capt Marn at BAPAUME. Capt Morre & BAC Bearer Lt Adams left for temp duty with 6th Australian field Amb, who have been having a very heavy time in front of MOEUVIE (C10c) Very cold wet day	
	17		Routine duties - Very cold day	

1875 Wt. W593/826 1,000,000 4/15 J.B.C. & A. A.D.S.S./Forms/C. 2118.

Army Form C. 2118.

WAR DIARY or INTELLIGENCE SUMMARY

MAP 57c 1-40,000

Place	Date 1917	Hour	Summary of Events and Information	Remarks and references to Appendices
N.11.c	May 18		Am instd BAPAUME + Achanay Casls Place to which I have attached a Car for the Conveyance of Sick to this Station from day.	
	19		Visited CHAPPAYE (VARENNES) c DDMS 1st Anzac Corps to Collect certain Surplus Equipment there - Mayous Skirhrie - Left horse released with 2 Reserve Veterinary from last day c 9th Australian Fd Aml & reported I new Kicked + have to evacuate.	
			Received news that Capt Howe had been awarded the Military Cross that Green the Indian horse.	
	20		Routine duties — weather fine	
	21		" " " Capt Harris (TF) proposed for permanent duty with the DAC vice Cuff.	
	22		Routine duties but heavy rain interfered with Constructional work	
	23		Inspected over the BAPAUME Post kite St Australian Fd Aml. A return of fine weather Enabled us & proceed with more Constructional work which is going ahead again. Several Marquees have been pitched + Stoves + bed boards + a good Latrine round are already completed.	
	24		Routine duties HQrs orders weather fine	
	25		" " "	
	26		" " weather fine. From today are taking in Sick of 1st Anzac on hands dates DDMS 1st Anzac Corps called -	
	27		" " " We are in 4th Corps from today	
	28		DDMS 4th Corps called round round "Camp" — Some rain and thunder at night.	

Army Form C. 2118.

WAR DIARY
or
INTELLIGENCE SUMMARY

(Erase heading not required.)

Instructions regarding War Diaries and Intelligence Summaries are contained in F. S. Regs., Part II. and the Staff Manual respectively. Title Pages will be prepared in manuscript.

Place	Date 1917	Hour	Summary of Events and Information	Remarks and references to Appendices
N.11.C	May 29		Routine duties in morning. In afternoon trialed Advanced Pere Gros Bois at SAPIGNIES (H.8.c) to get extra equipment for D.R.S. Weather fine.	
	-30		Routine duties all day - some rain in afternoon	
	-31		ADMS called - weather finer. A transport of which I am provided in training detachment detail of the division with a view to repleting in hand for front line work in otherwise	

J Algren Lt Col RAMC T.F.

OC 1/3 South Midland Fd Ambulance

Appendix 1.

List of Casualties occurring during the month

No 437527 Pte Knowles S.H. Killed in Action 17.5.17
3/1st F. Amb 7th Amb. Attached 1/3rd (South West 7th Amb) buried at NOREUIL (map 57d C.10.c)

No 439292 Pte Rackhan R.G. 1/3 C Mount 7th Amb Shrapnel Wd. Rt. Forearm 16.5.17
439026 Pte Young G.H.R " " " " G.S.W. face severe 17.5.17

These Casualties occurred during the time that 2 heavy bethernes [bearer sections?] of my unit were on detached duty with the 8th Australian Field Ambulance

J Alpren Lt. Col. RAMC T
OC 1/3 S Mid Fd Amb

31/5/17

Army Form C. 2118.

WAR DIARY
or
INTELLIGENCE SUMMARY

(Erase heading not required.)

Appendix II.

The following members of my Unit have received decorations during the period for
conspicuous gallantry & devotion to duty on various dates pr: March 30th &
April 25th 1917 while the Unit was attached for collection of wounded from the front
line during the Advance of the 48th Division from PERONNE to GUILLEMONT & TOMBOIS FARMS.

Capt. G. Moore RAMC TF — Military Cross

439013 Sgt. F.H. Cann S.V.
439042 L/Cpl. Upston J.H.
439050 Pte. Ward W.E.   } Military Medal.
439278   " Sainsbury R.W.
439332   " Davis C.L.
439419   " Russell J.S.

J Agnew Lt Col RAMC
OC 1/3 South Midland Fd Amb.

31/5/17

WAR DIARY

OF

1/3RD SOUTH MIDLAND FIELD AMBULANCE

FOR
THE
MONTH
OF
JUNE 1917.

WAR DIARY or INTELLIGENCE SUMMARY

Army Form C. 2118.

Maps Ref. France 57^e 1/40,000

Place	Date	Summary of Events and Information	Remarks and references to Appendices
N.II.C.	Jan 1. 1917	Routine duties. Continuing construction of DRSP. Weather fine	
	2	Visited Anzac Corps R.E. Workshops - MEAULTE - re material being supplied by them for the Rest Stn at MEAULTE & FAIRFAYE & arranged for further Equipment. Capt Moore M.C. went on leave. Capt KENYON returned from leave. Weather fine	
	3	Routine duties. Fine day	
	4	M&M's called. Received wire from MATHS 5th Australian Division that Pte W J Young J.B. Section had been awarded the Military Medal for gallantry & devotion to duty whilst attached to 8th Australian Fd Amb. Weather fine	
	5	Routine duties. Capt SOUTTER left for temp'y duty ? No 2 Aus Casualty Clearing Station - CANDAS. Weather fine	
	6	Routine duties. M&M's called. Weather fine	
	7	Still very bad. Some rain. The frogs J. a heavy thunderstorm	
	8	Dull & some showers - more thunder in distance	
	9	Still lots of rain - their cobble spark held lately	

WAR DIARY
or
INTELLIGENCE SUMMARY
(Erase heading not required.)

Army Form C. 2118.

Map Ref. France 57c. 1-40000

Place	Date 1917	Hour	Summary of Events and Information	Remarks and references to Appendices
N.11.C	June 10		Routine duties. Very hot day	
	11		" " Terrific thunderstorm lasting from midnight to 7 a.m. the camp flooded. Fine day after's + atmosphere fresher	
	12		Routine duties - very hot. ADMS called at midnight Weather Cooler	
	13		" " Fine day	
	14		Visited ADMS at DH Qs. Capt Hume returned from leave. Weather fine	
	15		to went on leave. Capt Heapath assumed Command of the unit.	
	16		Routine duties -	
	17		Scarlet worship (with 4 dental mechanics) was Joined	
	18		Capt SOUTTER returned from Temp'y duty at No 2 Aircraft Depot R.F.C. ADMS called	
	19		in morning	
	20		ADMS 48th + 20th DW called in morning. DMS Theory DDMS T.O Corp + ADMS 45th Div visited the Unit at 2 pm + inspected the Corp Rest Station. DMS Expressed his approval - weather fine	
	21		Routine Duties - ADMS called -	

WAR DIARY or INTELLIGENCE SUMMARY

Army Form C. 2118.

Map Ref. France 57d 1:40,000

Place	Date	Hour	Summary of Events and Information	Remarks and references to Appendices
N.11.C	June 22		Routine shell cases of 2nd Bn (who have been clearing the lines) admitted from their Fd Ambulance	
	23		ADMS called. Routine duties	
	24		Schening cenke at BATAVIA. Taken over from 2nd Bn Capt KENYON + 9 Ors rank. proceeded there for duty	
	25		Routine duties. ADMS called. GOC 9th called + inspected the Camp	
	26		Capt MOORE reported to IV Corps for temp duty as DADMS	
	27		Option of Routing Duty Medic Blkred Corps. Returns sent direct to ADMS	
			ADMS called. Routine duties	
	28		HQ returned from Lienne. A heavy thunderstorm accompanied by terrific wind + rain wrecked the camp at 7.45 pm. 14 marquees + several uniforms blown down + all patients saturated - no one hurt. Rain until 10 pm including marquees + Majors [illegible]	
	29		Fine day. Spent in repairing damage of last night. OC 7th Fd Amb called re taking over from us a 2nd proto	
	30		A/Section (two detail) proceeded to GONIE COURT where 143 Inf Bde is concentrating in relief by a Bde of III Div trenches. Weather cold	

J. A. Green
LT. COLONEL

WAR DIARY or INTELLIGENCE SUMMARY

Army Form C. 2118.

Appendix No I

The work this week has been of an uneventful nature. The Unit has continued to run the II Corps Rest Station. A large amount of Constructional work has been carried out and accommodation to Marquees provided for 350 patients - also a Shelter - Bath, Laundry & Fumigating rooms have been built & Separate dining tent & Recreation room (with stage) erected. Water has been laid on throughout the camp & a Storage tank (9,000 gallon capacity) provided - the water being pumped to this tank from a pumping station 350 yards away. This work was carried out by the 149 C.R.E (Army Corps - Water Engineer). This has been a great help to a Dental department has been built & opened at which the dentist has attended from No 29 C.C.S. on two days for the 48th Div. & the Dentist from No 3 C.C.S (English) on two days for the 20th Div from days week - A dental instrument workshop has also been opened at which repairs to plates & teeth dentures have been made. This workshop has been fitted out with Equipment presented to the 48th Div by the Citizens of Birmingham & supplied by Dental Mechanics on the Strength of the 48 Div. The Scheme has worked splendidly. Large number of patients

2449 Wt. W14957/M90 750,000 1/16 J.B.C. & A. Forms/C.2118/12.

Appendix I Cont'd

have been attended to (50 to 70 daily.) Trepan and diabetic provided much more satisfactory than is possible when these have to be sent to the base on Army opinion. This scheme is well worth an extensive trial with front armies.

As regards the routine work of the Rest Station - All patients are bathed & clothes fumigated before they are admitted to the General wards & they are issued with newly fumigated blankets. Blankets found by patients leaving the Station are all fumigated before they are re-issued.

Separate B.S.O.'s P.V.O. & Branshower wards have been kept. Rugs put between are used generally for the depôts of Branshower cases has been tried with the incinerator.

[signature]
LT. COLONEL
O.C.No.3/2nd STH. MID. FD. AMBULANCE

WAR DIARY
or
INTELLIGENCE SUMMARY

Army Form C. 2118.

Appendix No. II

Copy of letter received from A.D.M.S., 48th Division 1/20.6.17:-

"The D.M.S., Third Army directs me to convey to the Field Ambulance Commanders his entire satisfaction with all medical units of the 48th Division inspected by him yesterday.

He considers that the neat and orderly appearance of the premises, and the nature of the arrangements made for the treatment and evacuation of the sick and wounded at the various posts show that much good hard work has been done and reflect great credit on all concerned."

J A Quin
LT. COLONEL.
COMDG. 1/3rd STH. MID. FD. AMBULANCE.

Army Form C. 2118

WAR DIARY
or
INTELLIGENCE SUMMARY
(Erase heading not required.)

Instructions regarding War Diaries and Intelligence Summaries are contained in F. S. Regs., Part II. and the Staff Manual respectively. Title Pages will be prepared in manuscript.

Place	Date	Hour	Summary of Events and Information	Remarks and references to Appendices

Plan of Improvised Disinfector used by 13 South Midland Field Amb. Also can show will do all thorough + effectual in a period of 250 patients coats + effectings it Battn. uniforms

Appendix 'a'

STEAM DISINFECTOR
SCALE: HALF INCH EQUALS ONE FOOT

SECTION AB — FRONT ELEV. — SIDE ELEV.
PLAN

Labels: WATER, FIRE, COPPER, FELT STRAW TANK CAGE, 100 GALLON TANK LINED WITH FELT AND STRAW, PULLEYS, COUNTER WEIGHT, WOODEN CAGE WITH DOOR REMOVED TO INSERT CLOTHING, TANK RAISED, LINE OF CAGE COPPER UNDER, LINE OF TANK, A — B

Army Form C. 2118.

WAR DIARY
or
INTELLIGENCE SUMMARY

(Erase heading not required.)

Place	Date	Hour	Summary of Events and Information	Remarks and references to Appendices
			Appendix IV	
			Awards to —	
			The following decoration has been received during the month.	
			No 439074 Pte Irving b. J — Military Medal — for gallantry & devotion to duty on May 17th 1917 while attached for duty to the 8th Australian Field Ambulance.	
			Mentioned in Despatches (fifth Section)	
			No 439,018 S/Sgt (Acting Sup/Major) Creese J	
			J A Green	
			LT. COLONEL.	
			O/C 3rd. CDN. MED. FD. AMBULANCE.	

1/3rd South Midland
Field Ambulance

War Diary
for the month of
July 1917.

Army Form C. 2118.

WAR DIARY
or
INTELLIGENCE SUMMARY
(Erase heading not required.)

Instructions regarding War Diaries and Intelligence Summaries are contained in F. S. Regs., Part II. and the Staff Manual respectively. Title Pages will be prepared in manuscript.

Maj. Adjt.
France 87e 1-40-00
                  1-100-000
Lens,   1-150-000
Hazebrouck

Place	Date 1917	Hour	Summary of Events and Information	Remarks and references to Appendices
N.11.C.	July 1st		7th Fd Amb. (17 Div) arrived preparatory to taking over hospital site at N.11.C. ADMS went on leave & OC proceeded to 1st Div. to act in his absence - weather fine	
GOMIECOURT	2		The Unit (less A Section which had already gone) paraded at 2 p.m. & with the party at the detraining Centre BAPAUME supplies marched to form A Section at GOMIECOURT. Before doing so, the R.R.S supplies were handed over to 7/Fd Amb. weather fine	
BIENVILLERS	3		The Unit marched under Orders of D.D.M.S. 143rd Bde & O.C to BIENVILLERS when it bivouacked. weather fine	
	4		Army Section tents & bivouacs - The OC to training in this area - weather fine	
	5		Route march to FONCQUEVILLERS. OC went for staff ride c B.G.C. Divisional(?) weather fine	
	6		Field day & tactical Exercise c 143rd Bde - A.D.S. Established in BIENVILLERS Collecting post at MONCHY. On wheeling instruction in method of reinforcing Kenno & Rusping touch with R.M.O's weather fine	
	7		Experimenting with provision of improvised pack saddlery weather fine & hot.	
	8		Stables for the Division - Very heavy thunderstorm during night Cooler after.	
	9		Lecture in morning - Sectional Route march in afternoon - weather cold & wet.	

Army Form C. 2118

WAR DIARY
or
INTELLIGENCE SUMMARY
(Erase heading not required.)

Instructions regarding War Diaries and Intelligence Summaries are contained in F.S. Regs., Part II. and the Staff Manual respectively. Title Pages will be prepared in manuscript.

Place	Date	Hour	Summary of Events and Information	Remarks and references to Appendices
BIENVILLERS	July 10		Route march - km HAIE - SAILLY. TONQUILLERS in morning. In afternoon C/Os + Capts. KERR + NAPIER? Staff rode to view tactical Exercise. Fine day but cold	
	11		Am lectures + drill. 4/o Flag home rode over ground of less tactical Exercise preparatory to evening nonary arrangements. Weather fine	
	12		Field and field day - practised went behind in method of marching to from an attack + a totally ordinary into communication between East Pke - A useful Exercise - weather very hot.	
	13		Drill as before. Respecters listed and Lachrymators for so representation for return of M.O.N.S. Weather fine.	
	14		Field day with 143 Inf Bde. Relief between C/ forward Collecting posts + method of Gate pushing forward bearers with advancing infantry - a good day having weather fine. Capt. transferred Smith sent for temp? duties c/ 1/8th Women in Bn.	
	15		Several returns of lamb c TABs became - All Officers as present c went reminded weather fine.	
	16		Holiday after movement above - weather fine but hot.	

WAR DIARY / INTELLIGENCE SUMMARY

Army Form C. 2118.

Map: BELGIUM Sheet 28 1-40,000

Place	Date 1917	Hour	Summary of Events and Information	Remarks and references to Appendices
NEUVILLERS	July 17		Batiquie & Company on earth preparation of frost saddlery - Weather hot -	
	18		AMS' Circus. PM Attended GOC's Conference. Weather - hot.	
	19		Routine duties - PM received orders that we were to proceed tomorrow to CREMAS -	
	20		Paraded at 11 am & marched independently to CREMAS. As I for reacted for them I walked. I find 2 horses and one HCRU owing to shortage of horses have to leave 2 horse Ambulances behind to fetch them later. Weather fine	
CREMAS	21		Routine duties - visited AMS who has been appointed our ADMS / Corps - weather showery hot	
	22		Marched to AUTHEULE at 2 pm. Entrained there under orders of 143rd Inf Bde for PROVEN (Belgium). Train left at 6.40 pm. Weather fine. Capt Morris sent to No 3 Canadian Infantry Hospital = P. 14 D (Kin Loy) recovered. Col Jones rooms left Station to proceed DOMS 17 Corps -	
	23		Arrived PROVEN at 2.30 am - unit had breakfast - them doubly Bodies of ADMS. Detailed A Reed sub Bourn & Cy KENNON to attend to Siding 17 143rd Inf Bde at SIDING IN THE ZEN. Remainder of unit marched to XVIII Corps Main Dressing Station at A.23.C.29. When it remained closed along side it. Weather very hot. So have ADMS hard not arrived at	
A.23.C.29	24		went to DADMS to XVIII Corps Head Quarters. Factory Closed parked ADMS in afternoon - Weather fine -	
"	25		Her Meng. - Capt. Hereford + Keer Booked proceed HOSPS at C.25 L 31. Stephen for our Division when we go through the 39 Divn	

WAR DIARY or INTELLIGENCE SUMMARY

Army Form C. 2118.

Place	Date 1917	Hour	Summary of Events and Information	Remarks and references to Appendices
A.23.C.29	Apr 26	am	Capt Kerr left (n. temp) duty c/o 143 Inf Bde vice Capt KENNON who proceeded to XVIII Corps Reinforcement Camp at VOLKERINCKHOVE. 1 NCO + 3 men also proceeded to HOUTKERQUE for duty at Reinforcement Camp. Two Clerks detailed for duty at Corps Hd Main Dressing Station. Capt SOUTTER went round A.DS & C.C. Post with A.D.M.S. In the afternoon the new A.D.M.S (Col Rankine T.F.) called	
"	27		At 11.30 am attended Conference of OC's Fd Ambulances at ADMS Office. My Unit were allotted the new Main Dressing Station. Then the Scheme for throwing in Dressing Coy Personnel + Capt Herapath + Capt Soutter left for temp duty with Sp & R.E.M. Capt Herapath for K XVIII Main Dressing Station. Capt Soutter to 39th D.T.C. 1 NCO + men of officers left with the Unit. Weather fine	
"	28		Party working as parties for Sw W.Sta. Stated in the 2nd phase of Operations will be Tunnel at C 25 b. 3.1. Capt Smith Rame (temp) attached to 1/k Works his relieving Capt Kennon Returned at XVIII Corps Reinforcement Camp YOLKERINCKHOVE. Capt Kennon reported for temp duty 2/k Warwicks Bn. Weather fine	
"	29		Working on Scheme for the MDSIT. Capt KERR returned. Capt HERAPATH at XVIII Corps MDSIT + 1/k Ladders returned to the Unit - ADMS. Colonel weather update. Fauerschoehen -	
"	30		Capt KENNON reported for duty in relief by Capt Challenor i/c Warwicks Batt Cold wet day	

Army Form C. 2118.

WAR DIARY or INTELLIGENCE SUMMARY

Map BELGIUM Sheet 28 A 1, 40000

(Erase heading not required.)

Place	Date 1917	Hour	Summary of Events and Information	Remarks and references to Appendices
A.23.c.2.9	31/7/31		Today being Z day the XVIII Corps attacked along its front on 15, 21, & 22, at 3.50 a.m. The 39th & 51st Divisions were in the line, with the 48th & 11th Division in support. Several of my Officers & Other Ranks (being in reserve) wanted to open up news by main (enemy S.A.?) worked all day as Intermedium in the Corps main Dressing Station. Others were busy completing arrangements for our impending move. At night all objectives of the Corps were reported taken & held against Counter attacks. Capt. Harmer RAMC T.F. & Capt. Lincoln RAMC reported for duty with my unit. A dull but fine day.	

J Ayun. Lt Col R.A.M.C T.F
O.C. "/3" South Midland Field Amb

SECRET.
9/130

WAR DIARY
OF
1/3RD SOUTH MIDLAND FIELD AMBULANCE
FOR THE MONTH OF
AUGUST 1917

WAR DIARY or INTELLIGENCE SUMMARY

(Erase heading not required.)

Army Form C. 2118.

Maps Hazebrouck 5a 1 - 10000
Belgium Sheet 28. 1 - 40 000

Place	Date 1917	Hour	Summary of Events and Information	Remarks and references to Appendices
A 23 c. 2. 9. XVIII Corps Main Dressing Station	Aug 1		The Active Operations initiated yesterday were almost brought to a standstill by heavy rain. My unit continued to hold a line at XVIII Corps M.D.S. Through which about 1000 cases have passed since yesterday morning. At 5-30 pm attended a Conference of O.C. 2d Ambulances at A.D.M.S. Office where it was decided that when the 48th Div. relieved the 39th Div. the 2nd Division of my unit should relieve the 1st Division of the 39th Div at Corps Main Dressing Station. My Reserve division will proceed for duty in front line under orders of O.C. ½ No S. hunt. 2d Amb.	
	2		Wet weather continues. Everything to act a standstill. Captn HARNEIS & FULLERTON (R.A.M.C. T.F.) joined my unit for duty.	
	3		Again continuous wet weather. Still leading voluntary ambulance at C.M.D.S. Another Conference of O.C. 2d Ambulances at A.D.M.S. Office.	
	4		The 48th Div. relieved the 39th. Today my 2nd division with myself & 4 other medical officers reported for duty at Corps Main Dressing Station at 8 am. At 12 noon the Reserve Division proceeded for duty in front line under orders of O.C. ½ No S. hunt 2d Amb.	
	5		At 4.30 pm again at 10.30 pm May Camp & the Corps Main Dressing Station was shelled by H.V. shells. The first shelling gave me two casualties but at 10.30 - 3 men were killed & 20 wounded. Amongst the latter were two men belonging to my unit. Weather showery fine	

WAR DIARY or INTELLIGENCE SUMMARY

Army Form C. 2118

(Erase heading not required.)

Place: HQ HAZEBROUCK 1-100,000
Belgium Sheet 28 1-40,000

Place	Date 1917	Hour	Summary of Events and Information	Remarks and references to Appendices
XVIII Corps Main HQrs Merris Str A 23 c 2.9	May 6		The Corps Main H.Q. was again shelled at 5.30 a.m. but no damage was done. During the morning visited CWGT Farm ( ) with a view to camp? recovery Cushion - there but later it was decided to stay at present site. The army bearers of 1 H.T. ASC attached here wounded in front line. Weather fine	
	7		Lt Col Rowe PSO O.C. 1/2nd Highland tho Amb (T.F.) appointed O.C. XVIII Corps M.T.S. vice Lt Col Hitchcock O.C. 134th Fd Amb. I remain in charge of army Tent division. Weather fine but dull.	
	8		Fine morning but heavy thunderstorm at night. Two bearers wounded in front line	
	9		Routine orders all day. One army bearer killed. Two wounded + two shell concussion (W)	
	10		" " Heavy bombing raid by Germans at night. Shelled a lot? Casualties around us but none in Corps MASF. - Weather fine	
	11		Routine orders in morning. In afternoon attended conference of DDs Fd Ambs at ADMS Office. Thunderstorm at night. 1 Bearer Garage (wounded)	
	12		Routine orders. Visited MDMS Office in afternoon. Had B&M G + DADMS trouble by horse lines rearrangement of troops to weather fine. One bearer wounded	
	13		Routine duties all day. Weather fine.	
	14		ADMS called in morning. The 1/2 M.T. ASC attached killed + one wounded + 3 horses killed and 1 wounded at MDS/- SWALLOW( ) + 1 horses ? (M) Weather - Thunderstorm in afternoon	

WAR DIARY or INTELLIGENCE SUMMARY

Army Form C. 2118

Place	Date 1917	Hour	Summary of Events and Information	Remarks and references to Appendices
XVIII Corps M.R.S1 A.23.c.2.9	Aug.15		Spent all day preparing for attack tomorrow. The H.T.M.S.C Divn. advance temporarily wounded yesterday died at C.C.S today. Capt Soutter & replacements came down the line. Dick – Capts Donvillio. Weather dull – some showers.	
	16		After a short but intense bombardment the 5th Army attacked at 4.45am this morning with modified success. On my front the opposition of the German troops not participate to be a result on our own particular front thro ST JULIEN the infantry came up against very machine gun powerless. Perhaps as a result of this the number of walking stops came from thro's the C M.A.S.Q.n was not so great to a Jut. 32. About 500 cases passed thro in the 24 hours from the divisional front. Few Germs. Any tenors in the line. Had a large time & I had 1 killed, one wounded – and 1 general. Weather fine.	
	17		The front was comparatively quiet today. Lost cases from yesterdays fighting continued to pour thro the C M.A.S.Q. In my own unit I had one man killed, one 5 wounded. 1 M.T. A.S.C (our driver) wounded. Bombing raid by German on trestled road. Weather from front – escaped up by 3 Coys of CCS influence.	
	18		Quiet day at CM.N.S.Q. Sad on the front heavy shelling by German continues. Two of my bearers wounded. Capt Soutter R.A.M.C T.F. of my unit sent to Suffolk Red Hospital POPERINGHE. Weather fine	
	19		Quiet day. At night we again had escaped the effects of hostile bombing raid. 1 wheel & body of CCS Suffered. Capt FULLERTON R.A.M.C T.F. of my unit Evacuated F.C.C.S unduly changnons & debility. Never totally unfitted for front line work – weather fine.	

WAR DIARY or INTELLIGENCE SUMMARY

Army Form C. 2118

(Erase heading not required.)

Place	Date 1917	Hour	Summary of Events and Information	Remarks and references to Appendices
A 23.C.2.9 May 20th XVIII Corps M.D. Sn.			Quiet day at CANIZY. Capt KENNON Grey went at present attached to these lines in the line. Came down for 2 days rest. Weather fine	
	21st		Nothing arranged for possible attack tomorrow morning. Thomas Gerard Kreutler joined from Capt KERR left for duty. Capt CHERRY who joined us for duty	
	22nd		Sutherland morning. Another attack with the aid of Tanks on our left arranged & happening several machine gun positions were captured. The number of Casualties are as usual Maj Ellick was not very good. Fine day. Grand at night 3 of my Kerries wounded.	
	23		Routine duties - Quiet day - MONS CELLUE saw Thomas very high winds.	
	24.		" " " The thermos surrounded H.Q.S with kanik chair wound	
	25		" " " MONS CELLUE. Fine + Quiet day.	
	26.		A Quiet front day. In evening received telephone in line to 75 in rear of infantry alkali tomorrow. MONS cellu. Every heavy rain at night	
	27.		One Army known wounded on 24th died of wounds at 47 C.C.S. today. Capt Saddell received from officers Red Cross Hospital. Heavy rain all day this morning. But Bothrave share on my Bu From LOTR place. About 100 Casualties passed through Cap MOST. Received instructions that the Division would be relieved on the night of the 28/29th. Any	

WAR DIARY or INTELLIGENCE SUMMARY

Army Form C. 2118

Map HAZEBROUCK 1 – 100,000
Belgium Sheet 28 1 – 40,000

Place	Date 1917	Hour	Summary of Events and Information	Remarks and references to Appendices
A 23 C 2.9 XVIII Corps M.D.S.	Aug 24		Bell ho full day. Cases continued to trickle thro' CWASI. Withdrawing Equipment to from CWASI.	
	29		Relieved this morning at CWASI by 2/1 Home Counties Fd Amb (58th Div) All pieces (Offrs 1 NCO & 6 men) reported from duty with the Line. Capt Soutter left for temp'y duty c 58t Div at DUHALLOW M.D.S. At 2.30 p.m. the unit marched to SCHOOLS Camp. Lt JAN TER BIEZEN in which area the Infantry brigades are going into rest On arrival opened a Sick distribution Room for men of the Division half the unit in 48 hours. Wet day –	
	30.		During the morning visited the 3 brigade Camps re medical arrangement & collection of sick. In the afternoon A.D.M.S. called & informed me that two Officers had been awarded the military medal. Capt Soutter returned from M.D.S. DUHALLOW Weather dull & showery at intervals. The line from M.D.S. DUHALLOW	Appendix II
	31.		Sunday morning visited 114 Brigade Off[icers] D.H. Dresser & after Corps HQ Bearers to Bearers returned from duty in the line.	

J A Quinn Lt Col R.A.M.C. T.F.
C.O. 1/3 North Midland Field Amb.

Army Form C. 2118

WAR DIARY
or
INTELLIGENCE SUMMARY
(Erase heading not required.)

Appendix I

Summary of Events and Information

Battle Casualties to Personnel of 1/3rd South Midland Field Ambulance during the month of August 1917.

Place	Date	Hour	Regt. No.	Rank	Name	Casualty	Nature	Disposal
	5-8-17		439259	Pte	Cox. A.J.	Wounded	Shell Wd L Shoulder	To C.C.S.
			439011	2/St.Sgt	Rex. S.G.	do	do R.Leg (Slight)	Remd at duty
	6-8-17		439218 / T4/244916	Pte Dvr	Sparrow J.W. Best G. (No 3C 498 Bn Trans ASC attd)	Wounded do	Shrap. Wd Face do - L Shoulder	To CCS do
	8-8-17		439513 / 439537	Pte "	Eaton E.J. Dymond J.S.	Wounded "	Shell Wd R Upper Arm (Cpd street) do - L Thigh (Slight)	Remd at duty
	9-8-17		439345 / 439330	Pte "	Snook H.A. Robbins J.R.	Killed Wounded	Shell Wds abdomen Shell Wd L Side	do
			439216 / 439051 / 439347	" " "	Bird J.H. Jones D.M. Holton S.G.	do do do	do - R Hand Shell shock (w) do (w)	Remd at duty Evacd to duty 1117 do
	11-8-17		439158	Pte	James H.J.G.	Wounded	Shell Gas - Dermatitis	Evacd to duty 12Fd
	12-8-17		439376	Pte	Barrett J.	Wounded	Shell Wd Face	Remd at duty
	14-8-17		439216	Pte	Bird J.H.G.	Wounded	Gassed, shell (w)	To CCS
			T4/244171 / 7/28107	Dvr do	Cook WG No 2 Co 448 Div Train Todd WG ASC attd	Killed Died of Wounds	Shell Wd Multiple do - Thigho	Evacd to No 4 CCS - 15/8/17
	16-8-17		63994	Pte	Britton E.	Wounded	Gassed, shell (w)	To CCS
			439056	Sgt	Lambourn WE	do	Shell Wd L Forearm (Cpd Fract)	do
			439325	Pte	Burnett W.L.	Killed	Shell Wd Chest	

Date	Regt No.	Rank	Name	Date	Casualty	Nature	Disposal
17-8-17	439436 / 439097	Pte "	Locke E.R. Stone R.J.	17-8-17	Wounded do	Shell Wd L Thigh do Thigh do	To CCS do
	54628 / M2/154482	" Pte	Belshaw G. Martin H (ASC(MT) attd)		do do	do L Leg & Back do Thighs	Remd at duty
	439511 / 439133	Pte "	Rawlings A. Wall S.	17-8-17	Killed Wounded	Shell Wd Chest do R Hand	Remd at duty
	439426 / 439456	Pte "	Prince K.W. Horsey W.H.C	18-8-17	Wounded do	Shell Wd R Hand do - L Fingers	Remd at duty do
	435154 / 439351	Cpl "	Parker D.B. Birch W.H.	23-8-17	wounded do	Shell Wd L Shoulder Face & Scalp do - R Hand	To CCS do
	439551	"	Surtees W.H.		do	do - Buttocks	do
	439203	Pte	Townsend W.	23-8-17	Burst of Womb	Shell Wd Chest R.Arm & Legs	2/1 SW 2/17 47 CCS. 26-8-17
	M2/156275	Pte	Hammond J. (ASC(MT att.)	27-8-17	Wounded	Shell Wd Back	To CCS
	439093	Pte	Blampied R.J.	28-8-17	wounded	Shell Wd Neck	To CCS

1875 Wt. W593/826 1,000,000 4/15 J.B.C. & A. A.D.S.S./Forms/C. 2118.

Army Form C. 2118

Appendix II.

WAR DIARY
or
INTELLIGENCE SUMMARY
(Erase heading not required.)

Place	Date	Hour	Summary of Events and Information	Remarks and references to Appendices
			MILITARY MEDAL	
			Awarded the Military Medal by G.O.C. XVIII Corps, for gallant conduct and devotion to duty in the field. (Authority 48 Div. Wire N° Q.F 28 7/28.8.17)	
			13rd S Mid 3d Amb. 439211 Cpl Weeks L	
			do 439216 Pte Bird H.J.	

WAR DIARY

OF

1/3rd SOUTH MIDLAND FD. AMB.

FOR THE MONTH OF

SEPTEMBER 1917

Army Form C. 2118.

WAR DIARY
or
INTELLIGENCE SUMMARY.

(Erase heading not required.)

MAP HAZEBROUCK 1 - 100,000

Place	Date 1917	Hour	Summary of Events and Information	Remarks and references to Appendices
SCHOOL Camp Sept 1st			Routine Duties - ADMS Called. Weather fine	
ST JANTER BIEZEN	.2		Showers morning. Capt Soutter left on medical charge of the Woverghem Batt- after which he held a conference	
	3		ADMS called & inspected the Ambulance. Weather fine	
			OC's An Ambulances	
	4		Routine duties. Fine weather the allurent however night Camp heavily bombed at intervals during night but no casualties. Capt Carrel went on leave.	
	5		In afternoon attended a conference of RMO's + D.M. units of the Division which was addressed by ADMS tapt + 2M/S on health of the troops. Fine day but clear night. Capt C HARRIS RAMC (TC) joined for duty.	
	6		Routine duties. Thunderstorm at night. Capt HARRIS left for temp: duty with the 1/5 R Sussex Rott'n	
	7		Capt HARRIS left for temp? duty at XVIII Corps Infantry School. Capt HERBERT SMITH RAMC SR reported from XVIII Corps reinforcement Camp	
	8		fine day. Routine duties	
	9		Routine duties - fine day. Lt A.G. MOORE. USA Medical Service joined for duty Capt KENNON left for temp: duty at AIRST DUHALLOW C 58° BW.	
	10		" " ADMS called	

Army Form C. 2118.

WAR DIARY
or
INTELLIGENCE SUMMARY. MAP HAZEBROUCK 1 – 100,000
(Erase heading not required.)

Instructions regarding War Diaries and Intelligence Summaries are contained in F. S. Regs., Part II. and the Staff Manual respectively. Title pages will be prepared in manuscript.

Place	Date 1917	Hour	Summary of Events and Information	Remarks and references to Appendices
ST JAN TER BIEZEN	Sept 11		Routine duties – fine day	
	12		" " " "	
	13		" " " Capt SOUTTER returned from duty as M.O. 1/8 Worcester Batt'n	
	14		ADMS called in morning. In afternoon traded ADMS at WINNEZEELE in acting for him during his absence on leave. Weather fine.	
	15		Joined the Brakin of the Brown as A/ADMS. Capt CEKHERATATH took over the command of the Unit during my absence. Capt HERBERT SMITH having volunteered for duty in MESOPOTAMIA left for training Centre at BLACKPOOL	
	16th		Under orders of 144 Inf. Bde. Transport proceeded to new Area at 9 a.m. Lt L.G. MOORE U.S.A. left to report to A.D.M.S. 55th Div for temporary duty.	
	17th		Orders received that personnel were entrain at ABEELE at 5.30 p.m.	
	18 –		Train left 1.30 a.m. 3 trains at Audruicq marched to BLANC PIGNON.	
	19th		Small Venturin hospital opened for 144 Bde men	
	20 –		3 Bn. men Class A men replaced by P.B. men present to have. T/Capt C. HARRIS returned from European duty. Routine work.	

A5834 Wt.W4973 M687 750,000 8/16 D. D. & L. Ltd. Forms/C.2118/13.

Army Form C. 2118.

WAR DIARY
or
INTELLIGENCE SUMMARY.
(Erase heading not required.)

Instructions regarding War Diaries and Intelligence Summaries are contained in F. S. Regs., Part II. and the Staff Manual respectively. Title pages will be prepared in manuscript.

M/fo HAZEBROUCK 1-100000
BELGIUM Sheet 28 - 1-40000

Place	Date	Hour	Summary of Events and Information	Remarks and references to Appendices
AUDRUICQ	21st		T/Capt C. HARRIS left for temporary duty with 240 Bde R.F.A. Routine work.	
	22nd		Routine work.	
	23rd			
	24th		Capt T.W. MORGAN-HARNEIS returned from temporary duty at XVIII Corps Inf. School. 2 men lent to 58th Div were wounded in action. Two horses were destroyed by shell fire.	
	25th		Routine work.	
	26th		Orders from A.D.M.S. that transports proceed by road to GWENT FARM (Sheet 28.N.28.a 2.6.) Convoy to GWENT FARM.	
	27th		Personnel proceeded by train to BRIELEN station & marched to GWENT FARM. Went to DUHALLOW (Sheet 28 C.25 d.2.3) to arrange taking over 142th A.D.S. / front line posts on the 28th.	
DUHALLOW A.D.S.	28th	9.a.m.	Bearers went up the line in charge of Capt SOUTTER to take over front line posts from 2/3 H.C.F.A.	
		12.1 p.	Tent division marched to DUHALLOW under Capt. HARNEIS. Took over from 2/2 H.C.F.A. I went round front posts to see all correct. OC Norman command of unit on relief at 4H.2. The D.R.P. at California Trench at C 22.6.8.2. was badly shelled & shifted the morning & the M.O's removed to VENHEDLE Fm C.17.d.3.8 front company two squads slept there	

A5834   Wt. W4973 M687   750,000   8/16   D. D. & L. Ltd.   Forms/C.2118/13.

Army Form C. 2118.

WAR DIARY
or
INTELLIGENCE SUMMARY

MAPS BELGIUM Sheet 24 ¹/₄₀,₀₀₀

(Erase heading not required.)

Place	Date 1917	Hour	Summary of Events and Information	Remarks and references to Appendices
A.D.S. DUHALLOW	Sept 29	6 am	MOMS called round front line & Capt HERAPATH. Busy all day filling in trench with W.O.R. at this station weather fine - front fairly quiet but a lot of "mustard" gas coming through	
	30		Visited LA BELLE ALLIANCE Post this morning & after! busy at HQ31 - trench quiet - day in front. Capt HARNESS & KENNON relieved Capts SOUTTER & ST PIERRE (U.S.A.) at VENHEULE. weather fine	

J. Ager
Urban Ruwet
O.C. 13th P.Med Fd Amb

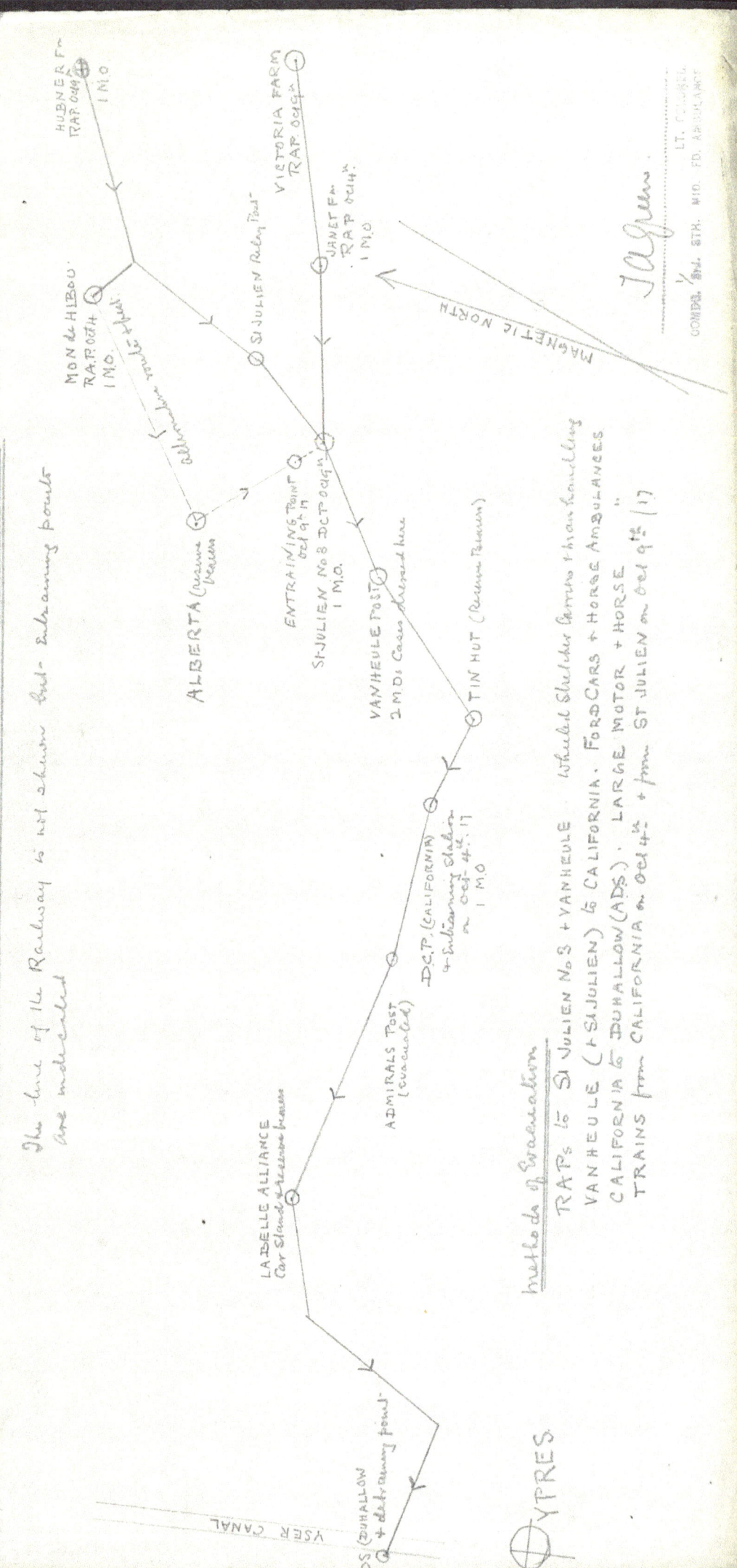

SECRET

WAR DIARY

OF

1/3rd SOUTH MIDLAND FIELD AMBULANCE

FOR THE MONTH OF

OCTOBER 1917

Army Form C. 2118

WAR DIARY or INTELLIGENCE SUMMARY

(Erase heading not required.)

Instructions regarding War Diaries and Intelligence Summaries are contained in F.S. Regs., Part II and the Staff Manual respectively. Title Pages will be prepared in manuscript.

Ref. Map. ST. JULIEN. 28. NW2. 1-10,000

Place	Date	Hour	Summary of Events and Information	Remarks and references to Appendices
A.D.S. DUHALLON C.25.d.30	1917 Oct/4		Routine duties at A.D.S. 1 man of my unit killed & 2 wounded at Admirals Cross Rd Post. C.22.c.5.5. This post was discontinued as it was of no value. Except for an intermittent shelling there + on Whitfeld in a very heavy shelled area.	
	.2		At 10 am attended a Conference of OC's Fd Ambulances at A.D.M.S. Office. When it was decided that the 1/1st S.Mid.Fd.Amb. should take over the A.D.S. during the forthcoming active operations and that I should be responsible for the forward line. Bearers of the 3rd S.M.F.A. were withdrawn from the front for 24 hours and-replaced by bearers of the 1st S.Mid Fd Amb. Weather fine.	
	3		OC 1/1 S.Mid Fd. Amb. took over the A.D.S. of DUHALLON. During the afternoon battle casualties were made for collecting wounded from the front line in accordance with R.A.M.C. (46 Div) Operation Orders of this date. Intensive Forward are diagrammatically shown in Appendix. Briefly wounded were to be taken over from the Regtl RAP at Mon du HIBOU (C.6.c.2.3) + Regtl RAP at JANET Fm (C.12.d.5.0) by R.A.M.C. bearers. Carried by hand on Wheeled Stretcher Carriers to ST. JULIEN No 3 Aid Post (C.11.c.4.8) thence by hand ambulance even at VAN HEULE Fm (C.17.d.2.6) — where wheeled carriers were reversed, thence by horse Amb Cars & the D.C. Post at CALIFORNIA TRENCH (C.22.6.7.1.) from this post they by Cars were to be transferred to the MAIN DRESSING STATION DUHALLON by large Motor Ambulance Cars detailed from 3rd M.A.C. for the purpose. + Walking Cases were to be guided of the lens avenue lying + worn by light Railway. To facilitate the landing of the trucks a Siding had been constructed at the Depot. All available Bearers from the Field Ambulances were used & not 60 were at first kept in Reserve. Capt. C.E.R. Sheppard was put in Charge of the Forward Posts and he had 5 other officers working under his orders. I myself remained at DUHALLOW where I could control both Road & train Evacuation the in touch with the A.D.M.S. Horse Ambulances were held in reserve for working wounded any to ease Camps. the light railway broke down. It was arranged that the first train should be at the Dep at 6 am. Weather fine	

Army Form C. 2118.

WAR DIARY or INTELLIGENCE SUMMARY

REF. MAPS — ST. JULIEN 28 N.W 2.1 — 10,000
POELCAPELLE 1-10,000

(Erase heading not required.)

Place	Date	Hour	Summary of Events and Information	Remarks and references to Appendices
A.D.S. DUHALLOW C.25.d.3.0	Oct 4th 1917		Rain had commenced before during the night & got worse as the day advanced. The troops attacked at 6 am after a short but very heavy bombardment. When the first news approached the D.C.Post it was found that the railway had been destroyed by the enemy shell fire & the enemy in 7 places may known to the friend & surprise work of 9 Plgr & Furlonger & the 29th Light Railway Operating Co. R.E. who was in charge of the Ambulance trains. It was repaired by 10 am & afterwards the Evacuation by this route continued to run smoothly. Bearers & three Ambulances were turned out to deal with the walking wounded & with 10 large Motor Ambulances also working – no Corporation of Cars took place in any of the Aid Posts. Three Ford Cars Supplied to bring the loaded Cars with N.C.O. Military Cases Either Walked both D.C.P. or came down on returning G.S. Wagons the Ford Car had arrived at the D.C.Post & from that time onwards a steady stream of Cases continued to come in. Altogether about 360 Cases were brought down with the first returns. The personnel Support consisted of 6 Officers & 240 Bearers (60 men were the Returns of Infantry who have been attached to run the Regt. Shelters Pioneers). The Enemy when advise fighting had ceased, in accordance with NDM's orders I advanced by Ambulance Bearer to new R.A.P's at VICTORIA Fm D.7.6.21. on the Right & MONT du HIBOU (D.6.C.2.3) on the Left. I advise my most original bearers for a short rest. Owing to the fact that there have already no suitable Cover at VICTORIA Fm & the inclemency of the weather the 1st and MO turned up the bearers subsequently returned to JANET Fm but the wounded continued to be taken over from the R.M.O at the former Post.	
		Oct 6	At 2 am several nurses arriving that the Bearers of the Front Line were exhausted & arrived carry on no longer – Also that, owing to communico news the Reinkins were in an apparently state. Making it very difficult for Capt Caro to run them D.C.P. turned out & horses Ambulances to work & interior & the Inf & between ST. JULIEN & the D.C.Post and these arrangements to deal with all the cases. All cases from Yesterday & today (about 800 all told) were cleared to the A.D.S. by .... today. The R.M.O's reporting all clear at 4 pm	

War Diary / Intelligence Summary

Army Form C. 2118.

Ref MAPS ST JULIEN 28 N.W. 2.
POELCAPELLE

Place	Date 1917	Hour	Summary of Events and Information	Remarks and references to Appendices
ADS in DUHALLOW C.25.d.3.0	Oct 6		A dull wet day - no active fighting. Troop had casualties coming in. It has been decided that for the next series of active operations the D.C. Post closer to at ST JULIEN. No 3 (C.18a..?) tramway cars will be loaded onto tram at (C.17.b.B.9.) Collected trench boards to lay double track from the No DCP to the Loading Point. The whole was done by turning off the SW Pa who had been withdrawn from line - they were employed with work of the removal and to GWENT Fm for a rest. 17.24 hrs	1 - 10000 1 - 10000
	7		Another dull wet day. French bath WE12 completed & in interchange of trays by M/S 54 & 9 and different identity recommended for 24 hours rest. No signs of siding from light railway at loading point - though it is hoped we shall have one	
	8		Under time commenced this morning. A fine morning but heavy rain at night. All lorries brought into line & dispositions made for next attack. The changes in dispositions so connected with these for Oct 4th were as follows. The left R.A.P. was moved to HÜBNER Fm (D.1.c.4.6) & the D.C.P. to ST JULIEN (C.18.a...7). Every possible thing made besides the Parge [battn?] ambulances [bituminous?] will not as a rule go further forward than CALIFORNIA POST (C.22.6.7.1). Evacuation from the left sector will be along the POELCAPELLE-ST JULIEN Road. An alternative route being across trench board track from march HIBOU and ALBERTA (C.11.C.9.7) to railhead at D.17.b.2.9. & thence at (if necessary) to ST JULIEN. The R Amb personnel is same as for the 4th unit & 3 Platoons of Infantry are available to help Reg. Stretcher bearers.	
	9		Zero hour was 5.20 am. No railway siding has been made at loading place for walking wounded but no difficulty was experienced in loading. Lorries wounded were fairly numerous though there was some delay in getting them away. In anticipation of this difficulty motor Amb Convoy were sent at 5:30 am to VAN HEULE (C.17.d.2..6) to convey men to CALIFORNIA	

WAR DIARY or INTELLIGENCE SUMMARY

Army Form C. 2118.

Maps S. JULIEN 28 NW 2. 1-10000
POELCAPELLE 1-10000

Place	Date 1917	Hour	Summary of Events and Information	Remarks and references to Appendices
AD SN AUHALLON C.25.d.3.0	Oct 9 Cont.d		Officers the Fd. Ams were able to attend with them. Changes in dispositions were made as follows. The Right R.A.P. was advanced to VICTORIA Fm (D7.b.3.2) The Route of Evacuation from Right sector was changed via Duckboard track in ALBERTA. Stk Bearers were again been brought in spite of congestion of traffic that road. The first Convoy reached the N.W.S.H. at 6.30 am & afterwards continued to come in a steady stream. At noon was ordered to Lieut Capt SOUTTER for duty with 8 Worcesters over 21 million came died of wounds. She weather remained fine during the day but the ground was in a bad condition. Officers of the 27th Fd Amb (I X Divison) came klowed round with a view to taking over from us tomorrow.	
	Oct 10		the my unit was relieved today in the Front line by the 27th Fd Amb. Two Officers & 72 O.R. were left behind until known to clear the wounded & the 49th Div - working party at S.JULIEN. The remainder of the unit marched to our base camp at GWENT Fm (Amb. End of PEPPERMITE. All sheets the Captains before remarked ever to the incoming Fd Amb. Weather dull but fine.	
GWENT FM.	Oct 11		The rear party returned to GWENT Fm. In the afternoon having cleared the field. 49th Div Wounded - Beb's 80.5 & 90.0 Cases were collected for the 9th & 11th Amb. A very wet day - 2 MB. Cattle appeared in the Hanston Fogleze as being appointed D.A.L. to Hon? Klaus. in my unit	
	Oct 12		Capt Humphreys went on leave. Bristol O.25.4.1/10.S.m. 2d Ambm with reference to recommendations for immediate rewards. Another wet day. Received orders that my unit would move to a new area vacated by 13 G.F. Cy 143 Inf Bde. Details of the Remarks of the Bn south reference to the situation	

WAR DIARY or INTELLIGENCE SUMMARY

Army Form C. 2118.

Ref Map. LENS 1–100000
HAZEBROUCK 1–100000

Place	Date	Hour	Summary of Events and Information	Remarks and references to Appendices
GWENT. EM	1917 Feb 13		Wet day. Coy Freeing up for move tomorrow. Interviewed my Corpl & Oven Slevin re OC South African Lt Amb. Sent to move 4 Ambulance party to new area at GWENT.	
	14		The Unit proceeded by train under orders of B.G.C 143 Inf Bde to the area behind LENS when HYTHGONNIN Coy will in due course relieve the 2nd Canadian Division. The transport proceeded all Noute. Marched to PESCHOEK where the Unit Entrained. Personnel left at 5 pm. (train to Decipole) I saw traffic the Railways journey was complicated. The transport (it away at 6.30pm but bivouac followed in 2 half trains. I travelled with motor ambulances by road via LOSTE to HYPT to TILQUES than at 5.30am arrived my journey. Detraining Station was at MAREUIL (4 miles N.W of ARRAS) the transport arrived at 8.30 am & the remainder of the Unit late in the day. The whole Unit went into Camps at MONT ST ELOI during the day itself. The H. Amb Sect at VILLIERS au BOIS. CHATEAU de la HAIE, LES 4 VENTS & ESTREE COUCHIE. All of which I have to take over from Veronia Canadian Fd Ambulance. Wet day	
	16		Lt MOORE t 'C' Tent Sub Division proceeded at 8.30am to take over Amb Sub at ESTREE OURMIC. 1 NCO 4 men with me at 4 VENTS as a holding party. Capt HARMEIS t 'B' Sed Sub division with me VILLERS au BOIS to take over Amb Sub at Chateau de la HAIE my duties at present are to collect t obtain stock in back area. Weather fine	
	17		Visited all posts during day - Weather fine	

WAR DIARY or INTELLIGENCE SUMMARY.

Army Form C. 2118.

R/MAP LENS 1-100 000

Place	Date 1917	Hour	Summary of Events and Information	Remarks and references to Appendices
Chateau de la HAIE	Oct 18		Routine duties – weather fine	
	19		Wet day – ADMS called in afternoon	
	20		Visited VILLERS au BOIS + DTM 2 in morning. Capt Robinson + Lt Greenless R.A.M.C. reported for duty.	
	21		Routine duties in morning. P.M. visited 1st ADMS, ESTREE COUCHIE + C.R.S. at FRESNICOURT	
	22		" Been R.E. Stores for alterations to Chateau de la HAIE	
	23		Visited 4th A.D.S. at CAMBLIGNEUL. ADMS called in afternoon. Saw 2nd ADMS V Corps when I have to take over tomorrow from a Canadian Fd Amb. 2nd ADMS notified be opened as a Corps Sick Hospital.	
	24		+Saw the ADMS V Corps had decided that the Amb Sect at ESTREE COUCHIE should be opened as a Corps Sick Hospital for the reception of Scabies, Impetigo + allied conditions. Wet day. Took over Amb Sect at CAMBLIGNEUL + put in a Section party 9/NCO + 6 men. Also took over whole of the 4 VENTS from another Canadian Fd Amb (less dental dept which remains for time being) Reference Estimate of Materials (R.E. + Red Cross) required for ESTREE COUCHIE + submitted them to ADMS. Capt Merrylees returned from leave.	
	25		Cleared all Fd Amb stores from CAMBLIGNEUL. Handed Area Stores over to Town Mayor. Capt Merryleeses + remainder of B Section proceeded to VILLERS au BOIS. Capt Robinson R.A.M.C. T.F. proceeded for duty c/w wrecked Batt'n viee Capt SOUTER (temp.) attached What unit.	

Army Form C. 2118.

WAR DIARY
or
INTELLIGENCE SUMMARY.
(Erase heading not required.)

Army Form C. 2118.

LENS – 1–100000 –

Place	Date 1917	Hour	Summary of Events and Information	Remarks and references to Appendices
Aubin au HME Oct 26			Routine duties – Capt Sooter reported from 1/7 Worcesters	
Aud. Station	27		" "	
	28		Met MOs 48th & 59th Divisions at 3rd Amb. Stn. near SAINS en GOHELLE - re distribution of Red Cross Stores required for V Corps Skin Hospital. Routine duties. Wet day	
	29		" "	
	30		RMS closed in afternoon. Lt Prestorea RAMC left for Temp. duty as MO 1/4 Staffs. Capt SOOTER went on leave.	
	31		Visited Corps Skin Hospital & afterwards CRE V Corps troops re materials for the hospital. Capt J Drew Temp RAMC TF from leave Reported for duty from Base. Weather fine	

J Agnew Lt-Col RAMC TF
OC 1/3 South Midland Fld Ambulance.

WAR DIARY
or
INTELLIGENCE SUMMARY.

Army Form C. 2118.

APPENDIX N° 3 TO WAR DIARY OF 1/3RD SOUTH MIDLAND FIELD AMB: FOR OCTOBER 1917

AWARDS

The Military Cross:-

Capt. C.F.K. HERAPATH (1/3rd S. Mid. Fd. Amb: T.F.) awarded the Military Cross by the Field Marshal Commanding-in-Chief. (Authority - XVIII Corps D1/360 d/24-10-17)

T/Capt. R. KENNON (RAMC attd. 1/3rd S. Mid Fd. Amb:) awarded the Military Cross by Field Marshal C.-in-C. 9-10-17 (Authority XVIII Corps R.O. 738).

The Military Medal

#39131. Cpl. F.G. LODGE (1/3rd S. Mid. Fd. Amb. T.F.) Awarded the Military Medal by Corps Commander (Authority XVIII Corps D1/363/367 d/22-10-17)

#39199 Pte F.G. CLARK - do - - do -

M2/032583 Cpl W. CLARKE (ASC. MT attd. 1/3rd S. Mid. Fd. Amb:) - Awarded the Military Medal by G.O.C. XVIII Corps (Authority 48 Division Order N° A506 d/28-10-17)

M2/288402 Pte D. MCILVENNY - do - - Awarded the Military Medal by G.O.C. XVIII Corps (Authority N° HR/3922 d/2-10-17)

Army Form C. 2118.

WAR DIARY
or
INTELLIGENCE SUMMARY.
(Erase heading not required.)

Summary of Events and Information

APPENDIX No 2. TO WAR DIARY OF 1/3RD SOUTH MIDLAND FIELD AMB: FOR OCTOBER 1917.

BATTLE CASUALTIES

Killed in Action:—

439109 Pte Johnson E.V. (1/3rd S: Mid Fd Amb) 1-10-17

Wounded in Action:—

439117	Pte Ford. W	(1/3rd S Mid Fd Amb) — Shell Wd R Leg (Cpd fract) + R Arm	— 1-10-17
439262	" Morrish. B	do — Shell Wd R Buttock	— do
439230	" Moore A.W	do — Shell Wd L Arm	— do
439217	" Fraser C.L	do — Shell Wd Scalp (slight)	— do
439108	" Pople A.H	do — Shell Wd L Hand (slight)	— 6-10-17
439199	" Clark F.G	do — Shell Wd R Hand (slight)	— 10-10-17

www.ingramcontent.com/pod-product-compliance
Lightning Source LLC
Chambersburg PA
CBHW080914230426
43667CB00015B/2680